THE MODERN
HORROR FILM

Other Books by John McCarty

You're On Open Line: Inside the Wacky World of Late-Night Talk Radio
Splatter Movies: Breaking the Last Taboo of the Screen
Alfred Hitchcock Presents (with Brian Kelleher)
Psychos—80 Years of Mad Movies, Maniacs and Murderous Deeds
The Films of John Huston
The Little Shop of Horrors Book (with Mark Thomas McGee)
The Official Splatter Movie Guide
Deadly Resurrection (a novel)

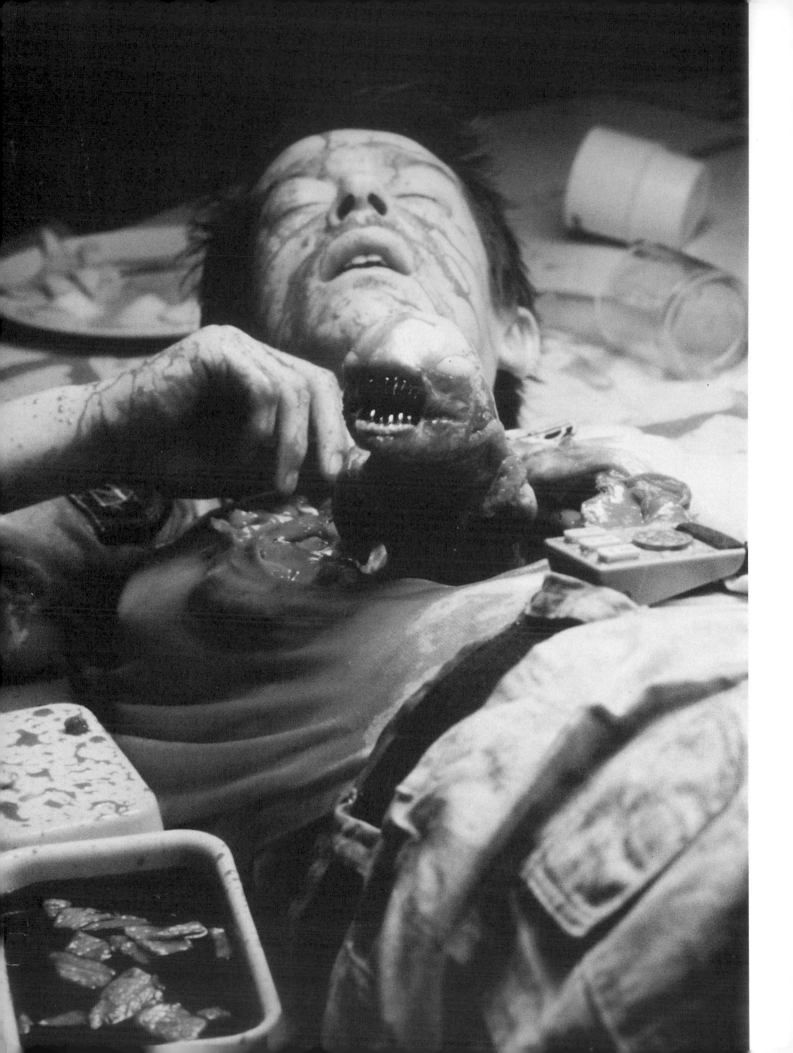

THE MODERN HORROR FILM

50 CONTEMPORARY CLASSICS

from

"The Curse of Frankenstein" to "The Lair of the White Worm"

by
John McCarty

A CITADEL PRESS BOOK
PUBLISHED BY CAROL PUBLISHING GROUP

Photo Credits

American-International Pictures
Avco Embassy Pictures
Blood Relations Company
Bryanston Pictures
Cinerama Releasing
Columbia Pictures
Dawn Associates/Katherine Kolbert
Dead Films, Inc./Richard & Susan Golomb
Empire Pictures
Hammer Film Productions Ltd.
Laurel Entertainment
London-Cannon Films Ltd.
Marianne Productions, S.A.
MGM/UA
New Century Vista Film Co.

New Line Cinema
New Sky Productions
New World Pictures
Paramount Pictures
Playboy Productions
The Rank Organization
Renaissance Pictures
Tri-Star Pictures
Twentieth Century-Fox
United Film Distribution
Universal Pictures
Vanguard Releasing
Vestron Pictures
Virgin Vision
Warner Bros. Inc.

Copyright © 1990 by John McCarty

A Citadel Press Book
Published by Carol Publishing Group

Editorial Offices
600 Madison Avenue
New York, NY 10022

Sales & Distribution Offices
120 Enterprise Avenue
Secaucus, NJ 07094A

In Canada: Musson Book Company
A division of General Publishing Co. Limited
Don Mills, Ontario

Queries regarding rights and permissions
should be addressed to: Carol Publishing Group,
600 Madison Avenue, New York, NY 10022

DESIGNED BY LESTER GLASSNER

Manufactured in the United States of America
ISBN 0-8065-1164-8

10 9 8 7 6 5 4 3 2 1

Library of Congress Cataloging-in-Publication Data

McCarty, John.

    The modern horror film : 50 contemporary classics.
    1. Horror films--History and criticism.
I. Title.
PN1995.9H6E94   1990   791.43'09'0916
ISBN 0-8065-1164-8

For Peter Cushing,

Boyhood hero, wonderful actor, gracious gentleman

Acknowledgments

I would like to thank the following people for their various contributions in helping this book see the light of day: Dominick Abel; John Brent—for his help in supplying me with photos and for giving me the opportunity to air my views (in slightly different form) on a couple of the films discussed herein in his excellent magazine *Phantasma*; Eric Caidin (Hollywood Book & Poster)—without whose dedication in finding and supplying me with rare photo material this film book (and most of my others) would be quite at a loss; Bruce G. Hallenbeck—for sharing his vast knowledge of Hammer Films with me and for contributing most of the chapter on *Hands of the Ripper*; Ken Hanke (my fellow Ken Russell enthusiast)—for keeping me entertained with his letters, for his insights into the creative world of Ken Russell, and for generously contributing most of the material on the *Psycho* films, *The Devils, Altered States, Gothic, The Lair of the White Worm, A Nightmare on Elm Street* and *The Re-Animator*; Dick Klemensen—for continuing to find the time to publish *Little Shoppe of Horrors* and for supplying me with some rare Hammer stills; Frank LaLoggia—for sharing some "insider stuff" about the making of *Lady in White* with me, and for supplying me with stills; Judith McGuinn at Virgin Vision—for supplying me with stills and some additional material from *Lady in White*; Allan J. Wilson (Citadel Press)—for having the interest and faith in the project to begin with; and last, but far from least, my wife Cheryl—for putting up with my movie madness.

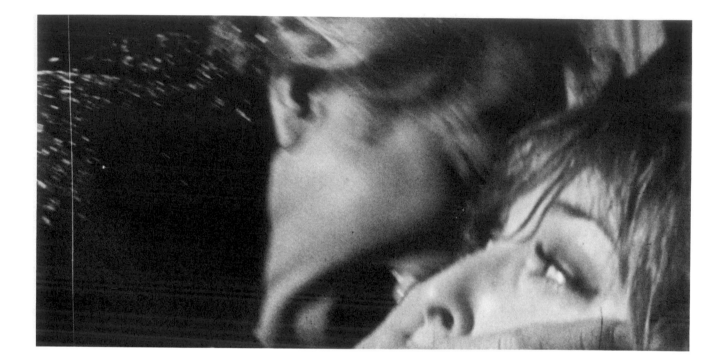

CONTENTS

THE MODERN
HORROR FILM

Hammer Films' *Horror of Dracula* (1958).

8

INTRODUCTION

It may be hard to believe—especially for young people—but there was a time not too long ago when there were very few opportunities to *read* about horror films. For a kid growing up in the Fifties—which is when I began tuning in to genre films—it was a real dry spell, believe me. Critical assessments of past or present horror films were as hard to come by as a unicorn. This is why the appearance of Forrest J. Ackerman's *Famous Monsters of Filmland*, the very first magazine devoted to exploring every facet of the horror, SF and fantasy film, caused such a stir—and proved to be such a formative experience. It literally opened the door for us teens with a thirst for knowledge about the genre's past and paved the way for the flood of horror film books and magazines that have come our way since—many of them written by "the children of *FM*."

In truth, *FM* was scarcely a scholarly publication. Nevertheless, it fostered a critical approach to assessing genre films that was quickly adopted by more serious writers. *FM* tended to take the genre films of the past a lot more seriously (albeit in its own pun-filled way) than those films that were being made at the time. Remarkably, this approach is still with us. And more remarkable still, even though more than thirty years have gone by since *FM* defined the list of the genre's past triumphs, very few writers since then have attempted to expand upon that list. It's almost as if criticism of the horror film got locked in some kind of time warp back in 1957, the year of *FM*'s debut, and has stubbornly refused to budge.

If you subscribe to the view that the passage of a considerable amount of time is necessary for judging the true merits of a film, there is something basically illogical about this phenomenon—for the fact is, at the present moment, we are as far away in time from the genre films of the Fifties and Sixties as *FM* was from the films of the Twenties and Thirties when it began venerating those older films as classics. Even allowing for the "broad view of time" approach, the genre must surely have contributed *something* of worth over the past thirty-odd years. And yet if you look at most books purporting to deal with the *best* horror movies ever made, you'll find very few post '57 films hailed as "classics." With only slight modification, the basic checklist is always the same.

This book takes a very different approach by exploring fifty *modern* horror films that, I feel, are equally deserving of classic status and boldly adding them to that list.

The arrival of *FM* coincided with the syndicated debut of Universal's legendary shockers of the Thirties and Forties on TV screens all across the country—and with the worldwide premiere of *The Curse of Frankenstein*, a seemingly minor but, as it turned out, revolutionary film made by a little known studio based in Britain called Hammer Film Productions Ltd. *Curse* launched the next great cycle of screen horror following the heyday of Universal and gave birth to the modern horror film. In terms of its influence on the evolution of the horror film, Hammer is second in importance only to Universal—though even today it seldom gets the recognition it deserves. Though clearly rooted in the genre's past—as most horror films are even to this day—Hammer's early productions beginning with *The Curse of Frankenstein* altered the look, style and, most importantly, approach to screen horror. This may be the main reason why so many critics stubbornly refuse to give the studio its proper due. Few people welcome change—and film critics tend to welcome it less than most. This is evident by how many critics are still tearing their hair and beating their breasts over the changes wrought to the genre—and to film in general—by the next, post-Hammer wave of graphically sexier and bloodier horror films typified by *Halloween* (1978) and *Friday the 13th* (1980). And yet without the emergence of a *Halloween* and a *Friday the 13th*, there might not have emerged David Cronenberg's superb remake of *The Fly* (1986), Stuart Gordon's hysterically original romp *The Re-Animator* (1985), or Frank LaLoggia's delicate and moving *Lady in White* (1988), a film whose effectiveness stems in large part from the director's attempt to alter the look, style and approach to screen horror yet again.

The fact that it influences change does not exclusively qualify a film for classic status, of course. The film must offer something more in the way of content, point of view and the relating of style to both. This is why you won't find *Halloween* or *Friday the 13th* included in this book on modern horror film classics. As influential as they may have been, my view is that they are fairly empty films that *don't* offer anything more. [You are certainly free to disagree with this view, as many will, I'm sure.] At the same time, I have included a good number of Hammer's early films precisely because they *do* offer something more—in some cases a whole lot more than previous writers have been willing to acknowledge.

No, not all of Hammer's output was great. But then, neither was all of Universal's. And yet most critical vol-

Ken Russell's *The Devils* (1971).

William Friedkin's *The Exorcist* (1973).

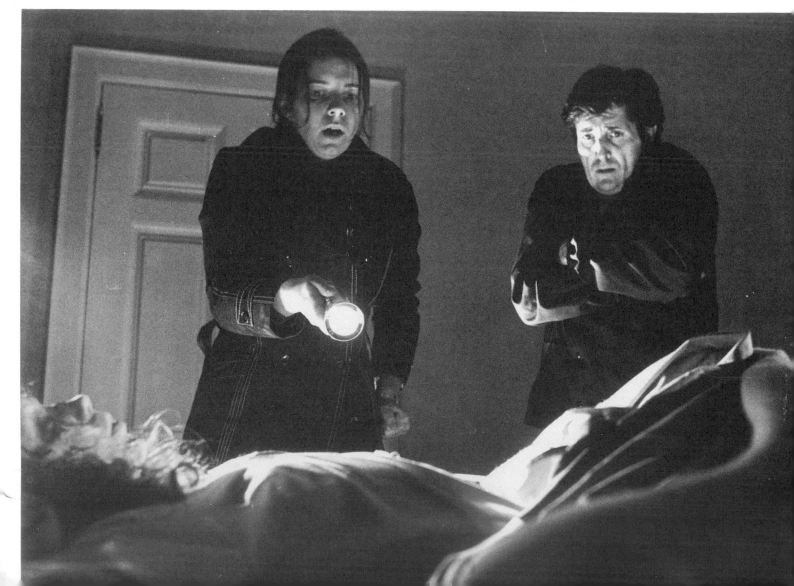

Stanley Kubrick's *The Shining* (1980).

umes have always given a lot more credence to even the least of Universal's shockers than they have to the best of Hammer's. Why is this? Well, nostalgia certainly has a lot to do with it, of course. But the more important reason, I think, is that the writers of these books have never been able to get past Hammer's graphic approach to mayhem (which certainly did break new ground, but was never all *that* graphic) to look beneath the surface. [They also tend to forget that even Universal's classic films—particularly *Frankenstein* (1931)—were initially greeted with a fair amount of disdain for being too ghoulish and violent as well.] This prejudice continues to exist and continues to cloud judgment of even newer films as well. My own view has always been that there is no virtue in subtlety unless the tale that is being told is best served by that approach (as ghost stories tend to be, for example—even though there are exceptions here as well.) Conversely, there is no vice in explicitly *showing* something if the story is best served by that approach— George Romero's *Night of the Living Dead* (1968), for example.

David Cronenberg's *The Fly* (1986).

No, Hammer's *The Curse of Frankenstein* may not be a better film than James Whale's *Frankenstein*. But in terms of what it says and how it goes about saying it, *Curse* is just as valid, unique—indeed *classic*—as Whale's grandly flamboyant out-of-the-closet horror/sex-capade. At the same time, Hammer's *Horror of Dracula* (1958) *is* better than Universal's *Dracula* (1931) in almost every way, bringing out far more nuances in Stoker's story (and offering some new ones) than the Lugosi version ever did. And I think it's high time somebody said so.

Having done that, however, I want quickly to add that my intention here is not to bolster the reputations of the fifty modern classics I've selected for this book by attempting to tarnish the reputations of the older ones. Nor do I suggest for a minute that film scholars should cease to explore these older films. As I wrote at the outset, study of the horror/SF and fantasy film genre is a fairly recent development. There are still a lot of aesthetic riches to be mined from the study of the elder classics—as well as films that are even older. For example, the horror/SF and fantasy films made before the coming of sound—an incalculably rich period in the genre's history—have not been explored in much detail at all.

But I'm also saying that it's time to look to the present as well.

And so, on the fifty films I've chosen as the classics of today—classics of the *modern* horror film. Some of the titles may be obvious, while others might possibly raise some eyebrows (I would be surprised, in fact, if they didn't.) Authors of books of this kind can't resist the temptation of being at least a bit unorthodox in their selection, of course—or playing a certain number of personal favorites either. I can only hope that whatever the film, I have managed to make a good case for it—a case that will inspire genre fans, whatever their age, to see or re-see these films, and inspire other writers to either re-evaluate their own opinions or take mine on. Debate is healthy. And it is for that very reason that while I firmly stand by the fifty films I've selected, I *don't* claim they are the only fifty. There are certainly others. Let's start giving them *all* their proper due.

—John McCarty
October 1989

Frank LaLoggia's *Lady in White* (1988).

Ken Russell's *The Lair of the White Worm* (1988).

THE CURSE OF FRANKENSTEIN (1957)

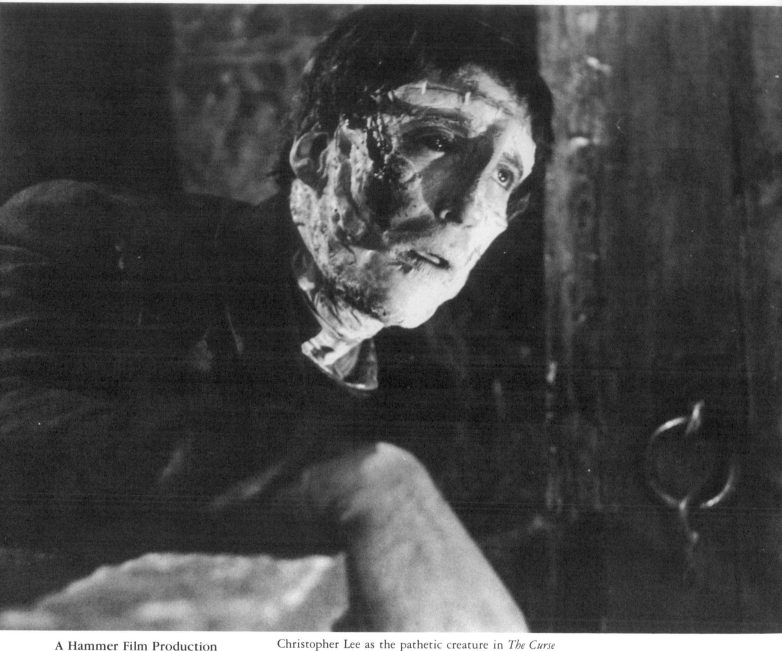

A Hammer Film Production
A Warner Bros. Release
Color/82 minutes

Christopher Lee as the pathetic creature in *The Curse of Frankenstein*. As if his facial features aren't bad enough, his right eye and cheek have been further destroyed by a bullet.

Credits

Director: Terence Fisher; *Producer:* Anthony Hinds; *Screenplay:* Jimmy Sangster, based on the novel *Frankenstein* by Mary Shelley; *Cinematographer:* Jack Asher; *Editor:* James Needs; *Music:* James Bernard; *Production Designer:* Bernard Robinson; *Videocassette source:* Warner Home Video.

Cast

Baron Victor Frankenstein: Peter Cushing; *Paul Krempe:* Robert Urquhart; *Elizabeth:* Hazel Court; *The Creature:* Christopher Lee; *Justine:* Valerie Gaunt; *Professor Bernstein:* Paul Hardmuth; *Aunt Sophie:* Noel Hood; *Young Victor:* Melvyn Hood; *Young Elizabeth:* Sally Walsh; *Grandfather:* Fred Johnson; *Priest:* Alex Gallier.

Hammer Film Productions Ltd. was the brainchild of British theatre chain owner Enrique Carreras and entrepeneur/comedian William Hinds, who joined forces in 1935 to form Exclusive Films, a domestic distribution outlet for films made by other companies. In 1948, Carreras and Hinds added a production arm to Exclusive and called it Hammer, after Hinds' stage name. Their goal was to produce a small number of their own pictures each year for domestic (U.K.) release via Exclusive. But they also sought to achieve a wider audience by linking up with a U.S. company that would not only co-finance their films, but distribute them to the lucrative American market. This was an unusual concept for a British company at the time, as most British films, even those financed by American companies with holdings in Britain, seldom achieved distribution outside the British Isles. The reverse was not true, however. Hollywood-made films not only got widespread release in Britain but often competed profitably for the same theater space. This obvious trade imbalance had kept the British film industry in a perpetual slump. To overcome this problem, Exclusive/Hammer made an arrangement in 1951 with Hollywood's Robert L. Lippert Productions to co-finance Hammer's productions and to release them through major American distributors in the U.S.

Hammer was crafty about choosing its material, often adapting popular British radio and television plays in order to guarantee a pre-sold domestic audience up front. This ploy didn't work as effectively abroad, however, as American audiences were unfamiliar with the works being adapted. To compensate, the company, possibly at Lippert's insistence, inserted at least one American "star" in the cast of its productions to soften the impact on American ears of "all those British accents." This policy continued for many years until the worldwide success of *The Curse of Frankenstein* clearly showed that "the yanks" were no longer needed.

Hammer did not stray too far from its past methodology when it launched its first outright horror film. It chose as the vehicle the most popular drama ever aired on British television: Nigel Kneale's science-fiction/horror thriller *The Quatermass Experiment*, which the BBC had broadcast as a six-part mini-series in the summer of 1953. For the starring role of Professor Quatermass, the studio selected American actor Brian Donlevy, a specialist in villainous roles—despite the

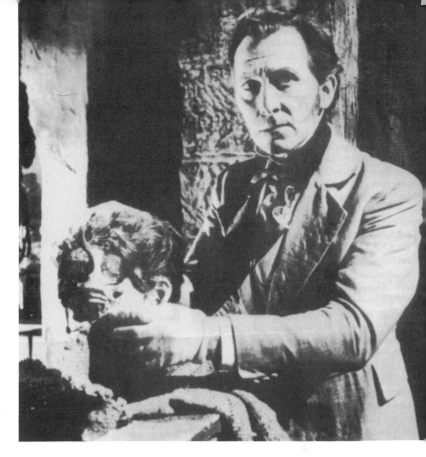

Frankenstein (Peter Cushing) discards the severed head of the body stolen from the gallows. Half eaten away by birds, the head is of no use to him—though compared to his later handiwork on the face of Christopher Lee, it doesn't look half bad.

With his customary lack of queasiness and aplomb, the obsessed Dr. Frankenstein (Peter Cushing) examines some grizzly offal.

Frankenstein (Peter Cushing) prepares to make some minor surgical adjustments as his creature (Christopher Lee) hangs about the laboratory.

Paul Krempe (Robert Urquhart) and his former pupil turned teacher, Baron Frankenstein (Peter Cushing), make a trip to the local gallows to steal a corpse for their experiment.

fact that Quatermass was a British scientist as well as the hero of the piece.

Production began at Hammer's sprawling manor house studio at Bray in Maidenhead near Windsor in late 1954, and the film was released in Britain the following year. Its instant success there was repeated when the film reached American shores in the summer of 1956. For the American release, however, the title was changed to the more lurid *The Creeping Unknown* and a few minutes of footage (mostly exposition) was trimmed from the print.

With *The Quatermass Experiment*, part of the key "Hammer team" began to form. Anthony Hinds, son of William Hinds, served as the film's producer—a chore he'd already handled on numerous other occasions almost from the studio's inception. An aspiring screenwriter, he would later achieve his goal by writing many future Hammer Horrors under his pseudonym John Elder. It was Hinds who hired a young composer named

James Bernard, fresh from BBC radio, to write the film's nerve-jangling music score. Bernard had never composed for the screen before and was paid just £100 for his score, which remains one of the film's most effective ingredients. Bernard's use of strings and percussion to create a powerful and brooding sense of Gothic atmosphere in this film and many subsequent Hammer Horrors would forever link him with the studio in the minds of fans.

For many, *The Quatermass Experiment* now seems quite dated. Surely, its subject—the invasion of earth by an alien intelligence capable of absorbing the energy of other life forms—has been treated many times since on the screen. In fact, it wasn't new when Nigel Kneale first tackled it for the BBC. But it wasn't the story or subject of the film that was important, but rather the style in which they were approached. This was Hammer's main contribution to the evolution of the modern horror film (and to British cinema as well): a no-

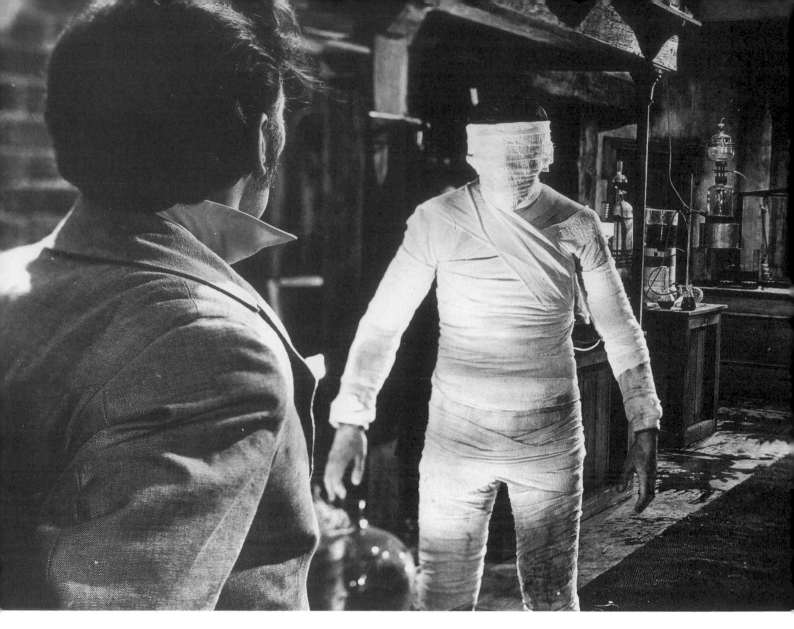

nonsense, visceral approach to moviemaking that stood in direct contrast to the almost stately style of most British movies (including Hammer's) up to that time.

With its unnerving, discordant score, brooding black and white photography that was, by turns, Gothic in atmosphere yet documentary in look, and naturalistic acting (reminiscent of Howard Hawks' *The Thing*), *The Quatermass Experiment* went straight for the gut. Brusque, brash and supremely self-confident, Donlevy's Quatermass steamrolls his way through the movie just as Hammer's *The Quatermass Experiment* steamrolled its way into theaters and British film history. As the film ends and the alien creature that returned astronaut Victor Carroon (Richard Wordsworth) has become smolders, dead inside Westminster Abbey, Donlevy, without pause for reflection, goes right back to work to start again. The film concludes with his next Q rocket taking off from the pad as the end title "A Hammer Production" is superimposed. There was no mistaking the message. Hammer, like Quatermass, was not about to go away. Hammer Horror had been launched.

Frankenstein (Peter Cushing) confronts the animated corpse of his creature (Christopher Lee) for the first time.

The overwhelming box office success of *The Quatermass Experiment* prompted Hammer to begin preparing a series of films with science-fiction/horror themes. These included a sequel to the first Quatermass film, *Quatermass II,* also based on a BBC serial by Nigel Kneale; *X the Unknown*, an original screenplay about a radioactive monster by longtime Hammer production manager-turned-writer Jimmy Sangster; and a remake of *Frankenstein*, also written by Sangster. Producer Anthony Hinds, director Terence Fisher and others connected with *The Curse of Frankenstein* have always maintained that they did not envision the project as anything special—it was just one of a series of films they were to make. And yet, if that was the case, why was the decision made to film *Curse* in color when Hammer's entire output up to that time had been shot in less expensive black and white? Indeed, *Quatermass*

II and *X the Unknown*, both made after *Curse*, were shot in black and white as well. Frankly, I think the decision to make the film in color, in period, and with an all-British cast indicates that Hammer *was* aiming at something special—they just didn't know if they would achieve it.

When *Curse* was finished, it was rushed to the States and screened for executives at Warner Bros.—another unusual move as Warners, one of Hollywood's leading studios, had never picked up a Hammer film before. Though it's been rumored that Jack Warner personally hated the film, his company agreed that the film had hot box office potential and acquired it for release in the summer of 1957. Despite mediocre reviews in the States and positively excoriating ones in the U.K. (the *London Observer* critic, on its release there in May, termed it, "...one of the half dozen most repulsive films I have ever seen..."), *The Curse of Frankenstein* outperformed everyone's expectations netting a cool $5 million worldwide (the film had cost roughly £160,000 to make.)

Today's horror fans tend to consider *The Curse of Frankenstein* rather tame stuff. The reality is: it always was—one U.S. critic even called it "tame stuff" in his review at the time. Yes, the film did show a bit more gore (as well as more cleavage) than filmgoers were used to seeing, but by no means was the film heavily laden with special effects—frankly, Hammer couldn't have afforded them. Nevertheless, *The Curse of Frankenstein* was a "turning point" film. Director Terence Fisher's decision not to avert the camera's eye as Dr. Frankenstein fondled various brains, eyeballs and severed hands was a watershed one. It not only shocked audiences at the time, but set the basic ground rules for all modern horror films to come.

The Curse of Frankenstein continues to endure not so much because of its bloody set pieces (which are minimal), but because of its updating of the Gothic Romance formula, cool style, flamboyant almost experimental use of color, and significant clarification and broadening of the Frankenstein theme. There was a reason for this. Hammer had initially intended the film to be an outright remake of the 1931 James Whale classic starring Boris Karloff. Universal, the owners of that film's copyright, had different ideas, however. Universal's *Frankenstein* still boasted considerable earning power, not only from its frequent theatrical reissues, but because it was about to be released to local television stations in the U.S. as part of a syndicated movie package called "Shock Theatre." Universal was not about to stand by and watch its profits diluted by this new, color "remake." Hammer was promptly notified by Universal's lawyers that should *The Curse of Frankenstein* lift any elements from the 1931 film—up to and including duplication of the Jack Pierce/Boris Karloff make-up—the studio would sue. Out of legal necessity, Hammer was compelled to look elsewhere for inspiration—and so it returned to the original Mary Shelley novel, which, being in the public domain, was fair game.

The fortuitous result was that Jimmy Sangster's screenplay was a lot more faithful to the theme and spirit (if not the letter) of Shelley's novel than Whale's film had been. In it, Christopher Lee's hapless creature, unlike Boris Karloff's sympathetic monster, is virtually reduced to a supporting role—in fact, the film is half over before he makes his first shambling appearance. Unlike Whale's film and its various sequels, Hammer's *The Curse of Frankenstein* is not about the creature—a mindless, motiveless humanoid thing that Christopher Lee has termed "a walking road accident;" it's about the Baron himself. This is fully in keeping with Shelley's novel, which was subtitled "A Modern Prometheus." The film, however, pushes the allegory into unsettling territory—for while the legendary Prometheus stole fire from the gods for the benefit of mankind, the motivations of Hammer's new Baron are not so humanistic. "Think of the lives we'll save," Krempe announces following the success of their initial experiment at animating a dead dog. The Baron, however, is little interested in the betterment of mankind. His single-minded purpose is not just to steal the secrets of the gods, but to *become* God by creating a man in his own image (which, in the sequel, *The Revenge of Frankenstein*, he will literally succeed in doing.)

Played to icy perfection by Peter Cushing (then a popular BBC television star who had actively sought the role of Dr. Frankenstein), Hammer's brand new Baron was something genre films hadn't seen before. No simple mad scientist, he is the ultimate narcissist—cold, ruthless, remorseless—and a murderer to boot. *He* is the monster of the film—not the pitiable, disfigured hulk played by Christopher Lee.

CURSE OF THE DEMON (1958)

(A.k.a. *Night of the Demon* in U.K.)
A Sabre Film Production Ltd.
A Columbia Pictures Release
B&W 82 minutes (U.S.); 95 minutes (U.K.)

The ferocious demon created for the film by production designer Ken Adam who would later design most of the James Bond films.

Credits

Director: Jacques Tourneur; *Producer:* Frank Bevis; *Screenplay:* Charles Bennett and Hal E. Chester based on *Casting the Runes* by M.R. James; *Cinematographer:* Ted Scaife; *Editor:* Michael Gordon; *Music:* Clifton Parker; *Production Designer:* Ken Adam; *Videocassette source:* RCA/Columbia Home Video [note: even though the video bears the U.S. title, it is the full length British print.]

Cast

Dr. John Holden: Dana Andrews; *Joanna Harrington:* Peggy Cummins; *Dr. Julian Karswell:* Niall MacGinnis; *Professor Harrington:* Maurice Denham; *Mrs. Karswell:* Athene Seyler; *Professor Mark O'Brien:* Liam Redmond; *Mr. Meek:* Reginald Beckwith; *Rand Hobart:* Brian Wilde.

In the hands of Jacques Tourneur, the use of understatement as the most effective method of sending chills up an audience's collective spine reached a sort of apotheosis. No one ever succeeded in scaring filmgoers so thoroughly and yet with such subtle sleight-of-hand as Tourneur. Even today, his masterpieces of the macabre retain all of their magic as well as much of their power to lift viewers off their chairs—and none more so than *Curse of the Demon*.

Tourneur's singular status derives from his aesthetic conviction that the only way to portray supernatural events on the screen was to keep as straight a face as possible and to show as little as you could get away with. Other giants of the genre both before and since have eschewed such an approach with equal effectiveness, but for Tourneur this approach was mandatory and as a result, his work remains not only distinctive, but, in many ways, unsurpassed.

Though born in France, Jacques Tourneur grew up in the U.S. where his famous father, Maurice Tourneur directed films for both Paramount and MGM. In 1926, Maurice Tourneur left Hollywood and sailed for France following a creative dispute with studio executives over a film he was to make based on Jules Verne's science-fiction classic, *Mysterious Island*. He remained in France making films until his retirement in 1948. He died in 1961.

It was in France where Jacques Tourneur began his own film career, starting out as an editor for his father. In 1932, he directed his first feature, *Tout Ca Ne Vaut Pas L'Amour* with Jean Gabin. He directed three more

Dr. Karswell (Niall MacGinnis) and Dr. Holden (Dana Andrews) have a friendly chat during a Halloween party Karswell is giving for the neighborhood children.

films in France before striking out for Hollywood. MGM hired him to do second unit work. There, he met Val Lewton.

Lewton had come to MGM as a writer and publicist, but he also served as a unit producer. When MGM launched its big budget production of *A Tale of Two Cities* (1935), Lewton was assigned to produce the storming of the Bastille sequence. Jacques Tourneur was appointed his second-unit director and they became close friends. In the next few years, Tourneur rose from second units to directing short subjects. In 1939, he made his first American feature, *They All Came Out*, a crime melodrama. Soon after, Val Lewton was put under contract by RKO to produce a series of low budget films and he immediately called upon Tourneur to direct the first one, *Cat People* (1942).

Holden (Dana Andrews) greets Joanna Harrington's (Peggy Cummins) admonitions with his customary skepticism.

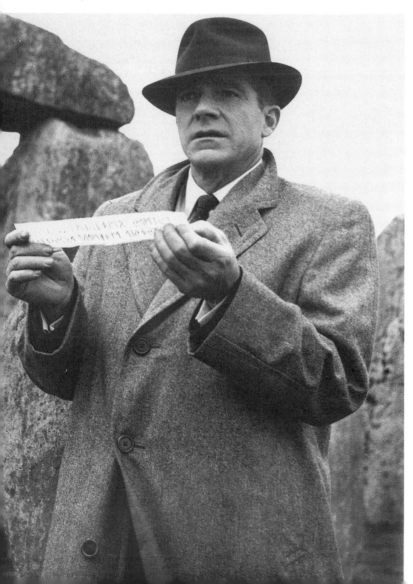

Confronted by the demon in the woods outside Karswell's estate—Holden (Dana Andrews) is forced to believe his own eyes—though later, he will attribute the pheonomenon to auto-suggestion.

Holden (Dana Andrews) matches the inscription on the parchment passed to him in secret by Dr. Karswell against similar writings on the runes at Stonehenge.

The now-famous style of *Cat People*, with its emphasis on atmosphere and understatement, was a far more subtle approach to the genre than audiences who had been weaned on *Frankenstein* (1931) and *Dracula* (1931) were used to seeing. Its innovation has largely been attributed to Lewton, and rightfully so. But comparisons to those Lewton films made by other directors and to films made by Tourneur in later years without Lewton reveal that the style and substance of *Cat People* belong very much to Tourneur as well.

Tautly written by DeWitt Bodeen from an idea by Lewton and Tourneur, *Cat People* is the story of a girl (Simone Simon) who weds a young draftsman (Kent Smith), then refuses to consummate their marriage because of a medieval curse condemning her to turn into a leopard if her passions are aroused. Smith seeks the help of a psychiatrist (Tom Conway) but to little avail and eventually looks for solace in the arms of a co-worker (Jane Randolph). When they fall in love, Simon's jealousy is aroused, she turns into a cat and attacks Randolph.

It is important to note that when Smith demands an explanation as to why Simon refuses to consummate their marriage, she hides nothing. She reveals her fears of what would happen should they go to bed together. At the end of the film, Smith remarks, "She never lied to us." This line characterizes not only Simon, but the "villains" in Tourneur's other macabre films as well.

Curse of the Demon is built upon this very concept. Dr. Karswell, a character patterned loosely after Aleister Crowley, is a professor of the black arts, who has dedicated his life to proving that supernatural forces exist. His opponent, Dr. Holden, a stubborn, pragmatic professor of occult sciences who has perversely dedicated his life to discrediting the very subject of which he is an expert, is Karswell's mirror image. Their contest of wills is fascinating to watch.

Like Simone Simon, Karswell lays all his cards out on the table and not until Holden starts dealing with Karswell on the black magician's own terms is he able to stem the supernatural tide—in fact, to survive, he even resorts to black magic himself. If Holden is *Demon's* hero, he is, like Kent Smith, a destructive one. Holden is destructive because of his almost pathological skepticism. His determination to prove that he isn't "a superstitious sucker like the rest of humanity" is built upon a profound negativism. The result: two deaths, a kidnapping, a medium's near mental collapse, and a close call with death for Holden as well.

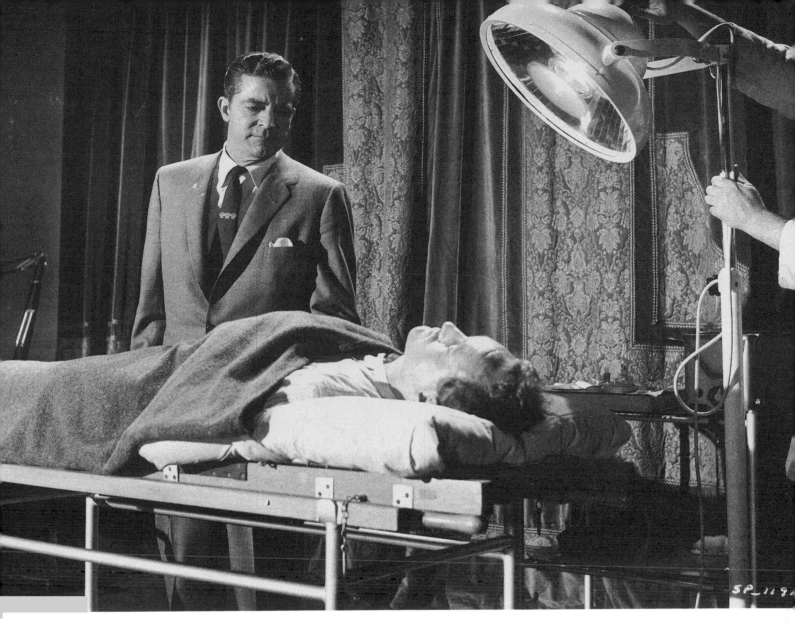

SP_1691

Revelations drawn from the hypnotized Hobart (Brian Wilde) finally convince Holden (Dana Andrews) that supernatural forces are indeed at work.

Similarly, if Karswell is a villain, he is, like Simone Simon, a sympathetic one. When he initially fails to convince Professor Harrington of his occult powers, he conjurs up a demon to demonstrate them, but is willing to call it off when Harrington finally gives in—except that by then it is too late. The demon must have its victim. Every effort is made to humanize Karswell, to turn him into a three dimensional, non horror-movie-type villain, and his personality and motivations are very carefully sketched in.

Karswell's basic motivation is a thirst for recognition, then to be left alone. And he will let no one stand in the way of achieving that goal, not even his own mother, whom he has turned into a doting slave. At one point, she rebels. On the sly, she takes Holden to a medium, Mr. Meek, who, in a trance, speaks in Harrington's voice, relating the horrific events that led to his death. Holden storms out of the seance, convinced the affair is a sham arranged by Mrs. Karswell to make him cease his professional attacks on her son. She pursues him into

23

Karswell (Niall MacGinnis) prepares to meet his grizzly fate at the hands of the demon.

the street, but Holden drives off before she can catch him, and she finds herself chillingly reprimanded by her son's off-screen voice—a superb touch used more than once to suggest Karswell's magic powers. The camera then cuts to Karswell sitting in his car and she wilts before him.

As *Curse of the Demon* begins, a narrator tells us that, "…evil, supernatural creatures *do* exist in a world of darkness." Moments later, we see the demon rising out of the trees to claim Professor Harrington. Tourneur said that showing the demon at the beginning of the film was a mistake, and he was right. It should have been saved for the fiery climax when Karswell becomes its victim. The same criticism applies to a scene where Holden breaks into Karswell's home and is attacked by a housecat that suddenly transforms into a leopard. A similar scene in *Cat People,* where Tom Conway kisses Simone Simon, arouses her passion, and does battle in silhouette with whatever she has become, is subtler and immeasurably more effective. Typical of Tourneur's passion for authenticity, the demon, which is probably the most fearsome beast ever created for a film, was patterned by designer Ken Adam (later of the James Bond films) on medieval woodcuts over 400 years old.

Though flawed, *Curse of the Demon*'s overall impact is more than satisfactory. Its salient image is that of darkness probed but never totally illuminated, either by the headlights of a car or the scope of man's knowledge. The Tourneurian theme is clear: to see in the dark, one must first turn out the lights.

As the demand for a more graphic approach to horror on the screen increased in the Sixties and Seventies, Tourneur's subtle approach held less and less favor with producers. To work, he turned to television, a medium he despised. "It's against everything I believe in," he told Charles Higham and Joel Greenberg in their book *The Celluloid Muse.* "If you don't bring some of your individuality and some of your experience to bear on a subject, you don't get more than a mechanical result." His only really happy experience in the medium, he told Higham and Greenberg, was a Richard Matheson episode he directed for *The Twilight Zone.* Titled "Night Call," it starred Gladys Cooper as an aging spinster who receives a series of late-night phone calls from her long dead lover. In his book *The Twilight Zone Companion,* Mark Scott Zicree termed the episode "a wonderfully creepy tale, a triumph of atmosphere in which the horror grows ever so slowly, bit by bit." In other words, pure Jacques Tourneur.

Jacques Tourneur died in 1977.

HORROR OF DRACULA (1958)

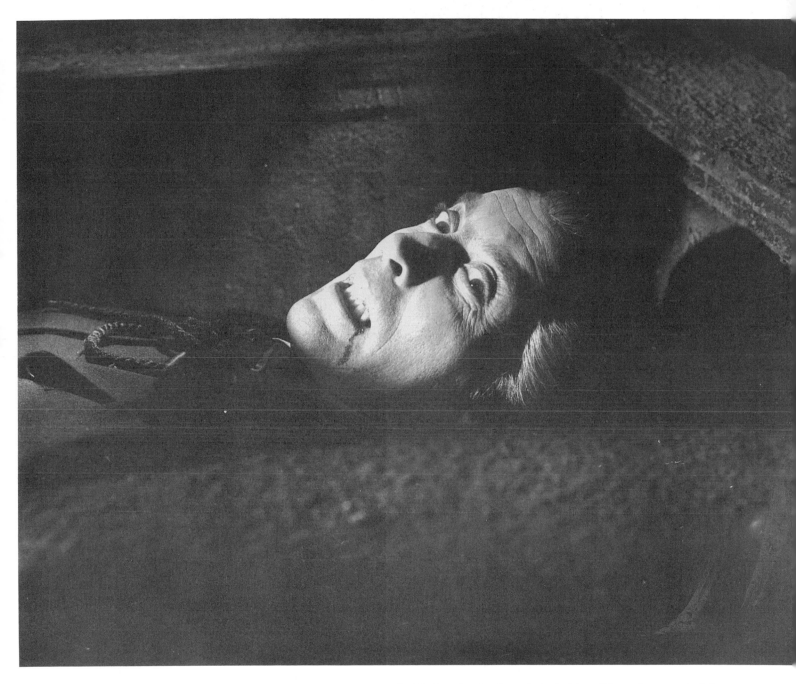

A Hammer Film Production
A Universal-International Release
Color/82 minutes

Dracula (Christopher Lee) awakens in his coffin at the sound of the vampire woman's screams.

Credits

Director: Terence Fisher; *Producer:* Anthony Hinds; *Screenplay:* Jimmy Sangster, based on the novel *Dracula* by Bram Stoker; *Cinematographer:* Jack Asher; *Editor:* Bill Lenny; *Music:* James Bernard; *Production Designer:* Bernard Robinson; *Videocassette source:* Warner Home Video.

Cast

Dr. Van Helsing: Peter Cushing; *Count Dracula:* Christopher Lee; *Arthur Holmwood:* Michael Gough; *Mina Holmwood:* Melissa Stribling; *Lucy Holmwood:* Carol Marsh; *Jonathan Harker:* John Van Eyssen; *Gerda:* Olga Dickie; *Vampire Woman:* Valerie Gaunt; *Undertaker:* Miles Malleson; *Dr. Seward:* Charles Lloyd Pack; *Tanya:* Janina Faye.

The success around the world of *The Curse of Frankenstein* did not go unnoticed by Hollywood. Hammer, which once had to go shopping for American co-financing deals, now had the major studios banging on its door. Agreements were quickly signed to produce a number of pictures each year for Columbia, Universal and United Artists—though curiously not Warner Bros., who, despite the phenomenal success of *Curse*, did not ask for a sequel. It was made instead for Columbia.

Hammer's first film for Universal (then Universal-International) was *Horror of Dracula* (*Dracula* in the U.K.). Hammer chief James Carreras had no intention of playing against a winning hand and recruited virtually the same team that had made *Curse* to bring *Dracula* to the screen. The film was to be made in color and was allotted a larger budget—though not much larger, about £200,000.

Production began at Bray shortly after the first of the new year (1958) and was concluded twenty-five days later. Released in the U.K. that spring, *Dracula* was treated even more harshly by the press ["This film disgusts the mind and repels the senses," said the *London Daily Worker*] than its predecessor had been—for this new Hammer Horror was by far the gorier and more intense one. Plus, it had another ingredient that turned critics off: sex. Unlike the Tod Browning/Bela Lugosi *Dracula*, which critics insisted on comparing the new film to—despite the fact that director Terence Fisher had publicly announced that he had neither sought to duplicate nor draw upon the earlier film in any way—Christopher Lee's Dracula exuded a blatant sexual charm. And the metaphor of giving in to vampirism as a release of sexual repression (so obvious in Stoker's book but quite muted in the Lugosi film) was brought clearly to the fore.

When it was released in the U.S. a few months later, American critics were more tolerant and on the whole more appreciative, though the inclination to compare the new film to the Lugosi version [sometimes un-

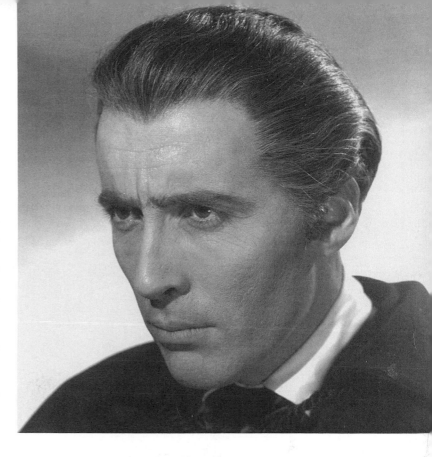

Christopher Lee's reinterpretated Dracula exudes a blatant sexual presence.

favorably] was still present. I suppose this was inevitable. Lugosi was then firmly identified in the minds of a whole generation of filmgoers as *the* Dracula because, until Lee's appearance, no one else had attempted the role in an all-out version of the Stoker story. Ironically, the same thing would happen to Frank Langella twenty years later when he assumed the role in an even more erotic version of *Dracula* and was dismissed by many critics and fans as not being on a par with Christopher Lee.

With filmgoers, however, *Horror of Dracula* was warmly welcomed and not only repeated the success of *Curse* around the world, but surpassed it. The film firmly established the Gothic Horror formula as sketched out in *Curse* as the studio's strong suit and forever altered the manner in which vampirism would be treated as a subject on the screen. After *Horror of Dracula*, there was no longer any question as to what the image of the predatory, long dead Count hunkering over the throats of his all-too-willing victims actually symbolized.

But there was more to Hammer's version of *Dracula* than sexual innuendo and graphic violence. In addition to the extra shadings given the character of Dracula and the nature of his menace, Jimmy Sangster's screenplay, Terence Fisher's direction, and, especially, Peter Cushing's performance as Van Helsing, Dracula's obsessive nemesis, brought out heretofore untapped resonances in that character as well. In most screen versions of Stoker's book (indeed, in the book itself), Van Helsing is portrayed as an aging, kindly Dutch physician whose knowledge of the undead comes in very handy when the time arrives to bring the story to a close. In *Horror of Dracula*, however, Van Helsing assumes a dominant role—and an unsettling one.

Terence Fisher later said of the character: "An individual who never goes out without his hammer and stake is hardly a sensitive soul." I'd put it even stronger.

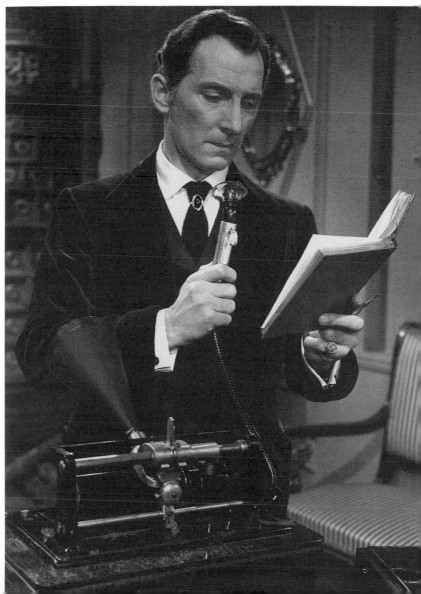

Van Helsing (Peter Cushing) reads a portion of Jonathan Harker's journal into a 19th century dictaphone (the relic was borrowed from a British museum). Moments later, his confounded servant asks him who he was talking to and Van Helsing answers, "I was talking to myself." Van Helsing probably does this often—even without a dictaphone—as he is obviously not "all there."

Dracula rots away in the sunlight.

6820-31

It is Van Helsing, much like Dr. Frankenstein, who is the real villain of the piece. [The Count, much like Frankenstein's creature, has no free will and acts mainly out of instinct.] In most versions of the story (as in the book), Dracula leaves Transylvania in search of new victims. In *Horror of Dracula,* he leaves because his domain has been intruded upon and his "bride" destroyed by Van Helsing's surrogate, Jonathan Harker. He seeks out Lucy to replace her and, when she too is destroyed (by Van Helsing) turns his teeth on Mina, sealing his own doom. Fisher called the film "nothing more nor less than a love story." That indeed it is—from Dracula's point of view. From Van Helsing's, however, it is a hate story. And nowhere is this subtext more clearly presented than in the much ballyhooed—and criticized—sequence where Van Helsing puts the stake to the undead Lucy. He doesn't just drive the stake in. He *pounds* it home with an almost ghoulish zeal as blood gushes from the screaming girl's collapsed chest. This sequence had a visceral effect on audiences that was unparalleled at the time. And it holds its own even today in the age of Splatter.

The blood and gore (which is not nearly so abundant as most people tend to recall) are not really what's important about the scene, however. It's the zealous manner in which Van Helsing goes about his job—which Fisher takes great pains to contrast with the reaction of Lucy's distraught brother, Arthur Holmwood, who is also present in the scene. As Lucy writhes and screams and Van Helsing pounds away, Holmwood covers his ears, then doubles over against the wall, sickened by the hideous act—even though the act's aim is purification. Not so Van Helsing, whose all consuming passion and fanatical purpose is "to rid the world of this unspeakable evil." Van Helsing is a madman, but one whose madness is just barely concealed by Cushing's inherently warm personality. The obsessive vampire hunter flinches only twice in the film—once when he discovers that his friend Harker has become a vampire (he should flinch as it was he who sent the ill-prepared Harker to his doom in the first place) and again when he traps Dracula and watches as the benighted nobleman crumbles to dust in the sunlight. And yet, as the film ends, we sense not a feeling of triumph on Van Helsing's part, but one of emptiness. For what will he do next—now that his disagreeable sense of purpose has been gruesomely and finally fulfilled?

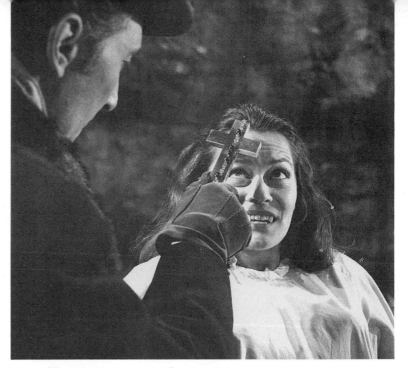

The vampire woman after Jonathan gets the better of her. Alas, he will prove a lesser match for Dracula.

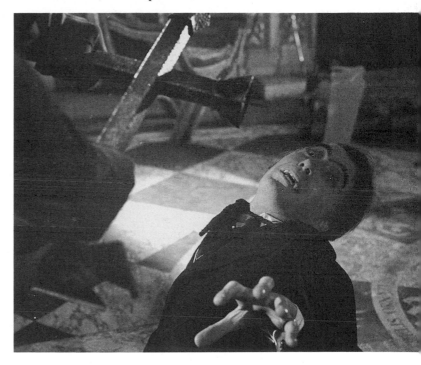

Van Helsing traps Dracula in the sunlight with a pair of candle holders formed into a cross. Note the look of pure terror on the Count's face as he realizes the end is near.

Just about everyone—even the film's one-time detractors—now tend to agree that with *Horror of Dracula,* Hammer achieved a classic. Some even rank it as one of the best British films of the past thirty years. One thing is for sure, it remains, as of this writing, the most ingenious big screen reworking of Stoker's antiquated novel so far—and certainly one of the most sumptuous.

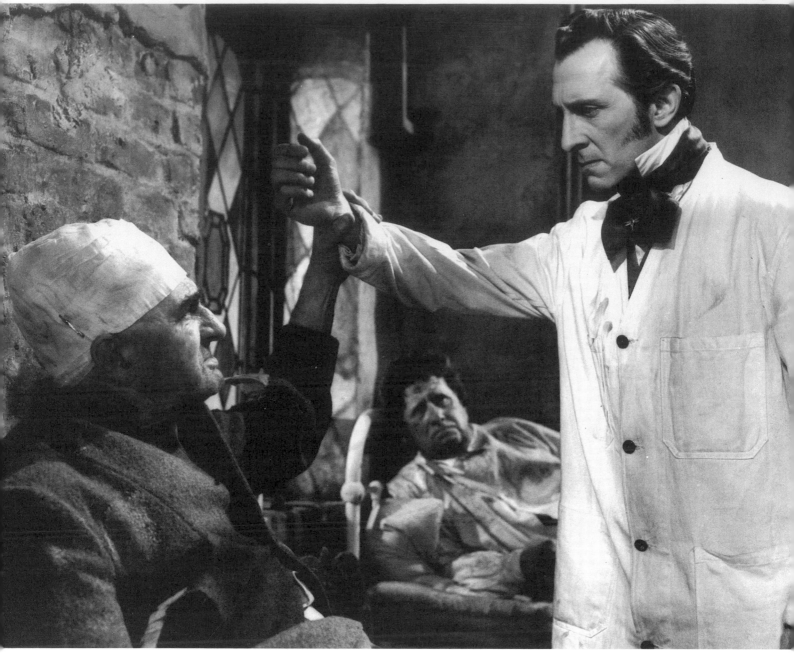

Baron Frankenstein (Peter Cushing) pays a visit to his clinic for the poor.

A Hammer Film Production
A Columbia Pictures Release
Color/89 minutes

Credits

Director: Terence Fisher; *Producer:* Anthony Hinds; *Screenplay:* Jimmy Sangster (with additional dialogue by Hurford James); *Cinematographer:* Jack Asher; *Editor:* Alfred Cox; *Music:* Leonard Salzedo; *Production Designer:* Bernard Robinson; *Videocassette source:* Unavailable.

Cast

Dr. Stein: Peter Cushing; *Dr. Hans Kleve:* Francis Matthews; *Margaret Konrad:* Eunice Gayson; *Karl #1:* Oscar Quitak; *Karl #2:* Michael Gwynn; *Janitor:* Richard Wordsworth; *Graverobbers:* Michael Ripper and Lionel Jeffries; *Medical Council President:* Charles Lloyd Pack; *Inspector:* John Stuart; *Lab Caretaker:* George Woodbridge; *Patient:* Michael Mulcaster.

Not only having satisfied the demands of Universal's lawyers but also having created a worldwide box office sensation with its own version of *Frankenstein*, Hammer immediately began thinking about a sequel. The monster played by Christopher Lee in the first film was dead and there was never any intention of trying to resurrect him as the Universal films had done with the Boris Karloff character. Hammer had intentionally established the Baron as the pivotal figure around whom any potential series would form—and as he was the monster anyway, the studio really had the best of both worlds.

Writer Jimmy Sangster was quickly asked to devise a new creature even more horrible than the first. His solution was ingenious. Thinking about what scared him most, he struck upon the idea of making the new creature a cannibal. Everyone at Hammer agreed that this concept was precisely right. One of the major hurdlcs the studio had to overcome in the first film was

Frankenstein (Peter Cushing) admonishes the Meddlesome Margaret Konrad (Eunice Gayson), who is helping out as a nurse, while the even more meddlesome janitor (Richard Wordsworth) looks on.

Frankenstein (Peter Cushing) and Dr. Kleve (Francis Matthews) prepare to transplant the brain of the misshapen Karl (Oscar Quitak) into a brand new body.

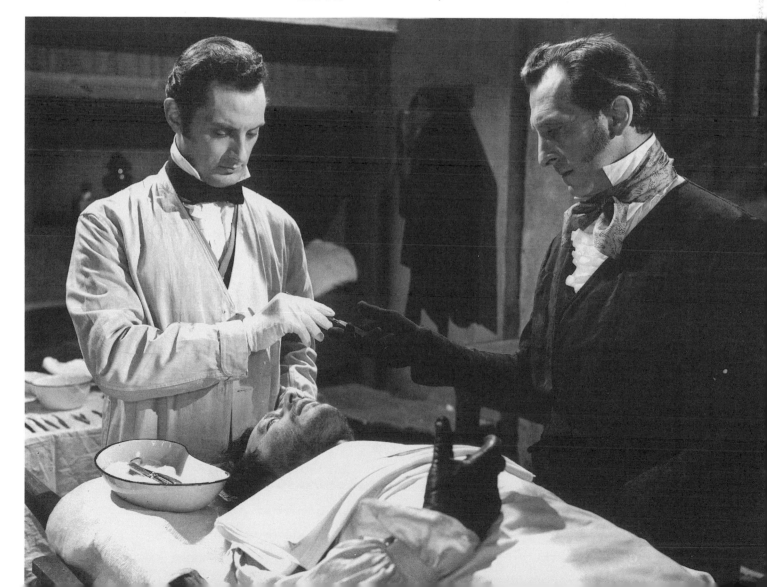

The suspicious janitor (Richard Wordsworth) observes Frankenstein's (Peter Cushing) secret the recovering Karl (Michael Gwynn) in a special room.

concocting a makeup for the creature totally unlike Karloff's. Sangster's concept eliminated this hassle in the sequel. The new monster wouldn't need a horrible makeup as its flesh-eating deeds would prove unsettling enough.

Like *The Bride of Frankenstein*, James Whale's own follow-up to *Frankenstein*, Hammer's sequel begins right where the first film left off. As a result, it, like *Bride*, isn't really a sequel at all so much as a full-blown second and final act. At the conclusion of *The Curse of Frankenstein,* the Baron is headed for the guillotine to be executed for his crimes. *Revenge* begins with the execution itself, adding a twist. With the help of a confederate, Karl, a misshapen fellow whom the Baron has promised a new body for his assistance, Frankenstein arranges for the priest delivering the last rites to be beheaded in his place. The film then skips forward

three years. The Baron, now calling himself Dr. Stein, has established a successful practice in another city, where he administers to the rich and poor alike. The rich provide him with the funds to continue his work while the poor provide him with the body parts to create his new creature. This situation offers an interesting metaphor, for, in a sense, the Baron—like the cannibal creature to which he is about to give life— feeds off his clientele (in the case of the poor, quite literally). Once again, the link between Frankenstein and his monster—that, in fact, he *is* the monster—is quickly established. By the end of the film, this theme will take an ingenious turn.

The Baron is recognized by another of the city's physicians, Dr. Kleve. In exchange for his silence, he persuades the Baron to take him on as an assistant. Though this amounts to blackmail, Kleve is not portrayed as an unsavory character—rather, he serves as an extension of the Paul Krempe character in *Curse*. He thirsts for knowledge so that he may better the lot of mankind. Like Krempe, he even says so. As before, the Baron is mum on the matter—for his goals are far more self-oriented. Despite his lofty ideals, however, Kleve is not above turning a blind eye to what's being done to achieve them—namely, that the poor and helpless are literally being mutilated for their body parts.

The operation proves a success. Without a hitch, the brain of the misshapen Karl is transplanted into the skull of Karl #2, a strapping, healthy young man. The original Karl's body is preserved with embalming fluid as it's the Baron's aim to give before-and-after demonstrations of his achievement when it becomes time to let the world know of his genius. In the interim, Kleve discovers that a lab monkey on whom a similar transplant operation was performed has turned cannibal, devouring its mate. He expresses his concern but the Baron says not to worry—as long as Karl gets sufficient rest and suffers no accidental blows to the head (as the monkey had) before recovery is complete, he will not turn into a cannibal.

Kleve mistakenly informs the convalescing Karl that he'll soon be the toast of all Europe. This disturbs Karl, for all his life he'd been stared at as a freak. He breaks free, returns to the lab and burns his old body. But before Karl can get away, the thug-like caretaker who keeps an eye on the place mistakes him for a burglar and breaks a chair over his head. Karl kills him and flees. Hungry, he soon murders a young girl for her flesh.

Degenerating fast (his new body soon becomes as twisted as his old one), the pitiable Karl breaks into an elegant dinner party that the Baron has also intruded upon and reveals his mentor's true identity ("Help me, Frankenstein!") before collapsing into his arms and dying. Later, the Baron returns to his clinic for the poor and is beaten to a pulp by the vengeful patients whose bodies he has destroyed. Kleve spirits him off to the lab and transplants the man's brain into a new body the Baron had been stitching together—a body whose face the Baron has sculpted entirely in his own image. The town officials arrive to arrest the notorious Frankenstein, but Kleve informs them that the Baron has expired from his wounds. In an epilogue, however, the scene shifts to London where Frankenstein, ably assisted by Kleve, has set up a new practice under the name Dr. Franck. In effect—and with great irony—the Baron has quite literally become his own creation. End of story.

Karl (Michael Gwynn) returns to the lab to find and burn his old body.

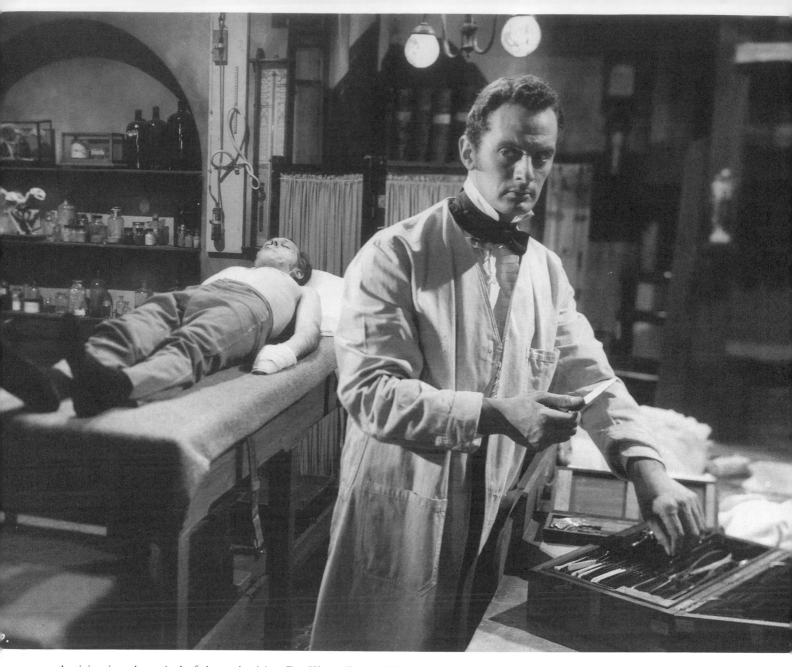

Anticipating the arrival of the authorities, Dr. Kleve (Francis Matthews knows he must act quickly if he is to save the life of the mortally wounded Dr. Frankenstein (Peter Cushing, on table).

As dramatically and thematically satisfying as this conclusion was, it also presented a problem, however. Like its predecessor, *The Revenge of Frankenstein* was a solid box office hit worldwide. Hammer was not about to kill the golden goose by laying the Baron to rest. And yet, with *Revenge*, Sangster and director Terence Fisher had taken the story as far as it needed to go. Sangster refused even to attempt writing another sequel ("The story's been done to death," he still maintains), though in 1970 he would return to the story, if only to parody it, with his amusing *The Horror of Frankenstein.*

Hammer's solution was to let a number of years go by and then, like the Baron himself, begin entirely anew. *The Evil of Frankenstein* (1964), written by John Elder

(Anthony Hinds) and directed by Freddie Francis, doesn't even attempt to take up where *Revenge* left off; instead, it pretends that the two earlier films never existed. In it, the Baron (played again by Peter Cushing, but with far less overt villainy) thaws out his original monster (Kiwi Kingston, whose makeup resembles Karloff's—apparently, as the film was made for Universal, that studio's lawyers had become far more lenient in the ensuing years). Then, in a flashback that bears no relationship to what happened either in *Curse* or *Revenge,* he recounts how his nefarious medical career all began. Though by no means a good film, *The Evil of Frankenstein* did prove one thing—that it *is* possible to have one's cake and eat it too.

THE MUMMY (1959)

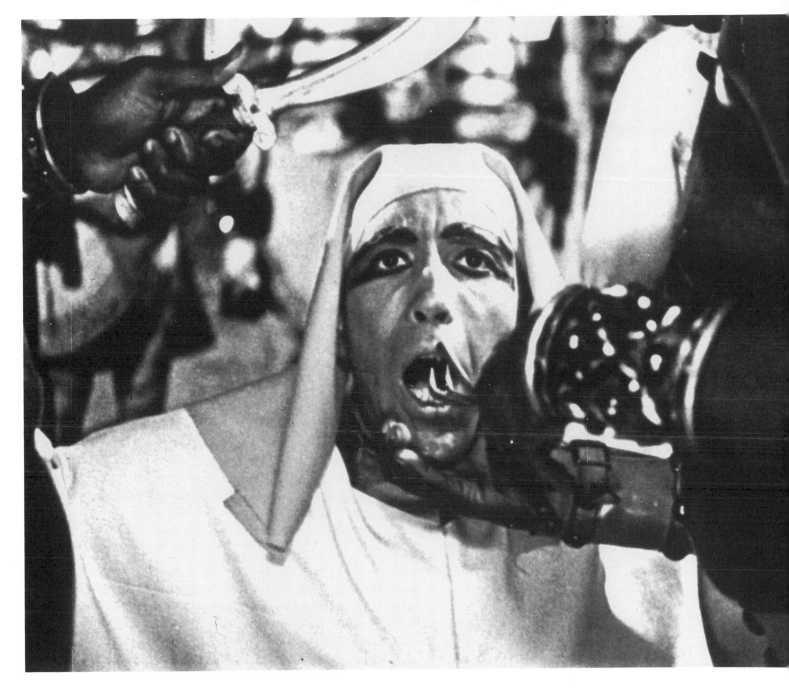

A Hammer Film Production
A Universal-International Release
Color/88 minutes

Prior to being walled up alive, Kharis (Christopher Lee) has his tongue torn out.

Credits

Director: Terence Fisher; *Producer:* Anthony Hinds; *Screenplay:* Jimmy Sangster; *Cinematographer:* Jack Asher; *Editors:* James Needs and Alfred Cox; *Music:* Frank Reizenstein; *Art Director:* Bernard Robinson; *Videocassette source:* Warner Home Video.

Cast

John Banning: Peter Cushing; *Kharis:* Christopher Lee; *Isobel/Ananka:* Yvonne Furneaux; *Stephen Banning:* Felix Aylmer; *Joseph Wemple:* Raymond Huntley; *Mehemet:* George Pastell; *Inspector Mulrooney:* Eddie Byrne.

I think most horror fans will agree that the mummy has never been found in the company of the most terrifying screen monsters—creepy, perhaps, but not terrifying. The reason for this, I think, is that up until Hammer tackled the subject, the mummy seldom had seemed particularly dangerous. It was always portrayed as a rather lumbering thing—deadly to be sure, but so slow moving that even a child would have little difficulty escaping its murderous clutches. In effect, one would have to be practically suicidal to be done in by such a creature. By choosing the 6′ 4″ Christopher Lee to play the part (Universal's mummies had all been shorter—and sometimes stockier—figures, thus diminishing their powers of intimidation even more) and making him able to rip through iron bars and crash through doors and windows with terrifying zest and speed, Hammer clearly rectified this situation. Lee's Kharis is a far more threatening presence than Karloff's, Tom Tyler's or Lon Chaney Jr.'s had been.

The Mummy marked the first time Hammer had actually set out to *remake* one of Universal's esteemed classics. Both *The Curse of Frankenstein* and *Horror of Dracula,* arguably classifiable as remakes, were, in fact, based more on the source Shelley and Stoker novels than on Universal's *Frankenstein* and *Dracula.* Universal's *The Mummy,* however, was an original screenplay (by John L. Balderston). So, when Hammer chose to film *The Mummy,* it signed a contract with Universal to do an outright remake. In fact, however, Jimmy Sangster's screenplay draws equally from the 1932 film's various sequels, particularly *The Mummy's Hand* (1940). The result is a sort of omnibus remake, or summation, of Universal's entire series of mummy

The ritual sealing of Ananka's tomb revealed in a flashback sequence. The High Priest Kharis (Christopher Lee), who is in love with Ananka, will re-enter the tomb later to revive her and be walled up alive for his blasphemy.

films—but totally rethought in terms of Hammer's Gothic Horror formula. This is an important point. Hammer's version of the classic tale has often been criticized for its *stagebound* sets, particularly those meant to represent the outdoors of ancient Egypt and the English bog where the mummy is finally killed. True, these sets were created in the studio and don't look naturalistic, but that's just the point. From *The Curse of Frankenstein* onward, Hammer sought to give its movies a distinctive look, or milieu, just as Universal

had done with its horror films. Universal had drawn upon the theatrical and cinematic traditions of German expressionism to create this look or milieu. Hammer sought to evoke a very different fairy tale world based on the closed-in atmosphere of the Gothic Romance. *The Mummy*'s stagebound sets are consistent with that concept. They are landscapes of the imagination. This concept is evident throughout the film (indeed, all of Hammer's Gothics), but especially so during the afore-mentioned bog scene. Instead of de-emphasizing the

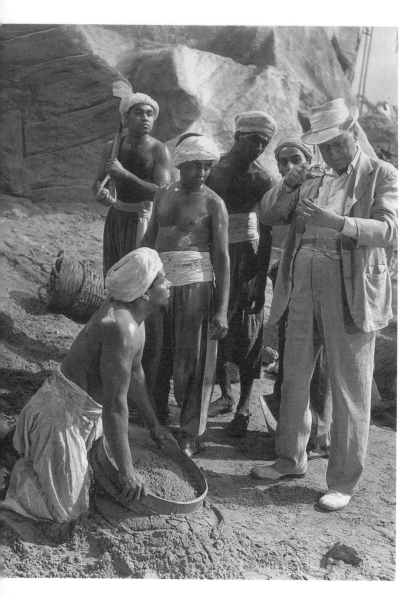

vaguely unreal look of this set, cameraman Jack Asher heightens its unreality by painting the set with unnaturally bright gold, green, blue and red lights. The net effect is almost ethereal and quite stunning indeed.

Sangster's plot centers around the exploits of a group of British archeologists bent on discovering the tomb of the Egyptian queen Ananka. The junior member of the team, John Banning, has been incapacitated due to a broken leg, so his father, Stephen, and his uncle, Joseph Wemple, carry out the rest of the dig. Just as the tomb is to be broken into, an Egyptian named Mehemet appears to warn them against desecrating it. The elder Banning ignores the warning, unseals the entrance with dynamite and goes inside. There amidst Ananka's ornate sarcophagus and many other ancient treasures, he discovers the sacred Scroll of Life. When he reads it aloud, he awakens the spirit of Kharis, the mummy that was walled up to guard the princess' remains. Banning's mind snaps when he sees the monstrous creature lumbering towards him, and when the team returns to England with all its treasures in tow, the old man is placed in a sanitarium. Mehemet, who has confiscated the Scroll of Life and is in control of Kharis, heads for England as well to reclaim the stolen body of the princess. The box containing Kharis' mummified form falls from the transport wagon enroute, however, and slips into a bog. Undaunted, Mehemet returns to the bog, reads the Scroll and the mummy rises from the mire to do Mehemet's murderous bidding. Kharis breaks into the sanitarium and kills the elder Banning. Then he slays Whemple. But when he attempts to strangle the final member of the team, John Banning, he is stopped by the timely intervention of Banning's wife, who bears a striking resemblance to the long dead princess. In fact, Kharis believes she *is* the princess. Banning calls the police and the house is surrounded in anticipation of another attack. But Kharis proves too powerful an adversary and, in an orgy of destruction, kills several policemen, as well as the villainous Mehemet, scoops up Banning's wife and heads for the bog. There, she manages to escape and Kharis, surrounded by police, is shot to pieces in a fusillade of gunfire and disappears into the mire for all eternity.

It's debatable, of course, whether Hammer's *The Mummy* is better than the Karloff version, but one point I don't think can be argued is that it is a much

John Banning (Peter Cushing) takes up arms to protect himself against the mummy that has broken in to kill him.

Kharis (Christopher Lee) approaches Isobel Banning (Yvonne Furneaux) whom he believes to be the reincarnation of his long dead love Ananka.

more exciting film (though its running time is longer, it seems to go by much faster). The main reason for this, I believe, is Sangster's wise decision to give the mummy much more screen time. In the Karloff film, the bandaged creature appears only at the beginning, then turns up later in a mysteriously more youthful (but just as wrinkled) guise to carry out his murderous retribution. In effect, following this preamble, the actual mummy disappears from the film. Sangster avoids this structural problem by separating the Karloff character into two distinct people—Kharis and Mehemet—thereby giving the mummy a featured role and its fair share of the horror spotlight. In the role, Christopher Lee is quite menacing indeed. But he also brings a significant amount of pathos to the character. When he gazes upon what he believes to be the reincarnation of his long lost love Ananka, there is a sad longing in his eyes never even hinted at in any of the Universal films—nor, it must be added, in any of Hammer's subsequent (and vastly inferior) mummy films.

39

THE HOUND OF THE BASKERVILLES (1959)

A Hammer Film Production
A United Artists Release
Color/81 minutes

Peter Cushing as Sherlock Holmes. He sought to
model his performance as closely to Conan Doyle's
conception (and to the Sidney Paget drawings of
Holmes) as possible. He even went out and bought
his own costumes.

Credits

Director: Terence Fisher; *Producer:* Anthony Hinds; *Screenplay:* Peter Bryan based on the novel by Sir Arthur Conan Doyle; *Cinematographer:* Jack Asher; *Editor:* James Needs; *Music:* James Bernard; *Art Director:* Bernard Robinson; *Videocassette source:* CBS/Fox Home Video.

Cast

Sherlock Holmes: Peter Cushing; *Dr. Watson:* Andre Morell; *Sir Henry Baskerville:* Christopher Lee; *Cecile:* Marla Landi; *Stapleton:* Ewen Solon; *Dr. Mortimer:* Francis De Wolff; *Bishop Frankland:* Miles Malleson; *Sir Hugo Baskerville:* David Oxley; *Barrymore:* John Le Mesurier; *Mrs. Barrymore:* Helen Goss; *Selden:* Michael Mulcaster; *Perkins:* Sam Kydd; *Servant Girl:* Judi Moyens.

Though a number of Sherlock Holmes adventures had been broadcast on radio and television during the Forties and Fifties, Sir Arthur Conan Doyle's venerable sleuth had not made a feature length appearance on the big screen since the demise of the Basil Rathbone/Nigel Bruce series for Universal in 1946. Hammer Films' *The Hound of the Baskervilles,* the umpteenth retelling of what is probably Doyle's most-filmed tale—though the first in color—was the studio's attempt to redress that situation as well as mine yet another rich vein of well known source material for the modern horror generation. The film was to be the first of a series of Hammer Holmes films—all to star Peter Cushing—but, alas, its poor box office showing (in comparison to the company's successful Frankenstein and Dracula films) doomed that prospect to failure. A decade later, however, Cushing did star in a series of sixteen Sherlock Holmes adventures for the BBC; one of them, yet another remake of *The Hound,* trimmed to an hour-long format.

One possible reason for the film's indifferent reception was its lack of full-throttle horror. It did possess overtones of horror and the supernatural, but it was essentially a Gothic mystery—although the film's advertising, which downplayed Holmes in favor of the blood-dripping hound, boldly suggested otherwise. Thus, audiences expecting to see an out-and-out horror film felt cheated when they didn't get it. Ironically, most critics voted thumbs down for much the same reason. Having

The film's advertising, stressing horror rather than Holmes, drew fans into the theater, but left them feeling somewhat disappointed, for Hammer's *Hound* was more of a mystery than a full-blooded horror film. Its poor box office showing sealed the doom for a proposed Hammer series of Holmes films to star Peter Cushing.

chided the studio's previous efforts for offering too much ghoulish content, they denounced *The Hound* for possessing too little. The film's hound (a reportedly docile Great Dane) was subjected to the greatest ridicule for being not some mythological beast but just an ordinary dog—even though this was precisely the key to the mystery Holmes succeeds in unraveling. The hound isn't a supernatural creature from hell. It *is* just an ordinary Great Dane—which the villain, Stapleton, has starved into viciousness so that it will attack and kill Sir Henry.

But enough of what audiences and critics thought at the time of the film's original release. Today, most horror film fans agree that *The Hound of the Baskervilles* is a bona fide modern classic of the genre—a beautiful looking film that in many ways ranks as the best screen version of the Conan Doyle tale yet produced. This opinion stands firm despite the five remakes (not including the Cushing/BBC retelling) that have followed since. They include an execrable made-for-TV version starring Stewart Granger filmed in 1972; a three-part BBC mini-series made in the Seventies starring Tom Baker of *Dr. Who* fame; Paul Morrissey's unfunny send-up of the story made in 1977 starring Dudley Moore and Peter Cook; a nicely mounted but overlong made-for-TV adaptation in 1983, directed by Douglas Hickox and starring Ian Richardson; and a two-part 1988 *Hound* which aired as a segment of Granada TV's popular Sherlock Holmes series starring Jeremy Brett.

Hammer's *The Hound of the Baskervilles* remains memorable for a number of reasons, not the least of which is that it marked a significant change from the manner in which the characters of Holmes and Watson had previously been played on screen—and were perceived by audiences. Peter Cushing's Holmes and Andre Morell's Watson owe absolutely nothing to Basil Rathbone and Nigel Bruce, but a lot to Sir Arthur Conan Doyle.

At the conclusion of the 1939 version of *The Hound*, Rathbone's Holmes says, "Quick, Watson, the needle!"—a daring reference to the character's legendary need for cocaine once the mystery has been solved and his ennui has begun to set in. Cushing's Holmes makes no such request, but the sleuth's addiction is evident in every nuance of the actor's performance. Cushing took

42

Sir Hugo "lets loose the pack" in pursuit of a peasant girl who refused to give in to his titled demands—namely sex.

Sir Hugo (David Oxley) kills the peasant girl (Judi Moyens)—only to be killed himself moments later by the legendary hound.

great pains to model his Holmes as faithfully as possible to Doyle's original character and to the Sidney Paget drawings of Holmes that had appeared in the *Strand* magazine. Reportedly, he even went out and bought his own costumes to make sure they had the right look. The crowning touch, however, was his depiction of Holmes as a man whose mental batteries are so supercharged by the excitement of the hunt *and* drugs that he can barely keep still. He makes Holmes behave higher than a kite. He scribbles appointments on his shirt cuffs, lights his pipes with coals from the fire, is flippant and irascible with practically everyone, and gets furious with himself when he fails to grasp the meaning of an important clue.

Cushing plays Holmes as an intellectual neurotic whose obsession with solving the mystery almost leads to Sir Henry's death. The screen had never presented Sherlock Holmes in such a light. But this was precisely as Conan Doyle had written the character. Thus, Cushing's performance was quite a groundbreaker. It paved the way for a host of similarly authentic Holmes interpretations in the years to come—culminating with Jeremy Brett's even more neurotic (and perhaps definitive) incarnation a quarter of a century later in the Granada TV series and as Holmes on the London stage. In addition to the BBC adventures (which the author has not seen and which some writers have reported

Dr. Watson (Andre Morell) gets stuck in Grimpen Mire.

Holmes (Peter Cushing) explains to Watson (Andre Morell) and Sir Henry (Christopher Lee) how he was first put onto the scent of "the hound of the Baskervilles." Sir Henry looks none too pleased—Holmes' obsession with solving the mystery almost cost Sir Henry his life.

were destroyed), Cushing played Doyle's immortal supersleuth one more time in a 1984 British-made television movie. *Sherlock Holmes and The Masks of Death;* Sir John Mills, a close Cushing friend, played Watson.

Likewise, the late Andre Morell's Watson is no bumbling teddy bear, but a perceptive and competent physician whose stiff-upper-lip demeanor is quite in keeping with the fact (per Conan Doyle) that Watson earned his medical spurs as an army doctor.

Christopher Lee's aristocratic and frequently short-tempered Sir Henry is also a bit of a departure from past (and even future) film interpretations of the character, who is most often portrayed as a fairly congenial type. Lee's Sir Henry very obviously enjoys his wealth and new-found station in life—though he is not at all above fraternizing with the lower classes, particularly

females. This change, together with screenwriter Peter Bryan's transformation of the Stapletons from an upper class squire and his dupe of a sister (as in the book) to a tenant farmer and his accomplice daughter lends the film the same note of class conflict evident in other Hammer Gothic Horror films.

In addition to these intriguing elements, the film, as I've already noted, satisfies because it is a beautiful looking picture. Bernard Robinson's sets, particularly the Abbey ruin where most of the film's murderous hijinks take place, are genuine Gothic landscapes of the mind—which cinematographer Jack Asher suffuses in brilliant reds, blues, golds and particularly greens with experimental abandon. The color in this film all but jumps off the screen at you—not unlike the hound of the title.

THE MAN WHO COULD CHEAT DEATH (1959)

A Hammer Film Production
A Paramount Pictures Release
Color/83 minutes

Margo (Delphi Lawrence) is angered when she discovers that Bonnet (Anton Diffring) is not the marrying kind. Overstaying her welcome, she sees his aging process start to set in and is locked in the cellar of his house to keep the secret.

Credits

Director: Terence Fisher; *Producer:* Anthony Hinds; *Screenplay:* Jimmy Sangster, based on the play *The Man in Half Moon Street* by Barré Lyndon; *Cinematographer:* Jack Asher; *Editor:* John Dunsford; *Music:* Richard Bennett; *Production Designer:* Bernard Robinson; *Videocassette source:* Unavailable.

Cast

Dr. Georges Bonnet: Anton Diffring; *Janine Dubois:* Hazel Court; *Dr. Pierre Gerard:* Christopher Lee; *Professor Ludwig Weisz:* Arnold Marle; *Margo:* Delphi Lawrence; *Inspector Legris:* Francis De Wolff; *Streetwoman:* Gerda Larsen.

In many ways, *The Man Who Could Cheat Death* is a throwback to the stately style of British moviemaking that predated Hammer Horror. In fact, as directed by Terence Fisher, it comes across almost as a comedy of manners, minus the comedy. The pace is leisurely, the chills muted. The film is almost purely an exercise in style—a harbinger of Hammer's *Brides of Dracula*—in which cameraman Jack Asher pushed his experimental lighting techniques even further than he had in Hammer's *The Hound of the Baskervilles* (1959), bringing out even more nuances in the color schemes of Bernard Robinson's lush Victorian sets. It is surely, as many critics noted, a splendid film to look at. "Few horror films have been presented with such Technicolored elegance and high production values," wrote the *Library Journal.* Even more laudatory was *Variety:* "Hammer is still the only production unit concentrating on class horror films. Like its past successes, *The Man Who Could Cheat Death* has nothing foolish about it. Sangster's intelligent screenplay is directed seriously and straight by Terence Fisher."

Unlike many other classic Hammer Horrors, *The Man Who Could Cheat Death* seldom turns up on television—though, fortuitously, it did appear on one of my local stations while I was preparing this book. My memories of the film were unaltered by the experience of seeing it again, but the print on view was a terrible disappointment. As with so many Technicolor films of the Fifties and Sixties, its hues had faded; the whole film looked grainy and muddy, which is a tragedy considering the care that had gone into the photography, the film's chief asset. Hopefully, the original negative is not in as bad shape.

Hazel Court as the beautiful Janine Dubois whom Bonnet, tired of the loneliness of immortality, decides to make his bride for all time.

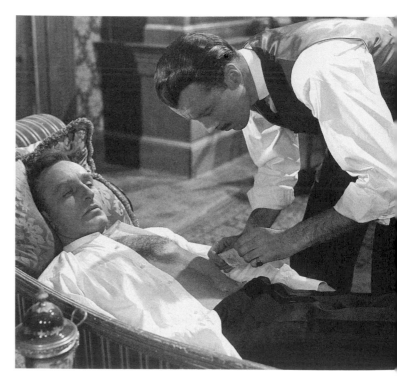

Dr. Gerard (Christopher Lee) patches up Bonnet (Anton Diffring). What Bonnet doesn't know is that Gerard, who is also in love with Janine, has not really gone through with the gland transplant.

Bonnet (Anton Diffring) confesses the truth about himself to Janine (Hazel Court), proposing that she undergo an operation as well and share in his immortality.

The Man Who Could Cheat Death, based on a stage play by Barré Lyndon, was likewise a remake—of Paramount's *The Man in Half Moon Street,* a "B" movie filmed in 1944 starring Nils Asther in the title role of the unbalanced sculptor who takes to murdering people to sustain his immortality. Those who feel *Cheat* is overly mannered and talky (which it is, but intentionally so) should see the first film version, which is little but a photographed stage play.

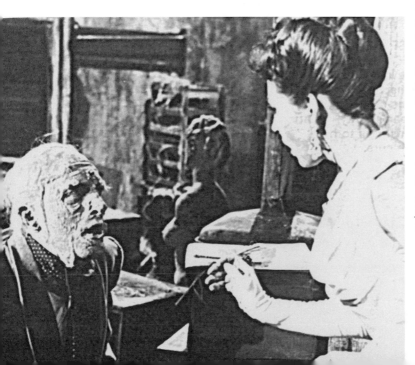

In the Hammer remake, the locale of the story is shifted from London to Paris. The sculptor, Georges Bonnet, is played by Anton Diffring, who took over for Peter Cushing when the latter had to bow out due to other commitments. Diffring had previously landed the Cushing role of Baron Frankenstein in the pilot for a proposed *Frankenstein* series Columbia Pictures had contracted Hammer to develop for American television. Though the pilot was shot, the series idea went no further. For the first time in a Hammer Horror, Christopher Lee not only gets the girl, he plays the hero (in *The Hound of the Baskervilles,* he played a good guy, but Peter Cushing's Sherlock Holmes was the hero.)

As scripted by Jimmy Sangster, who also novelized his screenplay for a publicity tie-in, *Cheat* is one part Jack the Ripper and two parts *The Picture of Dorian Gray* reworked as a medical thriller. As the film opens, Bonnet is seen stalking a victim through the Parisian mist, Gladstone bag in hand. He mutilates his victim in order to secure a gland required for his elixir of life, throwing the city into a panic and the police into a tizzy. At the showing of his latest sculpture, an old flame he'd run out on, Janine Dubois, shows up and determines to rekindle their romance. He not only takes her up on her offer, but, concluding that immortality has its lonely side, decides to have her operated on too so that she can be his bride for all time.

Professor Weisz, who performed the original experiment on the now 104-year-old Bonnet, has become too aged and infirm to carry out the next operation, however, and so Bonnet is forced to turn to a younger surgeon, Dr. Gerard, who not only dislikes and mistrusts Bonnet, but is in love with Janine himself. When Weisz learns that Bonnet has turned to murder to sustain youth, he balks and threatens to blow the whistle. Bonnet kills him and, by kidnapping Janine, blackmails Gerard into performing the operation. Gerard pulls a fast one, however, and Bonnet finds himself deteriorating rapidly.

Confronting Janine, he shrivels before her horrified eyes just as another of his lovers, Margo, who knows the truth about him and whom he has also locked away, goes berserk and sets fire to the house. Gerard rescues Janine just in time as Bonnet's virtually mummified remains are consumed in the inferno.

Bonnet (Anton Diffring) deteriorates before the horrified Janine (Hazel Court).

THE BRIDES OF DRACULA (1960)

A Hammer-Hotspur Production
A Universal-International Release
Color/85 minutes

The vampiric Baron Meinster (David Peel). "He was always self-willed and cruel," his mother says of him. Now, he's a whole lot worse.

Credits

Director: Terence Fisher; *Producer:* Anthony Hinds; *Screenplay:* Jimmy Sangster, Edward Percy and Peter Bryan; *Cinematographer:* Jack Asher; *Editor:* Alfred Cox; *Music:* Malcolm Williamson; *Art Director:* Bernard Robinson; *Videocassette source:* Unavailable.

Cast

Van Helsing: Peter Cushing; *Marianne Danielle:* Yvonne Monlaur; *Baron Meinster:* David Peel; *Baroness Meinster:* Martita Hunt; *Great:* Freda Jackson; *Frau Lang:* Mona Washbourne; *Herr Lang:* Henry Oscar; *Gina:* Andree Melly.

Perhaps more than any other motion picture he collaborated on for Hammer Films, *The Brides of Dracula* remains "A Terence Fisher Picture"—a grand Gothic fairy tale that succeeds almost exclusively because of its style and the emphasis Fisher places *on* style over content, the reasons for which will soon become clear.

Until his death in 1980, Fisher insisted that he was only a working director—a hired hand, as it were—who tried to bring the best out of each script he was given. And, he insisted, he was given *all* of them; he never initiated a single project with the exception, perhaps, of

Van Helsing (Peter Cushing) witnesses the wake of another victim of the vampire.

Turned into a vampire by her vengeful son, the Baroness Meinster (Martita Hunt) ashamedly conceals her fangs from Van Helsing.

Horror of Dracula, which, while not initiating it exactly, he specifically chose to do.

With the worldwide box office take of *Horror of Dracula* swelling Hammer's coffers, a sequel seemed inevitable—and it was equally inevitable that Fisher would be given it to direct. Hammer was still not about to tamper with its winning hand. The problem was that Dracula had disintegrated into dust at the conclusion of *Horror of Dracula*—and Christopher Lee, who was now firmly identified with the role in the minds of moviegoers everywhere, didn't want the character resurrected. He wanted to move on to other things. This dilemma was the main reason why it took Hammer a year longer to deliver a sequel to its first successful Dracula film than it had to its first successful Frankenstein film.

Jimmy Sangster wrote a script tentatively titled *Dracula II* which actually resurrected the Count. When the decision was made not to resurrect him—at least not yet—but go with a sort of "unofficial sequel" instead, screenwriters Peter Bryan and Edward Percy were

In one of the film's most chilling sequences, the crazed Greta (Freda Jackson) calls up one of Meinster's vampire victims from the grave.

brought in to rework Sangster's script. [Elements of Sangster's *Dracula II* script would subsequently turn up in *Dracula—Prince of Darkness* (1966), the "official sequel" to *Horror of Dracula,* in which Lee finally agreed to reappear as the Count and which begins with a reprise of the disintegration scene from the first film. Sangster wrote the script for that one too, under his pseudonym John Sansom.]

As developed by Sangster, Bryan and Percy, the revised *Dracula II* script, now called *The Brides of Dracula* (in a 1959 letter, Peter Cushing told me the title *The Mark of Dracula* was once considered as well), focused not on the now dead Count, but on one of his disciples, the fair-haired Baron Meinster, whose domineering mother keeps him chained up in the castle so that he won't disgrace the family name by putting the bite on all her neighbors. To satisfy his bloodlust, however, she occasionally imports a luckless village girl.

Suffering from the moral dilemma of keeping her

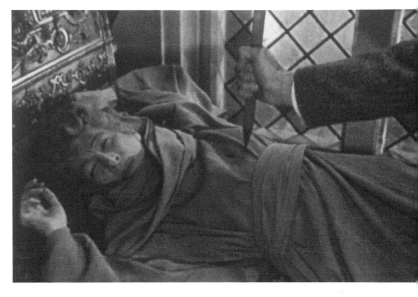

Though a lot less obsessive than he was in *Horror of Dracula*, Van Helsing (Peter Cushing) still drives a mean stake.

Two of the undead "Brides of Meinster" (Andree Melly and Marie Devereaux).

Meinster (David Peel) launches into a duel to the
death with Van Helsing in the bowels of the windmill.

as well. But Van Helsing once again comes to the rescue,
destroying the Baron in the shadow of a cross formed
by the blades of a burning windmill. [In the script of
Brides, a horde of vengeful vampire bats sets upon the
Baron for having committed matricide and contributes
to his downfall as well. Some critics have described this
scene as being in the final film. It isn't—though something very much like it does occur in Hammer's *Kiss of
the Vampire* (1963).]

Due to the constraints under which the project was
developed—and the patchwork methods of its writing,
the script of *Brides* is full of inconsistencies. For
example, Marianne is left stranded at the inn when the
coachman rattles off into the night with all her luggage.
And yet later, she makes reference to the fact that she
fled the castle without taking her luggage. Later, like
Count Dracula, Baron Meinster is able to transform
himself into a bat—if so, why does he need a key to
escape his shackles? And finally, as there is no Dracula,
just who are his "brides" supposed to be? [More than
one writer has suggested that the Count's disciples—in
this case, the Baron himself—are the "brides" the title
refers to, thus lending a hint of homosexuality to
Hammer's updating of the vampire myth. Indeed, there
are a number of elements to support this view, not the
least of them being the unhealthy psychological undercurrents that exist in the relationship between the
Baron and his domineering mother, plus David Peel's
blatant "pretty boy" looks and demeanor.]

So, what makes *The Brides of Dracula* a classic?

In an effort to bring out the best in what was a very
inconsistent script, Fisher set about turning the film
into a triumph of style—both his and Hammer's, which
had come to mean the same thing—over substance: a
definitive statement not on the Gothic Romance formula (he would do that in *The Phantom of the Opera*),
but on the Gothic *milieu.* In short, he turned *The
Brides of Dracula* into a dazzling visual showpiece—an
absolutely gorgeous tableau of Gothic sets and costumes and fairy tale colors that not only succeeded in
obscuring the plot's many inconsistencies, but turned
them into an advantage. *The Brides of Dracula* boasts a
dream-like quality in which the plot's lack of depen-
dency on logic seems integral to the experience—
much as the lack of logic in dreams seems integral to
that experience.

In terms of style, *The Brides of Dracula* remains
Terence Fisher's—and Hammer's—masterpiece.

only son alive by supplying him with victims, yet
knowing this is wrong, the fast dissipating Baroness
pushes the situation too far when she lures one victim
too many to the castle—in this case, a pretty young
teacher named Marianne, who has been left stranded
enroute to her job at a nearby girl's school. Instead of
becoming the Baron's latest victim, Marianne finds the
key to his shackles and releases him. When the monstrous Baron takes revenge on hated old mom by
turning her into a vampire, Marianne flees for her life
and is rescued by the intrepid Van Helsing, who delivers
her to the girl's school.

She is followed there by the Baron, who vampirizes
some of her associates, then attempts to claim Marianne

THE FALL OF THE HOUSE OF USHER (1960)

An American-International Picture
Color/79 minutes

6001 P-28

Roderick (Vincent Price) reveals the terrible truth of the Ushers' contaminated bloodline to Philip (Mark Damon).

Vincent Price as the benighted Roderick Usher in Roger Corman's superb production of Edgar Allan Poe's *The Fall of the House of Usher*.

Credits

Director: Roger Corman; *Producer:* Roger Corman; *Screenplay:* Richard Matheson, based on the story by Edgar Allan Poe; *Cinematographer:* Floyd Crosby; *Editor:* Anthony Carras; *Music:* Les Baxter; *Production Designer:* Daniel Haller; *Videocassette source:* Warner Home Video.

Cast

Roderick Usher: Vincent Price; *Philip Winthrop:* Mark Damon; *Madeline Usher:* Myrna Fahey; *Bristol [the butler]:* Harry Ellerbe.

In his 1982 book *The Films of Roger Corman,* Ed Naha wrote this about *The Fall of the House of Usher,* the first of Corman and American-International's now-legendary series of Edgar Allan Poe films: "*House of Usher* was a milestone for both AIP and Roger Corman. For AIP, it began a successful Poe series that was destined to stretch, in one form or another, until decade's end. For Corman, it gave him a certain amount of notoriety and critical acceptance in America. For movie audiences worldwide, it re-established a classic film genre: the Gothic Horror film."

While the first two parts of Naha's statement are certainly true, the last, clearly, is not. By 1960, the Gothic Horror film was already enjoying a worldwide resurgence due to the influence of Hammer Films, which, by the time *House of Usher* was released, had been making one successful Gothic Horror film after another for several years! I think it's quite fair to say—although Roger Corman and AIP founders Sam Arkoff and the late James Nicholson never did (not to my knowledge anyway)—that among the many motivations that prompted AIP to move into the realm of Gothic Horror, Hammer's success with the formula stood at the top. The reason I believe so becomes clear if one takes a look at the two companies, whose move into youth-oriented horror films occurred at roughly the same time.

The goal of both companies was most certainly the same: to drag us teenagers away from our television sets and back into the theaters by giving us something we just couldn't get on the tube. From the start, however, there were very obvious differences in approach. Both companies made low budget horror films with highly exploitable (and, in AIP's case, very youth-oriented)

Roderick (Vincent Price) tells his sister Madeline (Myrna Fahey) that she can never marry because of their family's history of mental illness.

Philip (Mark Damon) attempts to persuade Roderick (Vincent Price) that the curse of the house of Usher is nothing more than a figment of the man's sick imagination.

Bristol (Harry Ellerbe) quickly intervenes as the anguished Philip (Mark Damon) assaults Roderick (Vincent Price).

The deranged Madeline (Myrna Fahey) rises from the tomb in which she has been prematurely buried to kill her brother (Vincent Price).

titles. But AIP's horror movies *looked* cheap. Hammer's didn't. The actors and actresses in AIP's films were, in the main, *kids* themselves—not unlike those in the audience who flocked to see them. But Hammer drew upon the vast resources of British television and theater to create a stock company of seasoned professionals. Finally, AIP's films were shot in black and white whereas Hammer's were made in vibrant Technicolor. *That* was certainly something television wasn't offering us at the time. And so, fans began to divide into two separate, though not warring, camps: those who loved AIP and those who loved Hammer. I immediately fell into the latter camp. Undoubtedly, a certain amount of snobbishness entered into this division. Hammer's films were, after all, "European productions" and that meant "sophisticated" to our young eyes. But the reverse was also true. AIP fans touted as virtues the very same elements we Hammerphiles considered deficiencies in AIP's films.

The differences in approach between the two companies affected the appeal of their films in other ways too. Because of their sumptuous look and casts of top-flight British thesbians, Hammer's films appealed to *adults* as well as kids. Speaking from personal experience, my late father, a horror film fan since his youth, looked forward to each new Hammer Horror as eagerly as did his then teenaged son. But I couldn't get him to an AIP film on a bet—at least not until the Poe series appeared. With *House of Usher*, AIP succeeded in broadening its market and getting bookings in theaters, not just drive-ins. It had finally struck gold with the winning Hammer formula of Gothic Horror, but with a very homegrown touch: Edgar Allan Poe. And in Vincent Price, who had previously appeared in a variety of lesser horror films for William Castle and others, it found an American actor on a par with Hammer's Peter Cushing and Christopher Lee.

Corman and AIP lavished a larger budget ($350,000) on *House of Usher* than it had on any of their previous horror pictures—indeed, their budget for *Usher* was a larger one than Hammer had mustered for *any* of its films so far. And all the money shows on the screen. Corman also shot the film in CinemaScope, making very good use of the widescreen process with his "whip pan" and "mobile camera" directorial style. Much of the effectiveness of his use of the widescreen, however, is now lost in the "scanned" prints circulating on television and on videocassette. The studio-bound sets created by Daniel Haller, like those created by Bernard Robinson for Hammer's Gothics, were lush, lavish and fantastic—genuine landscapes of the imagination, which cinematographer Floyd Crosby, who had begun his career in the silent era working with such prestige directors as F.W. Murnau, lit in an over-the-top color style similar to that used by Hammer's Jack Asher.

Corman would go on to make seven more pictures in the Poe series (though his 1963 *Haunted Palace* would owe more to H.P. Lovecraft than to Poe) and AIP would go on to make several more without him. Fans of the series are very much divided as to which of Corman's contributions ranks best. Many opt for his 1964 *Masque of the Red Death*. But my personal preference is still his first, *The Fall of the House of Usher*. Perhaps because it was the first, there is a freshness to it that many of his subsequent Poe films lack (indeed, only a year later, Corman would begin to parody the formula in *Tales of Terror* and would do so again in 1963 with *The Raven*, a total send-up of the Poe series. Obviously, he'd grown tired of the series, but pressed on anyway.) But *House of Usher* remains one of the best gothic horror films America has ever made—and is therefore a bona fide modern classic. For all its imitativeness of the Hammer style and formula, it stands very nicely on its own as a genuinely striking, moody, eery (Madeline's premature burial and all that follows thereafter, a protracted sequence that evokes Val Lewton's 1943 *Isle of the Dead,* are particularly effective), well-written and performed (especially by Price) no-nonsense Gothic Horror film.

CURSE OF THE WEREWOLF (1960)

A Hammer-Hotspur Production
A Universal-International Release
Color/91 minutes

The luckless beggar (Richard Wordsworth) is teasingly wined and dined. Shortly after, the villainous Marquis will imprison him for making an off-color remark.

Credits

Director: Terence Fisher; *Producer:* Anthony Hinds; *Screenplay:* John Elder [Anthony Hinds] based on the novel *The Werewolf of Paris* by Guy Endore; *Cinematographer:* Arthur Grant; *Editor:* Alfred Cox; *Music:* Benjamin Frankel; *Art Director:* Bernard Robinson; *Videocassette source:* MCA Home Video.

Cast

Leon: Oliver Reed; *Don Alfredo:* Clifford Evans; *Teresa:* Hira Talfrey; *Cristina:* Catherine Feller; *Don Fernando:* Ewen Solon; *Mute Girl:* Yvonne Romain; *Marquis:* Anthony Dawson; *Beggar:* Richard Wordsworth; *Drunk:* Michael Ripper; *Pepe:* Warren Mitchell.

Languishing in the prison for years, the beggar (Richard Wordsworth) turns into something less than human.

58

With *Curse of the Werewolf,* Hammer, much as it had with *The Mummy,* injected some badly needed zip into another of the horror film's more uninspired sub-genres—the werewolf movie. Universal itself hadn't turned out a really good werewolf film since *The Wolf Man* (1941). And like the studio's Frankenstein and Dracula monsters, the fearsomeness of that film's central character had long since been diluted by the later Abbott and Costello parodies. For this reason, perhaps, Hammer chose not to introduce the werewolf to its new stable of monsters by remaking *The Wolf Man,* but turned instead to an entirely original source for inspiration—Guy Endore's classic 1933 horror novel *The Werewolf of Paris.*

Anthony Hinds, in an interview with a writer friend of mine, Bruce G. Hallenbeck, said that Hammer had to pay what was for them such an exorbitant price for the rights to Endore's book that there was no money left in the budget for a screenplay. So, Hinds wrote it himself—at no charge—under the pseudonym John Elder. It would be the first of many scripts he would write for Hammer in the ensuing years.

At the time, Hammer was also preparing a large scale horror film about the Spanish Inquisition. A script had been prepared and Bernard Robinson had already designed and constructed the sets for it on the Bray lot. But the project collapsed when the Catholic Church got wind of the project and announced that if the film was made, its film censoring body, The Legion of Decency, would condemn it—a decision that would severely affect the film's box office chances around the world. The project was scrapped, but the Spanish sets remained—so in a move born of economics more than anything else, producer-writer Hinds relocated Endore's Parisian werewolf to Spain and *The Werewolf of Paris* became *Curse of the Werewolf.*

These were just two of many alterations Endore's book underwent in being transferred to the screen. The book, while clearly a horror novel (and a very graphic, psycho-sexual one at that) was also a piece of historical fiction that climaxes with the bloody siege of the Paris Commune in 1871. In the book, the benighted main character, Bertrand Caillet, is condemned to werewolf-ism when his mother, a servant girl, becomes pregnant with him after being raped by a priest. He is born on Christmas Day, which, according to superstition, is "an insult to heaven." Raised by a guardian, Bertrand evidences signs of his inherent bloodlust very early on. In

The mute servant girl (Yvonne Romain) prepares to carry out her revenge on the lecherous Marquis (Anthony Dawson).

Possessed by full moon madness, young Leon attempts to break out of his caged room.

The murder of the prostitute.

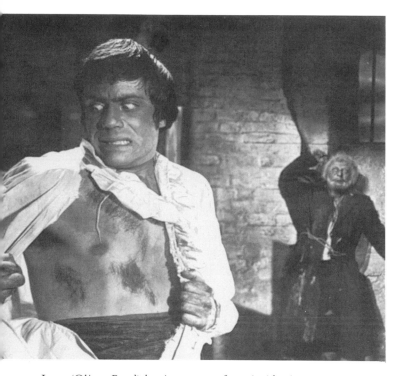

Leon (Oliver Reed) begins to transform inside the prison cell as a trapped drunk (Michael Ripper) looks on in terror.

His face transforming, Leon (Oliver Reed) turns to snarl at the drunk.

fact, it becomes all consuming. Even in his non-werewolf guise, he is compelled to drink blood and eat raw meat. He meets and falls in love with a girl named Sophie, who tempers his transformations by letting him cut her skin with a knife and drink from her wounds. Thinking himself cured, Bertrand heads for the embattled city of Paris to which the Germans are laying siege. There, surrounded by horrific daily examples of man's inhumanity to man, he quickly reverts, murdering a friend and killing a number of prostitutes.

Constantly at war with his inner urges, Bertrand tries to reduce his contribution to the growing body count by feasting on corpses he digs up from the local cemeteries. He's caught and tried, but his guardian arrives and attempts to defend him by attributing Bertrand's crimes to an inherited weakness of the soul rather than the kind of outright villainy demonstrated by the savage war. Bertrand is committed to an asylum where he subsequently dies. When his body is exhumed some years later, the skeleton of a wolf is found.

Hinds' script eliminates the rich religious and political backdrop of Endore's story, cuts or combines situations and characters and, despite the studio's reputation for indulging in sex and gore, does away completely with the sadomasochistic relationship between the werewolf and his lover. Much of the novel's graphic ghoulishness is also eliminated. Nevertheless, the movie does remain quite faithful to the spirit of the book's central tale—the tragedy of a man cursed from birth to be at war with himself, and who loses that war.

In the film, an evil Spanish Marquis imprisons a luckless beggar for making an off-color remark on the Marquis' wedding night. The beggar languishes in the castle dungeon for years, turning into something less than human. When a mute servant girl is thrown in with him for refusing to give herself to the Marquis, the beggar rapes her and expires from the strain. On her release, she kills the Marquis and escapes into the forest where she's discovered by the kindly Don Alfredo, who soon discovers she is pregnant. She gives birth to her illegitimate son, Leon, on Christmas Day. When the boy grows a few years older, signs of the curse begin to show. A wolf prowling the area, slaughtering sheep, is shot at one night by a hunter and Leon is found in bed the following morning with a bullet in his leg.

Don Alfredo puts iron bars on the boy's window to keep him in and, together with his housekeeper, lavishes love and affection on Leon over the years to help suppress his beastly urges. This seems to work and

Leon the werewolf (Oliver Reed) fully transformed.

when Leon reaches adulthood, he sets off to get a job, thinking he is cured. He falls in love with the daughter of a wine merchant, but the relationship is strained because she's being forced to marry someone else. Taken to a local brothel by a friend, Leon finds the wolf rising once again within him. He kills the friend and a prostitute. Arrested for the crimes, he pleads to be executed befores he transforms again, but the request is denied. That night, he once again turns into a wolf, breaks out of jail and wreaks havoc on the town until he is finally brought down by Don Alfredo, who shoots him in the heart with a silver bullet.

Because the film focuses so completely on the dilemma of its central character—Leon's inability to escape a fate he had no hand in defining—the film emerges as a very grim tale indeed (just as Endore's book does). And unlike most of his other Hammer Horrors, director Terence Fisher does not leaven the proceedings with any isolated bits of comic relief. The tone of the film is relentlessly grim because there is, quite literally, no hope for Leon at all. (What little there is—the love of the wine merchant's daughter—is iron-ically snatched from him by the girl herself.) This bleak

outcome is foreshadowed even in the film's opening credits where we see tears falling from the werewolf's blood-mad eyes. Because of this focus on character, *Curse of the Werewolf,* unlike *The Wolf Man* and most other werewolf films, is quite reticent about showing Leon in his werewolf guise—in fact, we don't see him fully transformed until the film's last ten minutes. Roy Ashton's horrific makeup and the powerful perfor-mance of Oliver Reed in his first lead (he had done only bits and walk-ons up to now) make these scenes worth the wait, but as horror fans go to monster movies mainly to see the monster, this reticence probably worked against the film. It was not a big box office success and Hammer never attempted another werewolf film.

Nevertheless, despite all the marvelous film trickery that has come our way since in such films as *An American Werewolf in London* and *The Howling,* Hammer's *Curse of the Werewolf* remains the last *good* werewolf film the screen has given us—and probably the best it has ever given us. It is certainly the most serious, boasting a conclusion that is not only full of high-powered horror but genuinely moving as well.

Director Hitchcock sits in for the unseen "Mrs. Bates."

PSYCHO (1960)

A Shamley Production
Released through Paramount Pictures
B&W/109 minutes

Credits

Director: Alfred Hitchcock; *Producer:* Alfred Hitchcock; *Screenplay:* Joseph Stefano, based on the novel by Robert Bloch; *Cinematographer:* John L. Russell; *Editor:* George Tomasini; *Music:* Bernard Herrmann; *Art Directors:* Joseph Hurley and Robert Clatworthy; *Videocassette source:* MCA Home Video.

Cast

Norman Bates: Anthony Perkins; *Marion Crane:* Janet Leigh; *Lila Crane:* Vera Miles; *Sam Loomis:* John Gavin; *Arbogast:* Martin Balsam; *Sheriff Chambers:* John McIntire; *Mrs. Chambers:* Lurenc Tuttle; *Psychiatrist:* Simon Oakland; *Cassidy:* Frank Albertson; *Caroline:* Pat Hitchcock; *Mr. Lowry:* Vaughn Taylor; *Highway Patrolman:* Mort Miles; *Used Car Dealer:* John Anderson.

PSYCHO II (1983)

A Universal Picture
Color/113 minutes

Credits

Director: Richard Franklin; *Producer:* Hilton A. Green; *Screenplay:* Tom Holland; *Cinematographer:* Dean Cundey; *Editor:* Andrew London; *Music:* Jerry Goldsmith; *Production Designer:* John W. Corso; *Videocassette source:* MCA Home Video.

Cast

Norman Bates: Anthony Perkins; *Lila Loomis:* Vera Miles; *Mary Loomis:* Meg Tilly; *Dr. Raymond:* Robert Loggia; *Toomey:* Dennis Franz; *Sheriff Hunt:* Hugh Gillin; *Mrs. Spool:* Claudia Bryar; *Young Norman:* Osgood Perkins.

PSYCHO III (1986)

A Universal Picture
Color/93 minutes

Credits

Director: Anthony Perkins; *Producer:* Hilton A. Green; *Screenplay:* Charles Edward Pogue; *Cinematographer:* Bruce Surtees; *Editor:* David Blewitt; *Music:* Carter Burwell; *Production Designer:* Henry Bumstead; *Videocassette source:* MCA Home Video.

Cast

Norman Bates: Anthony Perkins; *Maureen Coyle:* Diana Scarwid; *Dwayne Duke:* Jeff Fahey; *Tracy Venable:* Roberta Maxwell; *Sheriff Hunt:* Hugh Gillin; *Myrna:* Lee Garlington; *Ralph Statler:* Robert Alan Browne.

Marion Crane (Janet Leigh) and Sam Loomis (John Gavin) make illicit love during the poor girl's lunch hour.

Norman Bates (Anthony Perkins) with one of his stuffed birds.

As she listens to Norman talk about his own private hell, Marion (Janet Leigh) comes to realize the trap she has fallen into by stealing money from her employer.

Alfred Hitchcock's *Psycho* is probably the most famous, most written about and most over-analyzed horror film in movie history. Little new remains to say about it, but I feel compelled to give it a go because this book is about classics of the modern horror film, and *Psycho* is unquestionably one of them.

The ironic thing about *Psycho* is that Hitchcock's studio at the time, Paramount, had no faith in the project and didn't want him to make it. The studio executives thought the novel it was based on was little more than pulp fiction, cheap and tawdry, not worthy of the elegant Hitchcock treatment—and in black and white! Still smarting over the financial losses incurred by Hitchcock's last pet film for the studio, *The Trouble With Harry* (1955), Paramount vetoed the project. So, Hitchcock decided to finance it himself through Shamley Productions, his television production arm. To keep costs down, he shot the film on the Universal lot where the episodes of his television series, *Alfred Hitchcock Presents,* were made, using many members of his television crew, including cameraman John L. Russell and assistant director Hilton A. Green, who years later would produce the two *Psycho* sequels.

"Expect the unexpected from Hitchcock" was a familiar phrase in the ads for the latest Hitchcock picture. In the case of *Psycho,* it proved particularly apt, for at the time of the film's release, no one expected the screen's master of suspense (and king of the romantic comedy thriller) to unleash a fright flick as jolting as this one. As Paramount had suggested, there was no precedent for it—not in Hitchcock's work, nor anyone else's. [In fact, Paramount, after agreeing to distribute the film, didn't want it to be called *Psycho* because they feared audiences wouldn't have any idea what the word meant!] Younger horror fans to whom the film and its now famous set pieces (the shower murder, etc.) have become as familiar and perhaps old hat as *Frankenstein* can't imagine what it was like to experience *Psycho* with fresh eyes. It was, quite literally, 109 of the most nerve-wracking, nail-biting minutes as have ever been spent in a theater. The stories about people experiencing a shudder or two as they stepped into their private showers months and even years after seeing the film are true. The film left an indelible mark on the psyches of everyone who saw it. And to this day, *Psycho* continues to cast a very large shadow indeed—as witness the success of its two sequels, both made after Hitchcock died.

Norman (Anthony Perkins) reacts to mother's grizzly handiwork in the shower of cabin number one.

Two views of the Bates house—22 years apart.

The idea to do a sequel more than two decades after the original film's release belonged to executive producer Bernard Schwartz. "The idea of a *Psycho II* appealed to me," Schwartz said at the time. "It had a tremendous awareness; it was a classic, and it had a theme that interested me (the question of releasing the criminally insane from institutions) which was the basis to trigger a legitimate sequel to *Psycho.*" Hilton A. Green was selected to produce the film because of his experience working with Hitchcock on the original *Psycho.*

Casting Anthony Perkins was also a critical element. "For years, I'd resisted the whole idea of *Psycho* exposure," Perkins told the press. "I felt *Psycho* had been sufficient in itself. It was a well-constructed story. It never occurred to me there would be more juice in those characters. When I received Tom Holland's script, I liked it very much. It was really Norman's story...about how much he'd changed after twenty-two years in an institution. He was more educated about himself and had the knowledge that he had the potential of being dangerous. But he's also very trusting and generous of spirit. He's a likable guy with some very winning qualitites." So, Perkins signed on.

Other problems quickly presented themselves, however. When Universal Studios' backlot was redesigned to make way for the Universal City Tour Theme Park, the *Psycho* house, another critical ingredient, was moved from its original location and the motel torn down. Producer Green and director Richard Franklin found another site on the lot that best duplicated the original location, had a hill graded to resemble the landscape in Hitchcock's film, and moved the house there. Using photographs from the original film as well as old blueprints, production designer John W. Corso reconstructed the Bates Motel below the house from scratch. Only forty feet of the front side of the motel was filmed. The rest of it, as well as the neon sign, were completed optically by matte artist Albert Whitlock. Set decorator Jennifer Polito was then charged with finding props and set dressings to match those seen in the house and the motel in the original film. She was able to accomplish her task by screening the film several times, then pouring through Richard Anobile's frame-by-frame book of *Psycho* stills.

Psycho was legendary director Alfred Hitchcock's most financially successful (he got the last laugh on

Mary Loomis (Meg Tilly), daughter of Lila and Sam Loomis and niece of the slain Marion Crane, replays the notorious shower scene in *Psycho II.*

Paramount after all) and influential film. It opened the floodgates for much of what was to follow in the horror film genre. Its impact is all encompassing—not only on its direct series descendants, but on countless other, lesser films.

The reasons for the original's success are not difficult to understand. They come down to three factors: Alfred Hitchcock, the character of Norman Bates, and Anthony Perkins' realization of that character. It is unlikely that Hitchcock himself could have fully understood the import of his original creation. After all, Hitchcock's film came at a time very much before society had been inundated by the real life horrors of Charles Manson, Richard Speck, Albert DeSalvo (the Boston Strangler), John Wayne Gacy, Ted Bundy, et. al. What Hitchcock made was originally considered the last word in outrageous horror, when, in fact, it was only the beginning. What seemed so bizarre and so incomprehensible in 1960 has since become all too familiar indeed—offscreen as well as on.

The major difference between the *Psycho* series and its host of imitators lies in Norman Bates. In Hitchcock's original, Norman was as much a victim as any of the people he murdered, a fact that was quite lost at the

Anthony Perkins finds himself
descending once again into madness
in *Pyscho II*.

time in the rush to either attack or applaud the film's ability to scare and to shock. Hitchcock probably didn't realize that he was creating, if not a hero, at least a very viable portrait of a tortured and beleaguered mankind. Norman has since become very much an embodiment of our time—our own deepest, blackest fears made real on the screen—a link to the insanity of the world around us. Through him, we more readily understand that madness. As a result, he has very nearly become something of a "folk hero." Norman Bates himself put it best in one of his most famous lines from the original film (a line he would repeat in *Psycho III*): "We all go a little mad sometimes."

Anthony Perkins' Bates is no brain-dead killing machine. He is no *Friday the 13th*-style Jason Voorhees, nor a *Halloween*-style Michael Myers, nor a cartoonish Freddy Krueger figure, but a flesh and blood character with senses, perceptions and feelings of his own. This is the very reason why the idea was able to be revived and expanded upon twenty-two years after the fact. In terms of impact and directorial flourish (Australia's Richard Franklin mostly copycats the style of other, better directors), *Psycho II* was not the film *Psycho* was. But it did work. It worked because of Norman Bates and Anthony Perkins. *Psycho* is very much a Hitchcock film. The later entries, despite the undeniable influence of Hitchcock on them, are explorations of the character by Perkins. [One might even say that while Hitchcock was the undeniable auteur of the first film, Perkins has assumed that position in the two sequels—his decision to direct the third film being not only logical, but seemingly inevitable.]

This is not to denigrate or even downgrade Hitchcock's contribution to the series on the whole. The strict Catholic upbringing Hitchcock experienced (and which always lurked beneath the surface of his own work) found a ready voice in the subsequent *Psycho* films. Without question, Hitchcock led the way. He pointed the direction for the development of the Norman Bates character and the religious implications of the films as they have progressed.

As a series, the *Psycho* films simply could not exist without the potent contribution of Anthony Perkins, and not just in his having taken over the directorial reins for the third film. They simply could not exist without Perkins. In fact, it is almost entirely due to his performance—his center of gravity—that *Psycho II*, sans Hitchcock, worked as well as it did. Though extremely popular with audiences, *Psycho II* was scorned by most critics as not being up to the original. [Ironically, Hitchcock's film was also initially scorned by most contemporary critics as not being up to Hitchcock's usual high standard. And, subsequently, *The Birds* was critically drubbed upon its initial release as not being "as good as *Psycho*."] This is scarcely surprising, since *Psycho II was* a sequel (sequels generally tend to get a bad rap), and, moreover, a sequel to a (now) universally admired film. It was destined to suffer by comparison before it was even made. But, largely because the Norman Bates character had assumed a foreground position in the sequel, Perkins was even better here than he had been in *Psycho*. Approached to do a sequel for many years, he declined for lack of an innovative script. Tom Holland's screenplay for *Psycho II* appealed to him, he said, because it "had character." Indeed, *Psycho II is* Perkins' characterization. The sense of personal tragedy and torment brought to the film by Perkins (the part is admittedly well written) raised the film out of the realm of the standard sequel despite director Franklin's imitative style. Again, it is the character that made the sequel different—we are as much afraid *for* Norman as *of* him.

With Perkins taking over as director of *Psycho III,* it was only natural that the emphasis would shift entirely to the creation of a wholly sympathetic character. In so doing, Perkins created an even fresher and more pertinent film than the one that had preceded it. All of our understanding of *Psycho III* centers around Norman's character, much as it did in the second film, but the difference here being that our fears are now built upon the potential for Norman's actual salvation. If *Psycho II* was about Norman's character and his attempt to hold on to the nominal sanity afforded him by twenty-two years of psychiatric treatment, *Psycho III* is Norman's own battle to crawl out of the pit of madness into which he had returned by the end of the second film. It affords Norman the chance for redemption on his own, the chance to exorcise his own demons. In this film, his directorial debut, Perkins—reflecting his experience working with such screen greats as Hitchcock and Ken Russell—proves himself a far more daring and adventurous filmmaker than Richard Franklin. He con-

Two troubled souls, Norman Bates (Anthony Perkins) and Maureen Coyle (Diana Scarwid), find comfort in each other's arms in *Psycho III*.

It's back to the hoosegow for Norman (Anthony Perkins) as he contemplates yet another sequel.

sciously does not endeavor to recall Hitchcock or make a Hitchcock homage (though, inevitably, there is some of this), but rather strives to make a film that is worthy of Hitchcock on *thematic* grounds. What other horror film, especially the *third* in a series, has had the nerve and the wit to deliberately place an ambiguous situation at its center? Perkins' film can be successfully read two ways: as the tragedy of two people who might well have held the potential for each other's salvation, or as a particularly vicious satire of this same line of thought. The tormented ex-nun's (Diana Scarwid) vision of "Mother Bates" as the Virgin Mary manages to be perfectly valid religious symbolism and a parody of it all at once. It is the sort of complexity Hitchcock himself might well have admired. The essential Hitchcockian "rightness" of the approach is wholly evident if we recall that the original film was structured so that Marion Crane's (Janet Leigh) murder occurred immediately after her decision to redeem herself by returning the money she had stolen and facing the consequences of her actions—her shower, a symbolic washing away of her sins, cut short by the most famous murder in screen history. [Scarwid's physical resemblance to Leigh and the character's own name, Maureen Coyle (M.C.), further strengthen the parallel.]

Perkins himself has noted that the strength of the films lies in the fact that one genuinely wants to know what happened next. This is very true, particularly due to our own unfortunate growing familiarity with Norman Bates-like characters in real life. When Hitchcock made his film, Norman was so foreign to most of us that we never questioned that this was the whole story, that Norman would be forever locked away in an asylum. Events over the intervening years have proved that this was not necessarily so, that a murderer might very well be adjudged "restored to sanity" and sent back into the real world.

Indeed, *Psycho II* deliberately calls this once unthinkable situation directly to mind by having Mary Loomis (Meg Tilly) shown in bed reading *In The Belly of the Beast*, a book written by Jack Abbott, a supposedly reformed killer who turned out to be anything but. [The book reappears in the third film as well.] Time itself—and the occurrences in it—had made the once complete story incomplete and worthy of further examination. The glib explanation of the psychiatrist (Simon Oakland) at the end of the first film, which was never intended to be fully satisfying, became almost absurd with the passing years. Indeed, there *was* more to tell.

The Bates Motel itself [milieu and star of a proposed NBC television series with Bud Cort that did not come to pass] —is virtually a character in each film. At the very least, it is a perfect breeding ground for insanity. Its juxtaposition with the traditional "old dark house" behind it perfectly bridges the gap between the horror of yesterday and the very different modern horror explored in the series. Part of the shock of the first film was that the first direct horror, or assault on the audience's sensibilities and expectations—the notorious shower murder—did not take place in the old dark house, but in the brightly lit bathroom of the motel. Hitchcock had deftly set us up (as Robert Bloch had in the novel on which *Psycho* is based), forcing us to rethink our notions of where horrible, unspeakable things might take place. Following that idea, the subsequent films, especially *Psycho III,* were at pains to explore the concept that many of Norman's problems lay in his inability to recognize the failure of the Bates Motel, insisting on holding onto it even as it decays around him.

Plainly speaking, the *Psycho* films are not your average horror film series. There's more to them than meets the eye.

Norman (Anthony Perkins) hears "mother's" voice warning him about Maureen (Diana Scarwind). From *Psycho III.*

The fast deteriorating Norman (Anthony Perkins) is trapped inside his submerging car as he tries conceal the bodies of yet more victims in the swamp behind the Bates Motel. From *Psycho III.*

SCREAM OF FEAR (1961)

[A.k.a. *Taste of Fear* in the U.K.]
A Hammer Film Production
A Columbia Pictures Release
B&W/82 minutes

Susan Strasberg, the victim of a deadly psychological game of cat and mouse—and murder—lets loose with a *Scream of Fear*.

Credits

Director: Seth Holt; *Producer:* Jimmy Sangster; *Screenplay:* Jimmy Sangster; *Cinematographer:* Douglas Slocombe; *Editors:* James Needs and Eric Boyd-Perkins; *Music:* Clifton Parker; *Production Designer:* Bernard Robinson; *Videocassette source:* RCA/Columbia Home Video.

Cast

Penny Appleby: Susan Strasberg; *Bob:* Ronald Lewis; *Jane Appleby:* Ann Todd; *Dr. Gerrard:* Christopher Lee; *Spratt:* Leonard Sachs; *Marie:* Anne Blake; *Inspector Legrand:* John Serret; *Father:* Fred Johnson; *Gendarme:* Bernard Brown; *Plainsclothsman:* Richard Klee.

72

Director Seth Holt (seated to left of camera) sets up a shot for *Scream of Fear* on location near Cap d'Antibes in the south of France. Susan Strasberg is seated on the rock wall next to the microphone.

With *Scream of Fear,* Hammer Films entered another period in its evolution by producing a string of modern dress Gothics which would be dubbed "mini-Hitchcocks" by the press. The success of Alfred Hitchcock's *Psycho* had given the public an appetite for horror in a more realistic setting and for monsters drawn straight from the headlines rather than myths and legends. Shot in stark black and white, *Psycho* was a return to the expressionistic style of the Universal classics and the German silents—the film was even shot on the Universal lot. And so, those companies and filmmakers seeking to jump on the *Psycho* bandwagon began shooting their films in black and white too. For Hammer, this was a surprising reversal, for it had spent the past three years rejuvenating the horror genre by trumpeting the use of color.

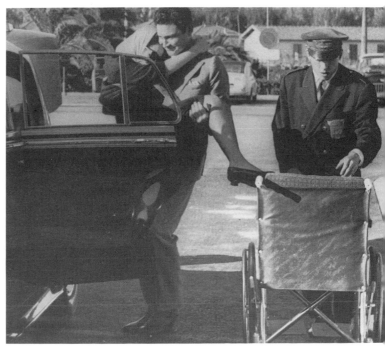

Bob (Ronald Lewis), her deceased father's kindly young chauffeur, helps the crippled Penny (Susan Strasberg) into the family Rolls.

Bob (Ronald Lewis) carries Penny (Susan Strasberg) back to her room—followed by Penny's stepmother (Ann Todd), whom Penny suspects of having murdered her father, and the equally suspicious family doctor (Christopher Lee).

Scream of Fear, the first of the Hammer shockers to be categorized by critics as "in the *Psycho* vein," was, ironically, not so much inspired by *Psycho* as by its success. Always interested in capitalizing on any new trend, the studio simply encouraged the connection. Actually, the script had been written well before the Hitchcock film was even released. Tired of writing period Gothics, Jimmy Sangster had submitted the screenplay to another studio. But when the deal fell through, Hammer—influenced no doubt by the notoriety *Psycho* was getting—picked up the option and launched the production the same year.

The antecedents of *Scream of Fear* really go back to a much earlier film, Henri Georges Clouzot's 1955 French shocker *Les Diaboliques,* which *Psycho* itself had drawn upon in no small way. The Clouzot film, also in black and white, was a contemporary murder mystery with overtones of madness and the supernatural which, in the end, prove to be bogus. Two women conspire to murder the overbearing husband of one of them only to find their victim seemingly reaching out from beyond the grave to get even. At the conclusion, the wife suffers a fatal coronary when the body of her supposedly dead husband rises out of the bathtub to threaten her. In a surprise twist, it is revealed that he and the other woman are lovers whose plan all along was to kill the wife for her estate. Sangster had already dabbled with this type of topsy-turvy plot in an earlier Hammer thriller, *The Snorkel* (1958), directed by Guy Green. *Scream of Fear* is cut from the same mold.

Ann Todd and Ronald Lewis as the scheming lovers in *Scream of Fear.*

In it, a high-strung young girl returns to her home in the south of France to recuperate from an accident that has left her crippled. Her beloved father is supposedly away on a business trip. She becomes increasingly unhinged, however, when she starts seeing his corpse pop up in unlikely places such as the bottom of the family swimming pool (a direct reference to *Les Diaboliques*) and grows convinced that he has been murdered. Full of unctuous concern, her stepmother calls in a sinister family doctor with whom the girl suspects her stepmother is in league in a plot to drive her insane. In the surprise twist, it is revealed that the girl and the doctor are actually working together to smoke out the real villains—the stepmother and the family chauffeur, lovers who murdered the girl's father and have since been trying to drive her out of her mind for her inheritance. In yet another twist, the girl turns out to be a friend of the dead man's daughter and not the genuine article. The real daughter, a manic depressive, had committed suicide.

Scream of Fear was suspensefully directed by Seth Holt, a former film editor who later would lend his meticulous craftsmanship to two equally noteworthy Hammer shockers, *The Nanny* (1965) and *Blood From the Mummy's Tomb* (1972), before his untimely death in 1971. The thriller evolved a new Hammer formula (the pull-the-wool-over-their-eyes shocker) which Sangster, as writer, producer and director, would repeat for the studio several more times in the years to come with varying degrees of success (*Scream of Fear* is the best of them). How much these films *do* pull the wool over your eyes depends very much on how closely you keep their model, *Les Diaboliques,* in mind. For Hammerphiles particularly, however, *Scream of Fear* offers another amusing tip-off. As a possible in-joke, the character of the supposedly sinister doctor played by Christopher Lee is named Gerrard. In Hammer's *The Man Who Could Cheat Death,* also scripted by Sangster, Lee's character (and first hero role for Hammer) is named Dr. Gerard. Surely this was not an unintentional clue.

After Bob (Ronald Lewis) rescues her from drowning in the family swimming pool, Penny (Susan Strasberg) finds herself falling in love with him. Or is she?

THE PHANTOM OF THE OPERA (1962)

A Hammer Film Production
A Universal-International Release
Color, /84 minutes

When he confronts the villainous D'Arcy about stealing his music, Professor Petrie (Herbert Lom) is knocked into the street.

Credits

Director: Terence Fisher; *Producer:* Anthony Hinds; *Screenplay:* John Elder (Hinds), based on the novel by Gaston Leroux; *Cinematographer:* Arthur Grant; *Supervising Editor:* James Needs; *Music:* Edwin Astley; *Production Designer:* Bernard Robinson; *Videocassette source:* Unavailable.

Cast

The Phantom: Herbert Lom; *Harry Hunter:* Edward De Souza; *Christine Charles:* Heather Sears; *Lord Ambrose D'Arcy:* Michael Gough; *Latimer:* Thorley Walters; *Dwarf:* Ian Wilson; *Ratcatcher:* Patrick Troughton.

The almost hostile accusations of banality and unoriginality that Hammer's *The Phantom of the Opera* drew from critics at the time of its release has always puzzled me. But then, Hammer fans didn't much care for it either—despite the fact that it was and still is one of the most elegantly mounted of all Hammer Horrors and certainly the most romantic Gothic Terence Fisher ever directed.

Consistent with Hammer's pattern, it was not so much a remake (of Gaston Leroux's twice-filmed novel, which was made yet again in 1983 with Maximillian Schell and in 1989 with filmdom's infamous "Freddy Krueger," Robert Englund) as a rethinking of it. Comparisons with the earlier screen incarnations—one of which (the Lon Chaney silent) was considered a classic—were inevitable. Frankly, I couldn't help comparing the trio myself, but unlike others, I didn't find this new *Phantom* to be anywhere near as wanting. In the first place, the Lon Chaney silent, while perhaps the most faithful to the Leroux novel, remains famous primarily because of Chaney's mime and makeup. It certainly doesn't play anywhere near as well with audiences today as it must have back in 1925 when it debuted. As for the Claude Rains version, that was certainly no classic. In it, the character of the phantom was effectively reduced to a supporting role—for large chunks, he all but disappears as the film focuses instead on the tepid romantic contest between Nelson Eddy and Edgar Barrier for the affections of opera star Susanna Foster (for whom the film was obviously meant as a showcase). At the very least, the Hammer version put the phantom back at the center of things.

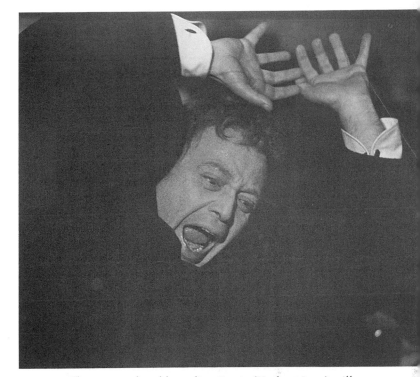

The wronged and brooding Petrie (Herbert Lom) will soon become *The Phantom of the Opera*, after accidentally dousing himself with acid, thinking it was water.

The Phantom (Herbert Lom) introduces himself to Christine (Heather Sears) who has just awakened in his underground lair.

The Phantom (Herbert Lom) works Christine (Heather Sears) to the point of exhaustion in order to turn her into a star in his opera based on the story of Joan of Arc.

Hammer lavished a larger budget on *Phantom* than its previous Gothic Horrors because it was clearly aiming for something special. And to a large degree, I think, producer Anthony Hinds and director Terence Fisher succeeded. The film's opera house (actually a Drury Lane theater) is not as opulent as the reconstructed Paris Opera House (Hammer's *Phantom* is set in London) of the Chaney and Rains versions, but the lack of opulence contributes strongly to the film's closed-in, gothic atmosphere. Remember, this was not a film apart from, but of a piece *with* the fairy tale world of the Gothic Horror that Hammer had so meticulously defined in its previous films. A spectacular opera house full of milling ticket buyers and a labyrinth of tunnels and rooms would have ruptured this gothic world, the claustrophobic nature of which is aimed at drawing viewers in, not getting them lost.

In director Terence Fisher's words, *Phantom* is, like Hammer's *Horror of Dracula,* "nothing more nor less than a love story." It is a tale of failed fortunes and realized dreams. The tear that falls from the phantom's eye when he sees his *Joan of Arc* opera come alive in the voice of Christine is not (as critic Bosley Crowther stated in *The New York Times*) an "inspired moment" but the summation of what the film is all about. Yes, the phantom is a menacing figure, but he is not an evil almost supernatural creature (like Chaney) nor a vengeful ogre (like Rains). He is a wronged man whose music has been stolen by a villainous impresario. Michael Gough's D'Arcy—much like Cushing's Van Helsing and Dr. Frankenstein—is in fact the real villain of the piece. The phantom does not try to drop the opera house chandelier on unsuspecting and innocent patrons, but is killed by it himself in an attempt to protect Christine when his dwarf assistant, fleeing the police, accidentally rips it from its moorings. This violent turnabout is perfectly in keeping with the film's very romantic tone, for it allows the phantom not only to repent with an act of heroism, but to exit vindicated and with dignity, having heard his music played and appreciated at last.

Herbert Lom is superb as the phantom—no better, perhaps, than Chaney and Rains, but equal to them in his own way. Like Richard Wordsworth's character of Victor Carroon in Hammer's *The Quatermass Experiment* and Chris Lee's creature, Dracula and mummy characters, he perfectly conveys that sense of sadness so much a part of Hammer's gothic monsters. But he is also overbearing, and demanding as he struggles to turn Christine into a star. He knows the clock is running out on his artistic assault on heaven and is determined not to be defeated. And he isn't. In important contrast to Chaney and Rains, Lom is not just a "nice guy phantom" (as *Newsweek*'s reviewer called him), but a heroic figure indeed.

With *The Phantom of the Opera,* Hammer and Terence Fisher reached an apotheosis of their Gothic Horror formula, leaving few other avenues to explore. As a result, the film is worthy of more attention than it invariably gets. But there is, perhaps, a reason for this. Since its theatrical debut, Hammer's *Phantom,* which now circulates primarily on television, has rarely been shown in its original form. The TV prints eliminate several scenes or portions of scenes—such as the grisly murder of the rat catcher, who is stabbed in the eye by the phantom's dwarf assistant. Simultaneously, new ones of a police investigation (shot by Universal with other actors) have been inserted which not only rupture the film's mood (and pad out its length) but treat the viewer with disdain by "explaining" what's going on.

The late Eighties outbreak of "Phantomania" courtesy of Andrew Lloyd Webber has caused some TV stations to start showing Hammer's original theatrical print, so a sharp eye should be kept. For Hammer's *Phantom* is worthy of reappraisal by those who've years ago seen and probably dismissed it. And worth getting to know by those who haven't as yet had the pleasure.

Opera producer Harry Hunter (Edward DeSouza) confronts The Phantom (Herbert Lom) about kidnapping Christine (Heather Sears).

The unmasked Phantom (Herbert Lom, or rather, his stunt double) faces what might be a fiery end as his underground lair goes up in flames.

THE BIRDS (1963)

A Universal Release
Color /120 minutes

Melanie (Tippi Hedren) as the ultimate damsel in distress.

The birds launch their first full scale on a group of children attending Cathy Brenner's (Veronica Cartwright) birthday party.

Credits

Director: Alfred Hitchcock; *Producer:* Alfred Hitchcock; *Screenplay:* Evan Hunter, based on the short story by Daphne du Maurier; *Cinematographer:* Robert Burks; *Editor:* George Tomasini; *Sound Consultant:* Bernard Herrmann; *Art Director:* Robert Boyle; *Videocassette source:* MCA Home Video.

Cast

Mitch Brenner: Rod Taylor; *Lydia Brenner:* Jessica Tandy; *Melanie Daniels:* Tippi Hedren; *Annie Hayworth:* Suzanne Pleshette; *Cathy Brenner:* Veronica Cartwright; *Mrs. Bundy:* Ethel Griffies; *Sebastian Sholes:* Charles McGraw; *Mrs. MacGruder:* Ruth McDevitt; *Traveling Salesman:* Joe Mantell; *Deputy Malone:* Malcolm Atterbury; *Drunk:* Karl Swenson.

A murderous crow attacks one of the children escaping from the schoolhouse in Bodega Bay.

More havoc prompted by *The Birds*.

The runaway success of *Psycho,* his first venture into horror film territory, prompted Hitchcock to be somewhat cautious about what his next project should be. *Marnie,* an adaptation of a suspense novel by Winston Graham about a female thief with psycho-sexual problems, was already in the planning stages. Hitchcock was hoping to lure Grace Kelly, his definitive ice-cool blonde, away from her palace in Monaco and back to the silver screen with the project. Kelly was interested, but then backed out [some sources say she was forced to back out by her husband, Prince Ranier, and other royal advisers], forcing Hitchcock to put the project on temporary hold.

Feeling that on the heels of *Psycho,* the subject matter of *Marnie* might prove a bit tame to audiences, Hitchcock immediately began considering the prospect of making another horror film—but one very different from *Psycho.* A Daphne du Maurier short story called *The Birds* in one of the periodic collections put out by the publishing wing of Hitchcock's entertainment empire struck him that the subject matter might be ideal for his purposes. The tale itself, however, would have to be considerably expanded upon in order to turn it into a feature length film.

Hitchcock hired novelist Evan Hunter (who also writes under the pseudonym of Ed McBain) to flesh the story out for him. Set in Cornwall, England, du Maurier's very brief tale recounts the efforts of a Cornish farmer and his family to defend themselves against the unexplained onslaught of flocks of killer birds by barricading themselves in their farmhouse. The tale's "nature gone mad" theme and du Maurier's choice of flocks of birds—the most harmless of creatures—as the suddenly murderous vehicle of nature's wrath appealed strongly to the director, whose films had always strived to expose the terror that lurked in the shadows of the commonplace. The technical challenges the film would present also appealed to him.

Together with Hunter, Hitchcock mapped out a story that retained little of du Maurier's original except the birds' final, murderous assault on the farmhouse. He and Hunter also transposed the setting of the film from England to San Francisco and California's northern coast. Released in 1963 with a memorable advertising slogan ("The Birds Is Coming!") devised by Hitchcock himself, the film was a solid box office success—though, like *Psycho* before it, it received less-than-

Melanie (Tippi Hedren), Mitch (Rod Taylor) and Mrs. Brenner (Jessica Tandy) fend off an attack of birds entering the house through the chimney.

rapturous reviews. Most of the negative notices focused on the romantic sub-plot that prefaced the film's final hour when flocks of birds descend upon the Bodega Bay area and its terrified inhabitants. Even the film's detractors admitted that the film's multitude of optical and other special effects and suspenseful set pieces during this final hour were handled by Hitchcock as deftly and expertly as ever. But for the majority of critics, the first hour seemed a concoction that severly diluted the impact of the climactic bird onslaught. Hitchcock disagreed, believing that the film not only required a slow build-up in order to put the audience on edge, but that the build-up itself was central to the

film's theme. "I believe that people are too complacent," he told *Cinefantastique* magazine in 1980, the year of his death. "People like Melanie Daniels [the initially vacuous heroine of the film] tend to behave without any kind of responsibility, and to ignore the more serious aspects of life. Such people are unaware that catastrophe surrounds us all. But I believe that when catastrophe does come, when people rise to the occasion, they are all right. Melanie shows that people can be strong when they face up to a situation, like the people in London during the wartime air raids. The birds basically symbolized the more serious aspects of life."

Mitch (Rod Taylor) attempts to force out one of the invading birds.

Though the first half of the film *is* slow—and seems even slower on repeated viewings—I tend to agree with Hitchcock's assessment. The low key first hour does put the audience on edge by making them impatient. But, more importantly, it sets up the film's theme in very intricate detail. Regardless of its shortcomings as drama (or comedy), if the first hour of the film were removed, the thematic aims of *The Birds* would be dissipated. Melanie, Mitch, Lydia Brenner and Annie Hayworth lead very empty lives, making mountainous problems out of their molehill insecurities. Worse still, they take their lives for granted. The attack of the birds—which comes out of nowhere and, as in du Maurier's short story, is never explained—pointedly reveals to them how shallow they'd allowed their lives to become and how fragile and tenuous, and therefore precious, life is. Apart from Annie Hayworth (who does develop *some* insight into herself before being killed by the birds), all the main characters evolve and grow throughout the film to the point where they are no longer frivolous, self-important or self-obsessed characters, but mature people who, upon deciding to take Cathy's "lovebirds" with them at the movie's tense conclusion, have finally embraced what Hitchcock called "the serious aspects of life."

Audiences didn't flock (as it were) to *The Birds* for edification, however. They went to be scared and shaken up by the promise of its winged pyrotechnics—and in this department the film clearly did not disappoint, nor does it today. *The Birds* (though shamefully ignored in the special effects category come Oscar time) remains one of Hitchcock's most sophisticated and technically ingenious accomplishments. The latter half of the film is full of set pieces that reveal Hitchcock at the top of his form as the screen's "master of suspense"—set pieces that remain memorable today. For example: the playground scene where one bird after another silently lights upon the swings, jungle gyms and other schoolyard paraphernalia with Melanie remaining blissfully unaware of their presence until she spots one lone crow and turns to see that the creatures have massed in the hundreds behind her; the bird attack on the schoolhouse itself; the devastation of the town of Bodega Bay; the birds' attempts to smash through the glass of the telephone booth (the metaphoric "gilded cage") in which Melanie has sought refuge; Lydia Brenner's discovery of the dead farmer Dan Fawcett, whose eyes have been pecked out; the birds' repeated assaults on the barricaded farmhouse in which Hitchcock sometimes uses sounds alone to convey their murderous presence (composer Bernard Herrmann, continuing his long association with Hitchcock, here received "Sound Consultant" credit); and Melanie's venture up to the attic swarming with birds, where she is almost torn to pieces as wave upon wave of clawing, shrieking, pecking creatures assail her. This last sequence particularly is as brilliantly shot and edited as the celebrated shower murder of Janet Leigh in *Psycho*—a scene it is clearly meant to recall, and almost equals in power and technical virtuosity.

The Birds remains along with *Psycho* one of Hitchcock's most influential and oft-imitated films. Following its success, the screen became surfieted with one "nature gone mad" film after another in which just about every commonplace, though not necessarily "meek," creature imaginable massed and trained its vengeful sights on complacent mankind—from bees, cockroaches, wasps, locusts and other bugs to rabbits, rats, bears, snakes and, of course, sharks. *The Birds* is still the best of them though, not only because it's the archetype for this sub-genre of the modern horror film, but because it's still the most thoughtful—a near-perfect melding of humor, horror, personal statement and "pure cinema," Hitchcock-style.

REPULSION (1965)

A Compton-Cameo Film Production
A Columbia Pictures Release
B&W /105 minutes

The mentally deteriorating Carol Ledoux (Catherine Deneuve).

Carol (Catherine Deneuve) gazes upon her distorted reflection.

Credits

Director: Roman Polanski; *Producer:* Gene Gutowski; *Screenplay:* Roman Polanski and Gerard Brach; *Cinematographer:* Gil Taylor; *Editor:* Alastair McIntyre; *Music:* Chico Hamilton; *Art Director:* Seamus Flannery; *Videocassette source:* Unavailable.

Cast

Carol Ledoux: Catherine Deneuve; *Michael:* Ian Hendry; *Colin:* John Fraser; *Helen Ledoux:* Yvonne Furneaux; *Landlord:* Patrick Wymark; *Miss Balch:* Renee Houston; *Madame Denise:* Valerie Taylor; *John:* James Villiers; *Bridget:* Helen Fraser.

Roman Polanski was born in Paris in 1933, the son of Polish parents, who returned to Poland when he was three and settled in Krakow. When the Nazi invasion came, Polanski's parents were sent to concentration camps, where his mother subsequently perished. Young Roman meanwhile escaped into the country to live with strangers.

After the war, he became a child performer in radio. This job and the contacts he made in it led him into the theater where he worked as an actor, stage manager and jack-of-all-trades for six years. When his father remarried, Polanski chose to continue his pursuit of a career in the arts rather than move back home. Financial support from his father, together with funds he was earning as an actor, enabled him to enter school to study painting and graphics. Simultaneously, his theater work began to carry over into films, a medium for which he'd always had a special fondness. Polanski's associations with Andrzek Wajda and other aspiring directors fired within him the goal of becoming a film director himself. He succeeded in gaining entrance to the National Film School at Lodz, an aesthetic and practical training ground for filmmakers that remains today one of the best schools of its type in the world.

His thesis film, *Two Men and a Wardrobe* (1958), was a surrealistic short about two men who emerge from the sea carrying a large chest, encounter a world that is hostile not only to them but to itself, and return with despair to the sea from whence they came. It afforded Polanski the opportunity to make additional films, and a series of equally surrealistic shorts—*When*

Angels Fall (1959), The Lamp (1959), The Fat and the Lean (1961) and Mammals (1962)—followed in fairly rapid succession. These gained him the opportunity to make his first full length feature, Knife in the Water (1962), which brought him international acclaim. It was invited to be shown at the first New York Film Festival and was later nominated for an Oscar as Best Foreign Film of the year [it lost to Federico Fellini's 8½]. Polanski attended the New York Film Festival screening and the later Oscar ceremonies as well, and his exposure to the opportunities that existed in the West convinced him that this was where his filmic fortunes lay.

Despite the acclaim Knife in the Water had earned him, Polanski did not find the studio doors of the West opening before him. Together with Gerard Brach, a film publicist-turned-screenwriter he'd met on a visit to Paris, Polanski wrote a script for a segment of a French

On location in South Kensington with Repulsion. Director Polanski can be seen peeking over Catherine Deneuve's left shoulder.

omnibus film called Les Plus Belles Escroqueries Du Monde [The Beautiful Swindlers] (1963), and also directed the segment, which was shot in Amsterdam. Like his previous work, the film, which was not widely distributed, did little to open additional doors for him. With Brach again, he wrote another script, Cul-De-Sac, a throwback to his surrealistic shorts, which found little enthusiasm among potential producers. A fellow Polish expatriate, Gene Gutowski, who was living in England, encouraged Polanski and Brach to develop a more commercially viable project—which Gutowski, who had some contact in the British film industry, agreed to produce.

Then, as now, making a low budget horror film seemed an ideal solution. Britain's Hammer Films (with

87

Carol (Catherine Deneuve) imagines the walls her flat beginning to crack.

The sexually frustrated Colin (John Fraser) prepares to break down the door to Carol's flat.

which Polanski was familiar) had made box office waves with this genre and was still very much in its heyday at the time. Meanwhile, Hitchcock's *Psycho* (1960), which had scared the pants off the world, was still influencing aspiring filmmakers everywhere. Polanski and Brach, inspired by Hitchcock's film, but even moreso by Michael Powell's controversial *Peeping Tom* (1960)—a personal favorite of Polanski's, set about writing a contemporary shocker about a beautiful but sexually repressed and mentally unhinged young girl whose fantasies turn to murder. They called it *Repulsion* and with Gutowski's help, they interested Michael Klinger and Tony Tenser's Compton-Cameo Films in Great Britain to put up the money. Interestingly, *Repulsion* would have been an ideal subject for Hammer to have made, for at the time, the studio was turning out a series of similar contemporary shockers, though none as potent, scary or influential as *Repulsion* would prove to be. Had Hammer made the film, it not only would have had a substantial critical and commercial hit on its hands (most of its own films in this vein were neither), but also added a very talented and innovative new director to its roster. Writer David Pirie, an expert on Hammer, has suggested that this type of missed opportunity was what led to Hammer's downfall. Instead of finding directors like Polanski to make a *Repulsion* for them, the studio continued to force even its younger talents to adhere to tried-and-true formulas, not recognizing that public taste was changing.

Unlike Hitchcock's *Psycho*, Polanski's *Repulsion* unfolds not from the viewpoint of the psychopath's victims, but from the psychopath herself. This is what ties it more closely to Powell's *Peeping Tom*. The two films are probing psychological case studies—although *Repulsion* probes the demented mind of its protagonist far more intimately than Powell's film does by placing the viewer *inside* that mind. Virtually the entire film is told from Carol's psycho-sexual point of view. Even when the scene shifts away from her, it does so to provide an additional insight into the nature of her problem. For example, when her frustrated lover, Colin, is kissed on the mouth by a male friend, he reacts with disgust and abhorrence, thereby providing us with a clue as to how Carol felt when he kissed her.

The phantom rapist invades Carol's bedroom.

Carol's dilemma—like Rosemary's in *Rosemary's Baby* (1968) and Trelkovsky's in *The Tenant* (1976)—stems from her inability to reconcile two warring aspects of her personality: in her case, the fact that she is both attracted to the idea of sex, yet repelled by it at the same time. When her sister goes on an Italian vacation with her married boyfriend, leaving Carol all alone in the bleak, cluttered and foreboding South Kensington flat they share together, Carol's inner turmoil reaches critical mass. Fantasizing a tryst with a phantom lover (who walks with a limp like her sister's boyfriend yet looks like one of the London construction workers who'd earlier made a pass at her), Carol puts

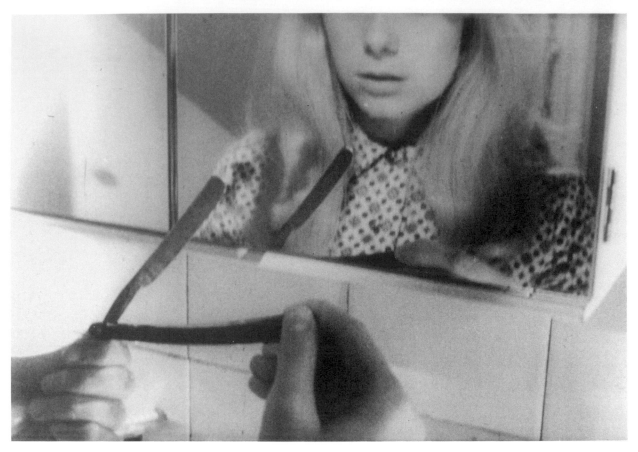

Carol (Catherine Deneuve) comes upon Michael's razor in the bathroom.

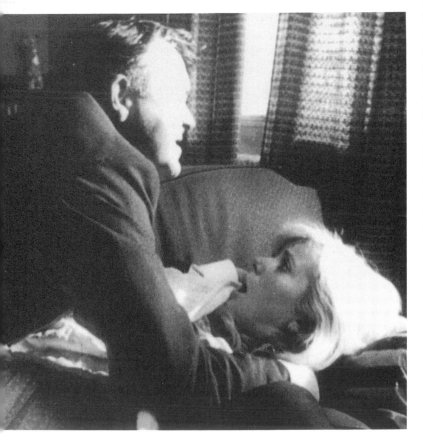

Carol (Catherine Deneuve) is assaulted by the landlord (Patrick Wymark); she defends herself by cutting him to ribbons with Michael's razor.

on lipstick in anticipation—then imagines herself being brutally raped instead. As her madness soars out of control, she imagines the walls of the flat cracking asunder. Hands burst from walls to fondle her. Rooms grow distorted and unfamiliar—as does her reflection when she gazes upon it in a teapot. When Colin, her sister's boyfriend, breaks into the locked apartment to find out why she hasn't been answering his calls, she misinterprets his advances and brutally clubs him to death with a candle holder and deposits his body in the bathtub. And when the landlord appears to collect the long overdue rent and sees the attractive girl in a semi-nude state, *he* misinterprets her appearance as a come-on, tries to make love to her and gets sliced up with a straight razor. By the end of the film, Carol's inner conflict is finally resolved when she retreats into a somnambulistic shell of total, irrevocable catatonia.

Repulsion is a disturbing film and Polanski makes no attempt to pretty it up. Today, the director tends to dismiss it as both slightly amateurish and technically shoddy, lacking the surface gloss of his two subsequent psychological case study films, *Rosemary's Baby* and *The Tenant*. True, *Repulsion* does lack the polished veneer of those later films, but, in my opinion, is all the more potent because of that. Nor is it even *slightly* amateurish. Its atmosphere throughout is suffocating and totally convincing. It remains to this day one of the most clinical studies of mental aberration and breakdown the screen has given us—and one of the scariest as well.

THE FEARLESS VAMPIRE KILLERS (1967)

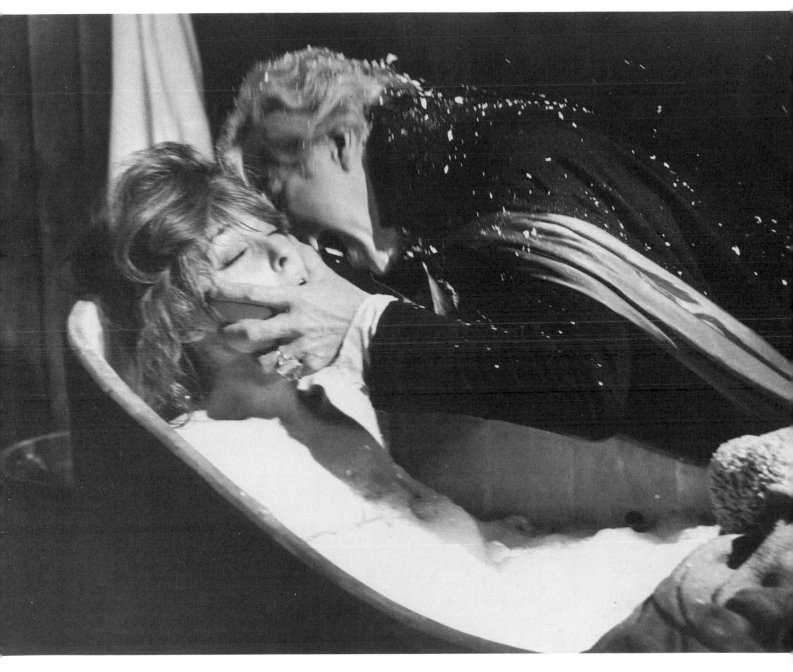

[A.k.a. *Dance of the Vampires* in U.K.]
A Cadre Films—Filmways, Inc. Production
Released through Metro-Goldwyn-Mayer
Color /91 minutes [U.K. version 107 minutes]

Count Von Krolock (Ferdy Mayne) puts the bite on Sarah (Sharon Tate) while she's taking a bath and spirits her away to his castle.

Hiding from the
vampires, the naive,
waif-like Alfred
(Roman Polanski)
finds himself falling
for a girl at the inn
(Fiona Lewis).

A moment of
slapstick from *The
Fearless Vampire
Killers*. Alfred
(Roman Polanski)
uses a stick to stop
Abronsius (Jack
MacGowran) whose
skis are running
away with him.

Ferdy Mayne cuts a
frightening figure as
the head vampire,
Count Von Krolock.

Credits

Director: Roman Polanski; *Producer:* Gene Gutowski; *Screenplay:* Roman Polanski and Gerard Brach; *Cinematographer:* Douglas Slocombe; *Editor:* Alastair McIntyre; *Music:* Christopher Komeda; *Production Designer:* Wilfred Shingleton; *Videocassette source:* Unavailable.

Cast

Professor Abronsius: Jack MacGowran; *Alfred:* Roman Polanski; *Shagal:* Alfie Bass; *Sarah:* Sharon Tate; *Rebecca:* Jessie Robins; *Count Von Krolock:* Ferdy Mayne; *Herbert:* Ian Quarrier; *Koukol:* Terry Downes; *Maid:* Fiona Lewis; *Village Idiot:* Ronald Lacey.

Repulsion had firmly established Roman Polanski as a master of the modern horror film. His follow-up film, the bizarre, absurdist *Cul-De-Sac* (1966), was not a genre film, however. In fact, it defies categorizing on almost every level. Polanski had hoped the film would elevate his chances of being invited to make a film in Hollywood. As the film was a critical success but a box-office failure, this didn't happen. So, for his next one, Polanski returned to the commercial genre that had served him so well with *Repulsion*—the horror film.

A fan of the genre since his youth, Polanski was also an aficionado of Hammer Horror. He particularly liked Hammer's bizarre and provocative *Brides of Dracula*. He decided to make a Gothic vampire film himself—one that would not only provide fans with the chills they desired, but appeal as well to his own absurdist tendencies by parodying the genre. The result, written with his longtime colaborator Gerard Brach, was the distinctive *The Fearless Vampire Killers* (subtitled *Pardon Me But Your Teeth Are in My Neck*), a comic/horrific extravaganza shot in the Dolomite Mountains of Italy with interiors at London's Shepperton Studios for a major studio—Metro-Goldwyn-Mayer.

The plot is simple and straight forward—and quite comic (in the vein of *Cul-De-Sac*):

Bumbling Professor Abronsius and his naïve, faint-hearted assistant Alfred infiltrate the Translvania retreat of Count Von Krolock with the intention of exterminating a nest of Undead. Unable to complete the mission due to its incredible ineptitude, the pair manages to escape, taking with them Alfred's newly acquired girlfriend, Sarah (a village girl who had been

Alfred (Roman Polanski) attempts to disguise himself as one of the Undead during the climactic "Dance of the Vampires."

kidnapped by Von Krolock). [Sarah was played by Sharon Tate, who would become Roman Polanski's wife and two years later became victim to Charles Manson and "family" in one of Hollywood's most notorious killings.] Both are unaware that she has become a vampire by now as well. As their sleigh spirits away from the castle down the snowy slopes, Sarah bares her fangs and sinks them into Alfred's throat. Abronsious, who is driving the sleigh, is oblivious to this—as he is to almost anything. Nevertheless, the implication is that he will be next and that the two fearless vampire killers will ultimately help spread the very plague of vampirism they had set out to restrain.

The Fearless Vampire Killers, like *Brides of Dracula*, reveals more than a trace of Krafft-Ebing with its depiction of vampirism as a fundamentally sexual perversion. Indeed, Alfred's seductive girlfriend Sarah and Count Von Krolock's homosexual son Herbert, each using sex to ensnare blood victims, begin as parodies of a type. They wind up owing more to such real life "vampires" as Countess Elizabeth Bathory (who slaughtered some 600 virgins and bathed in their blood to keep her complexion creamy and smooth) and Gilles de Rais (who slaughtered an almost equal number of children for equally nefarious purposes) than to the fictional fiends of Bram Stoker and Sheridan Le Fanu. This subtext adds greater thematic dimension to the

Thinking he's dancing with Sarah, Alfred (Roman Polanski) turns to find his partner is one of the Undead.

film—not to mention horror, but the strength of its bite does not diminish, or prove lethal, to the parody. Some of Polanski's gags are quite funny. For example, the Jewish vampire, Shagal, who proves undaunted by the cross ("Oy, have you got the *wrong* vampire!") and the quantities of protective garlic strung everywhere that prove useless in defending against vampires while practically suffocating everyone else.

The finale in which the vampires rise from their tombs to engage in a pre-conquest dance and celebration in the castle ballroom is a stunning set piece that successfully combines elements of horror and humor in equal measure. Alfred and Abronsius pose as vampires, clumsily groping their way through the swirling crowd of waltzing Undead to find some route of escape. They give themselves away, however, when their reflections and no one else's appear in the ballroom mirror—leading to a final madcap chase. Juxtaposed with the comedy—some of which borders on slapstick—are the figures of the real vampires themselves. Dressed in moldy burial rags, their dead-white flesh in varying

stages of decomposition, they're nightmarish—as frightening looking a group of monsters as any horror film has ever offered. The result of all this is that Polanski succeeded in having things both ways. His unique film emerges as frightening as the kind of film it is consciously trying to jest.

Executive producer Martin Ransohoff didn't think so, however. He believed the comic elements didn't quite come off—or that the more horrific elements succeeded in drowning them out. Polanski's contract with Ransohoff gave the director full control over the cut of his film in Europe, but not in the United States, where, Ransohoff believed, audiences would not catch onto the fact that the film was essentially a comedy unless some major surgery was performed. For U.S. release, Ransohoff replaced Polanski's existing title, *Dance of the Vampires*, with the more cartoonish *The Fearless Vampire Killers*—even adding a cartoon featuring caricatures of Abronsius, Alfred and Von Krolock to accompany the opening credits. He likewise cut sixteen minutes from the film and redubbed many of the actor's voices (including Polanski's) to eliminate the Yiddish and East European accents. Despite these efforts (or, perhaps, because of them), the film fell flat at American box-offices—whereas Polanski's version, which retained its original title of *Dance of the Vampires*, played to great success all over Europe.

Polanski had the last laugh. In the late Seventies, the European print (though it bore the American title, *The Fearless Vampire Killers*) was at last released in the United States, playing at universities and repertory movie houses all across the country to great success. It has become very much a cult film.

Some years later, Polanski, again in collaboration with Gerard Brach, attempted to rework the same formula with *Pirates*, a big budget send-up of swashbucklers featuring a bumbling, Abronsius-like pirate (Captain Red, played by Walter Matthau) who works in cahoots with a naïve, waifish assistant called the Frog, who is identical to Alfred in *Vampire Killers*. In fact, Polanski, who had been trying to make *Pirates* for almost ten years, had once planned on playing the role of Frog himself, but by the time he got the film bankrolled, he considered himself too old for the part (it was played by French actor Chris Campion). This time, however, the formula failed to work. Though occasionally amusing, *Pirates* was mostly just plain dull.

Alfred (Roman Polanski) looks on admiringly as his boss, Count Von Krolock (Ferdy Mayne) attempts to tell Sarah (Sharon Tate)—whose gotten the attention of two of the Undead—that they're playing "their" song at the "Dance of the Vampires."

ROSEMARY'S BABY (1968)

A Paramount/William Castle Enterprises Production
A Paramount Pictures Release
Color /136 minutes

Credits

Director: Roman Polanski; *Producer:* William Castle; *Screenplay:* Roman Polanski, based on the novel by Ira Levin; *Cinematographer:* William Fraker; *Editors:* Sam O'Steen and Robert Wyman; *Music:* Christopher Komeda; *Production Designer:* Richard Sylbert; *Videocassette source:* Paramount Home Video.

Cast

Rosemary Woodhouse: Mia Farrow; *Guy Woodhouse:* John Cassavetes; *Minnie Castevet:* Ruth Gordon; *Roman Castevet:* Sidney Blackmer; *Hutch:* Maurice Evans; *Dr. Sapirstein:* Ralph Bellamy; *Dr. Hill:* Charles Grodin; *Terri:* Angela Dorian; *Laura-Louise:* Patsy Kelly; *Mr. Nicklas:* Elisha Cook, Jr.; *Man at Telephone Booth:* William Castle.

Rosemary's Baby marked the first time Roman Polanski based one of his films on someone else's material—in this case a best-selling novel by Ira Levin. Levin's book was a watershed. Its enormous popularity cued publishers to the fact that horror fiction was no longer a genre of cult appeal but one with mass market potential. In effect, the book, which lifted formula horror elements such as devil worship out of their traditional gothic settings and thrust them into the bright contemporary urban landscape, gave birth to the modern horror novel. It paved the way for a host of new writers and books, including Tom Tryon's *The Other*, William Peter Blatty's *The Exorcist*, the work of Stephen King, Peter Straub and Clive Barker, among others—creating a whole new cycle of horror fiction.

Naturally, Hollywood couldn't help but take notice. Film rights to the book were snapped up by William Castle, a specialist in gimmicky low budget horror films (*House on Haunted Hill, The Tingler, Homicidal,* et al.), who planned on directing the film himself. Robert Evans, production chief at Paramount, the studio for which the film was to be made, declined Castle's services as director, however. His feeling was that the film, though not intended as a big budget, prestigious offering, still cried out for a more sophisticated approach than Castle's. Though Polanski had never made a film in Hollywood, he had established a reputation as a more upscale horror director with *Repulsion* and *The Fearless Vampire Killers*. He was sent the galleys of Levin's novel, read them in one sitting, and signed on

Rosemary (Mia Farrow) examines the charm given to Terri (Angela Dorian) by the Castevets. The charm contains an offensive smelling herb used in magic rituals. Terri, the Castevets' first choice to bear the devils' child, will soon commit suicide—and Rosemary will take her place.

Guy (John Cassavetes) and Rosemary (Mia Farrow) explore their new apartment in the Bramford—the previous tenant, now deceased, had a fondness for strange herbs.

Minnie (Ruth Gordon) and Roman (Sidney Blackmer) virtually adopt
their new neighbors Rosemary (Mia Farrow) and Guy (John Cassavetes).

right away, agreeing to adapt the novel himself. His screenplay adheres to the novel with uncommon fidelity.

Rosemary is a deeply religious girl at sea in an increasingly amoral as well as immoral world where the concensus is that God is dead. [*Time* devoted a cover story to this "new theology" at the time and Polanski includes a shot of that issue of the magazine in the film.] Naïve and unselfish, she is (again, characteristically of Polanski) married to the wrong mate: the agnostic and ambitious Guy, an aspiring actor. The pair moves into a new apartment in a gothic wonderland called the Bramford, a building with an unsavory reputation. [New York's Dakota Hotel, outside of which John Lennon was shot many years later, served as the model and the location for the Bramford.] This reputation proves well-founded for the place is crawling with devil-worshippers. Two eccentric members of the cult, Minnie and Roman Castevet, virtually adopt Rosemary and Guy. At first, the Castevets seem innocent enough, but their motives are quite devious. They offer Guy a Faustian pact. If he will help them secure Rosemary's services as

surrogate mother to the anti-Christ, he will be granted success and riches beyond his dreams. He takes little persuading. Rosemary is drugged and her body offered to the devil in an unholy, nightmarish ritual. Delighted at first that she is pregnant (by Guy, she believes), she soon becomes convinced that all is not as it should be. Only an author friend named Hutch believes her but he is quickly dispatched by the devil worshippers via black magic. She expresses her fears to her doctor, but he turns out to be a member of the Castevets' coven as well. She gives birth to the devil's spawn. Realizing what she's been a party to, she grabs a knife and sets out to kill the baby. But her maternal instincts get the better of her and she accepts the baby instead.

The film that emerged, though it *was* an adaptation, was pure Polanski, a chilling modern horror tale and a fascinating psychological case study as well. In a sense, it can be viewed as the second installment in what would be a trilogy of Polanski psychological case study films that begins with *Repulsion* and concludes with *The Tenant*. Each film is very similar in that it centers around a character who suffers from a psychological

98

conflict—one that is represented by and reaches critical mass within the claustrophobic walls of a closed-in environment the characters cannot seem to escape. The psychodrama at work in *Rosemary's Baby* is Rosemary's conflict at being unable to reconcile her strict religious upbringing with her adult agnostic desires. The events that befall her at the Bramford spur—in typically bleak Polanski terms—the resolution of her conflict. When she embraces the devil's child, she renounces God at last.

Rosemary's Baby was a phenomenal critical and box office success worldwide that succeeded in propelling Polanski into the front ranks in Hollywood. It is buoyed considerably by strong, believable performances from all concerned. Even under the tutelage of Woody Allen, Mia Farrow has never been better. She is the perfect Rosemary. John Cassavetes also registers solidly as the villainous but likable Guy. (Reportedly, Cassavetes and

Hutch (Maurice Evans) expresses his fatherly concern. The only one who believes Rosemary (Mia Farrow), he will soon be gotten out of the way via black magic.

Rosemary (Mia Farrow) shows Guy (John Cassavetes) a book Hutch gave her that offers proof of the Castevets' satanic background. He dismisses it as nonsense—but, of course, he already *knows* the truth.

Rosemary (Mia Farrow) confesses her fears to Dr. Sapirstein (Ralph Bellamy)—but he turns out to be a member of the coven as well.

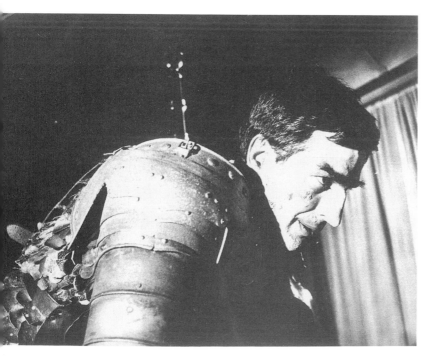

Guy (John Cassavetes) appears briefly as the devil during the hallucinatory "baby night" sequence.

Polanski were constantly at loggerheads during filming, but none of this shows on screen.) A whole new audience would be introduced to veteran Ruth Gordon, who won a Best Supporting Actress Oscar for her performance as the eccentric Minnie—a role she would repeat in several non-horror films in years to come. Polanski was also nominated for his screenplay, but he didn't win.

The real showpiece of the film, however, is Polanski's direction—for which, curiously but perhaps not surprisingly, he was not nominated. Like *Repulsion* before it and *The Tenant* later (and, indeed, all of Polanski's early films), *Rosemary's Baby* exudes a powerful sense of atmosphere. He makes the Bramford not just a setting, but a palpable presence—almost a character. In one scene, Guy is sitting in the living room engaging in small talk with Rosemary, who can be seen in the background bedroom packing an overnight bag to take to the hospital. The phone rings, Rosemary answers it, and her high spirits are suddenly crushed by the news of Hutch's unexpected demise. All the while, through the open bedroom window, we can see those of another apartment across the way. The gothic arches above the windows together with the surrounding wall of gingerbread form a pair of eyes. The building is literally watching Rosemary—waiting to strike like some malevolent demon. Which, of course, it does.

NIGHT OF THE LIVING DEAD (1968)

An Image Ten Production
Distributed by Continental Films
B&W /96 minutes

Credits

Director: George A. Romero; *Producers:* Russell Streiner and Karl Hardman; *Screenplay:* John A. Russo and George A. Romero; *Cinematography:* George A. Romero; *Editor:* George A. Romero; *Music:* Capitol Records stock music library; *Production Director:* Vince Survinski; *Videocassette source:* Various public domain sources.

Cast

Ben: Duane Jones; *Barbara:* Judith O'Dea; *Harry Cooper:* Karl Hardman; *Johnny:* Russell Streiner; *Helen Cooper:* Marilyn Eastman; *Tom:* Keith Wayne; *Judy:* Judith Ridley; *Karen Cooper:* Kyra Schon; *Graveyard Ghoul:* Bill Hinzman.

Ben (Duane Jones) uses a torch to push back the horde of invading ghouls.

The ravenous ghouls descend upon the farmhouse in *Night of the Living Dead*.

DAWN OF THE DEAD (1979)

A Laurel Production
A United Film Distribution Release
Color/126 minutes

Credits

Director: George A. Romero; *Producer:* Richard P. Rubinstein; *Screenplay:* George A. Romero; *Cinematographer:* Michael Gornick; *Editor:* George A. Romero; *Music:* The Goblins with Dario Argento; *Production Manager:* Zilla Clinton; *Videocassette source:* Thorn/EMI Home Video.

Cast

Stephen: David Emge; *Peter:* Ken Foree; *Roger:* Scott Reiniger; *Fran:* Gaylen Ross; *Dr. Foster:* David Crawford; *Mr. Berman:* David Early; *Biker:* Tom Savini; *TV Director:* George A. Romero; *TV Assistant Director:* Christine Forrest.

DAY OF THE DEAD (1985)

A Laurel Production
A United Film Distribution Release
Color/102 minutes

The re-animated corpse of Johnny (Russell Streiner) attacks his sister Barbara (Judith O'Dea) as the zombies overwhelm the farmhouse.

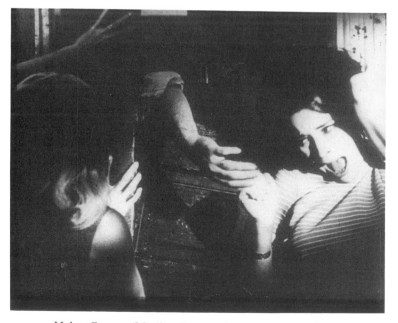

Helen Cooper (Marilyn Eastman) is overcome as the zombies break into the farmhouse in *Night of the Living Dead*.

Credits

Director: George A. Romero; *Producer:* Richard P. Rubinstein; *Screenplay:* George A. Romero; *Cinematographer:* Michael Gornick; *Editor:* Pasquale Buba; *Music:* John Harrison; *Production Designer:* Cletus Anderson; *Videocassette source:* Media Home Entertainment.

Cast

Sarah: Lori Cardille; *John:* Terry Alexander; *Captain Rhodes:* Joseph Pilato; *Dr. Logan:* Richard Liberty; *Bub:* Howard Sherman; *McDermott:* Jarlath Conroy; *Miguel:* Antone DiLeo; *Steele:* G. Howard Klar; *Rickles:* Ralph Marrero; *Fisher:* John Amplas.

1968 was one of the most turbulent and traumatic years in modern American history—even *more* turbulent and traumatic than the year that seemed to start it all, 1963, when President John F. Kennedy's life was claimed by an assassin's bullet, an act that stunned the world, but appalled Americans especially because, until then, we'd all held on to the naïve belief that "such things just don't happen here." A short five years later, the sound of the bullets that killed JFK reached a crescendo that is *still* ringing in our ears. The fabric of American society—indeed, world society—began to unravel. Nothing has been the same since.

In the midst of all the chaos of the time, a lower than low budget black and white horror film churned out over a long series of weekends by a bunch of Pennsylvania feature filmmaking hopefuls received its premiere (on October 2, 1968) in Pittsburgh, the city near which it was made. And like everything else that happened that year, this event too had a rippling effect. The influence of the film, *Night of the Living Dead*, is still being felt.

But it did more than, in effect, alter the face and form of true modern horror film. *Night of the Living Dead* managed to reflect the era in which it was made better than any film I can recall. Quite frankly, if future generations want to get some sense of what the traumatic Sixties—and particularly 1968—were like, they need look no further than *Night*. Whether the film's makers intended to or not (and to some degree, they did), *Night's* disturbing plot, gruesomely effective black humor, and nightmarish yet cartoon-like excesses serve as a potent metaphor—exaggerated and over the top, perhaps, but not by much—of what society *seemed* like during that dreadful but memorable period.

In *Night of the Living Dead*, an ill-defined [intentionally] space experiment goes awry and results in the dead coming back to life. These suddenly animated corpses turn on the living, the minority, quite literally devouring anyone who crosses their path. As a result, dead relatives turn on living relatives, dead oldsters turn on living youngsters (and vice-versa); the partially eaten victims—and anyone else killed for whatever reason—become animated as well as the nightmarish cycles keeps repeating itself.

A group of survivors led by a black man named Ben hole up in an old farmhouse where they succeed in stemming the zombie onslaught, at least for a time. Their only source of information as to what's happening in the "outside world" is a television set, which chatters away throughout the film, giving the microcosm survivors a (perhaps distorted?) macro view of a world now gone completely mad. This encourages them to stay indoors and therefore out of potential trouble.

Conflicts among the survivors soon flare up and they are eventually overwhelmed by the zombie menace. Only Ben manages to stay alive—ironically by hiding out in the cellar, the very place in which he'd protested against hiding out for most of the film. Adding to the irony, Ben is accidentally killed at the end of the film by members of a police and civilian posse with orders to shoot anything that moves. Not that they need such orders as they're gun-happy to begin with. The film grimly concludes with the message that there is no hope of escape or salvation from the engulfing cannibalistic madness.

One might cynically observe that writer-director George A. Romero and his cohorts were just setting things up for a sequel by concluding the film in this manner (and, of course, two sequels did follow a number of years later), but as they really had no idea that their horrific little film would become the cause célébrè and success that it became, I doubt this was the case. Regardless, the "no hope" ending works quite powerfully and disturbingly—especially in view of the year in which it was made.

Picked up for distribution by a relatively small firm, Walter Reade's Continental Films (a specialist in foreign language and British imports), *Night of the Living Dead* did not exactly receive a widespread release. Initially, it popped up mostly at drive-ins. Nevertheless, its impact was immediate. Audiences were astonished by the film's explicit, and plentiful, gore sequences of zombies consuming human entrails, the undead taking bullets in the brain (according to the plot, the only sure way of destroying them), and even more outrageously ghoulish images. Apart from some obscure gore films, then being made by exploitation mogul Herschel Gordon Lewis, American filmgoers had not been exposed to such fare on the screen before. *Night of the Living Dead*, as its makers intended it to be, was a full blown *modern* horror film that went straight for the gut. It was scary, funny and shocking all at the same time. And audiences loved it.

As might be expected, critics didn't, however. In fact, most were outraged. *Variety*, usually more savvy than most film journals, called the film "an unrelieved orgy of sadism...[that cast] serious aspersions on the integrity of its Pittsburgh-based makers, [distributor] Walter Reade, and the film industry as a whole."

Negative, indeed scathing, reviews of this kind worked for the film rather than against it, however. Still not a runaway success, it began making regular appearances at theaters in Boston, New York and other major cities, where it became a "midnight movie" cult favorite—the kind of word-of-mouth film people told other people, "You just gotta see!" *Night of the Living Dead* didn't really catch on though until it traveled to Europe, where French and British critics started raving about it. The prestigious British Film Institute's highbrow publication *Sight and Sound* even went so far as to put the film on its annual ten-best list.

Due to the film's relatively poor American distribution, I didn't catch up with it until three years later—by which time, its notoriety had spread considerably. Like most people, I was shocked and amazed by the film's over-the-top gore—though by 1971, *Night's* influence had spread and such blood-and-gore sequences were beginning to ooze into mainstream movies as well. But I was also very impressed by the film. Unlike the output of H.G. Lewis, which existed solely for the gore effects contained within them, *Night of the Living Dead* has a lot more going for it. It was a taut, extremely well paced and edited (and, for the most part, quite well acted) shoestring budget horror film. Writer-director-editor-photographer (and bit player) George Romero, I quickly decided, was a genre filmmaker of tremendous ingenuity and promise and I eagerly looked forward to more Romero.

The SWAT team blows the head off one of the zombies during
the opening moments of *Dawn of the Dead*.

A zombie feast from *Dawn of the Dead*.

The next film of his I did see [Romero made two obscure films in between] was *The Crazies* (1973). It was picked up by an even smaller distributor than Walter Reade and received even fewer bookings than *Night of the Living Dead*. I didn't catch up with it until 1978, when I saw a cut version of it on television called *Code Name Trixie*. Though not as impressive as *Night of the Living Dead*—and certainly not the groundbreaker that film was—*The Crazies* proved to me that my initial assessment of Romero's talents was not premature. In the film, a U.S. biological warfare weapon accidentally gets into the water supply of a small Pennsylvania town, reducing many of the residents to hallucinating, violent crazies. As government and local law enforcement officials cordon off the town and try to quell the madness, scientists search for an antidote. Graphic murder and mayhem fill the screen. *The Crazies*, like *Night of the Living Dead*, ends on a bleak note when the scientist who discovers the antidote is accidentally killed before he can reveal it.

Survivors of the zombie menace take up arms to protect their turf, a fabulous shopping mall, in *Dawn of the Dead*. From left to right: Scott Reiniger, Gaylen Ross, David Emge, Ken Foree.

A zombie gets it in the head with a machete in *Dawn of the Dead*.

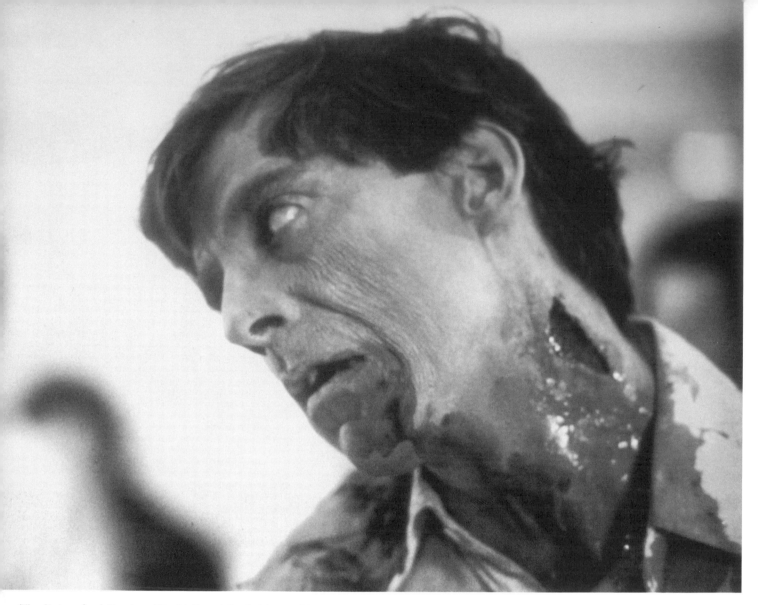

The living dead Stephen (David Emge) leads his zombie cohorts to the hiding place of his former friends in *Dawn of the Dead*.

Lining up a shot of one of the invading bikers in *Dawn of the Dead*.

The Crazies, befitting its title, is an extremely fast film. Romero, a brilliant editor (as *Night of the Living Dead* already showed), *never* lets the pace slacken—though I found myself at times wishing he would so that I could catch my breath. I don't think it's as good a film as *Night of the Living Dead*, but it *is* worth seeing, and it further crystalized the Romero trademark: suspense, gore, black humor (of the EC horror comics variety) with an underpinning of satire and metaphor. I hoped that with his next film, Romero would secure a larger budget and a better distributor so that I wouldn't have to wait another five years to catch up with it. As it turned out, however, by the time I saw *The Crazies*, Romero, who had since formed a partnership with an aspiring producer named Richard P. Rubinstein, already had another film in the can, a modern vampire movie called *Martin* (1978), which was, again, poorly distributed [I saw it a year later]. As frustrated as I felt about this situation, I can only imagine how Romero felt. He hadn't had a solid box office success since *Night of the Living Dead*, which was now a decade old!

In an attempt to recapture that success, Romero returned to the milieu that first had earned him his cult reputation and began preparing a bona fide sequel to *Night of the Living Dead* called *Dawn of the Dead*. This time, however, he was determined not to make the film "on the cheap." His aim was to outdo *Night* in every way. Financial backing for the more ambitious $1 million-plus production was secured from a variety of sources, including Italian horror film director Dario Argento, a strong supporter of Romero's and a big fan of *Night of the Living Dead*.

Dawn of the Dead, shot in color, takes up right where *Night of the Living Dead* left off—though with a new cast of characters (those in the first film were all dead) and in a different, though equally claustrophobic, location. The film begins in one of the TV studios that had been broadcasting news of the zombie menace in *Night of the Living Dead*. Chaos reigns supreme as the zombies overrun the city. Roger and Peter, survivors of a decimated SWAT team, and two other people, a pregnant girl named Fran and her lover, Stephen, flee in a helicopter and later set down on the roof of a suburban shopping mall, deserted except for a few zombies roaming about. The mall's multiplicity of food, clothing, furniture, drugs, electronics, and sporting goods shops provide the quartet with everything needed to survive—at least for a time. To separate themselves from the starving zombies, the four burrow deep within the bowels of the massive complex, venturing out into the stores only when supplies are running low. Things go awry when more and more zombies begin infiltrating the mall. (Though brain-dead, the undead are instinctively drawn to the mall as a place where they had once spent many happy hours.)

Frequent battles between the four survivors and the zombie invaders ensue—and two of the four, Roger and Stephen, are wounded. A gang of marauding bikers breaks into the mall to pillage the place and briefly capture the zombies' attention. When most of the bikers are dispatched, disemboweled and eaten, the zombies set their sites (and their appetites) once more on the original four. By this time, Roger and Stephen have become zombies as well. Roger is put out of his misery, but the disappeared Stephen soon leads his fellow zombies to Peter and Fran's hidden lair. As the spot is overrun, the latter two flee to the roof and escape in the helicopter just in time. Thus, unlike its long-ago predecessor, *Dawn of the Dead* concludes not on a bleak note, but a positive one—the implication

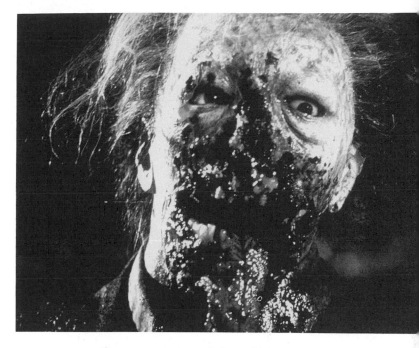

Cat got your tongue? One of Tom Savini's grizzly zombie makeups in *Day of the Dead*, the concluding episode (as of this writing) of George Romero's zombie trilogy.

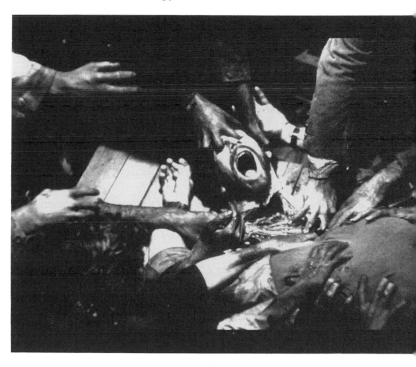

The zombies attack one of the soldiers, turning him into mincemeat in *Day of the Dead*.

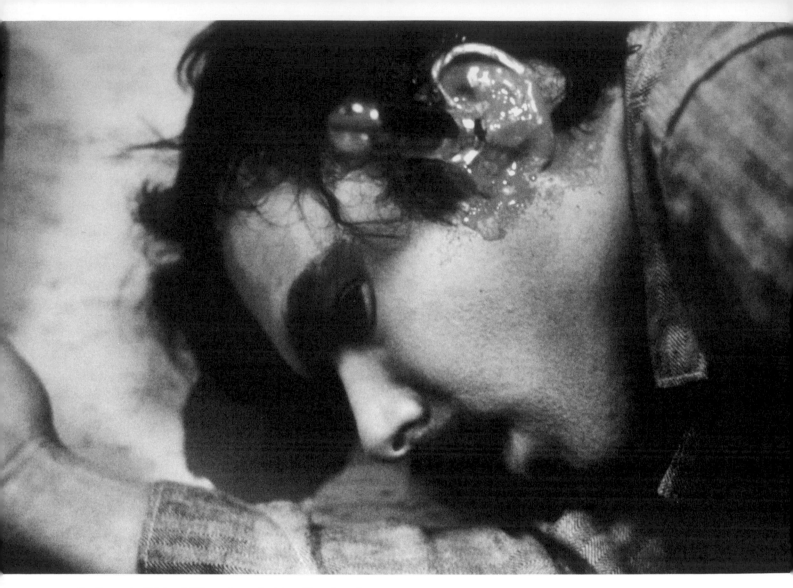

Dr. Logan's (Richard Liberty) surgical handiwork as he attempts to find a way of controlling the zombies in *Day of the Dead*.

being that Fran's impending baby will keep the living population going.

As influential as *Night of the Living Dead* was on the modern horror film, *Dawn of the Dead* proved even more so. It's wall-to-wall array of graphically spectacular splatter effects [the term "splatter" springs from this film], all brilliantly brought off by makeup man Tom Savini, who also doubles in a bit part as one of the marauding bikers, set the tone for much of what the horror film has since become. Carnage runs rampant in *Dawn of the Dead*, but in Romero's hands, the sheer volume of horrific effects produces a different reaction than most similar films made since. Yes, audiences were (and continue to be) amazed and grossed out by them, although the over-the-top style of the film—and the effects are very much a part of that style—has a comic bite to it that makes *Dawn* less repellent than amusing. Romero calls *Dawn of the Dead* a "filmic pie in the face." I call it something else: "splatstick," a mixture of all-out gore and all-out slapstick. The abundance of

exploding heads, mutilations and other mayhem in the film is so overabundant that the film emerges as a mega-EC horror comic brought to 35mm life. This is not to say that the film doesn't work on other levels too. Edited by Romero at his usual breakneck pace, it is both tremendously exciting and quite suspenseful as well. Romero's propensity for allegory and metaphor is also present. *Night of the Living Dead* may have unconsciously reflected the times in which it was made. But *Dawn of the Dead* consciously reflects them. the idealistic, turbulent Sixties were past. The American psyche was focusing once more on materialism and consumerism—as witness the building of more and bigger shopping malls (like the one in the film) all across the country. Though not at all heavy-handed, Romero offers this as a subtext in his film. Mass (and mad consumerism—which would explode in the Eighties—is metaphorically represented most specifically by the mindless, yet voracious zombies, but also by everyone else in the film, who see the mall as a sort of paradise where their every materialistic wish can be easily fulfilled.

There was never much question that *Dawn of the Dead*'s array of gruesome set pieces and effects would incur the wrath of the MPAA rating [Motion Picture Association of America] rating board and that unless substantial cuts were made, the filmed would be slapped with an "X" rating (no one under 17 admitted), which was sheer poison to exhibitors. So, Romero, Rubinstein and their distributor, United Film Distribution, decided to release the film without any rating at all—albeit with a disclaimer notifying patrons of the film's spectacularly violent content.

Dawn was a huge success not only in America but the world over, cementing Romero's reputation and providing him with a fair degree of financial security. A sequel was surely in his cards. After making two interim films (*Knightriders* [1981] and *Creepshow* [1982]), Romero quickly launched into writing the script for what he envisioned as the spectacular third and final act of his "zombie trilogy."

His completed script ran into budgetary problems, however, and he was forced to scale it down considerably. Romero and many fans of both *Night of the Living Dead* and *Dawn of the Dead* were disappointed with the result when the film, called *Day of the Dead*, was released in the summer of 1985. Though a box office success, it was not the bonanza its predecessor had been. The film's multitude of gory special effects (again supervised by Tom Savini, assisted by a small army of technicians) proved even more spectacular and inventive than those in either *Night of the Living Dead* or *Dawn of the Dead*. But *Day of the Dead*'s scaled-down presentation (it is even *more* claustrophobic than the first two films) lacked the flamboyance, outrageousness and gusto of *Dawn* especially, making it seem like it should have been the middle film in the series rather than the capper to it.

Despite much negative reaction from fans and critics alike, *Day of the Dead* has a lot going for it. The film takes place in an underground military installation (possibly an abandoned nuclear silo) located somewhere in Florida. By now, the zombies have overrun the earth. A small band of military men and scientists is struggling not only to survive but find a way of "taming" the flesh-craving creatures. The team's resident egghead (nicknamed "Dr. Frankenstein") succeeds in controlling a zombie named "Bub" by tapping into the ghoul's latent human memory. The foul-mouthed, gun-happy military types in arguable control of the project flip out, however, when they learn that the doctor has been feeding the flesh of their dead comrades to Bub and other zombie specimens as Pavlovian rewards for "good behavior." The project collapses and the installation is overwhelmed by rampaging zombies. Everyone is killed and devoured except for Sara, the female leader of the scientific team, a Jamaican pilot named John and his technician assistant, McDermott—all of whom flee by helicopter to an unpopulated tropical island free of the zombie menace.

Strongly acted—by Lori Cardille (Sarah), Terry Alexander (John) and Howard Sherman (Bub) especially—tautly written and excitingly staged and edited, *Day of the Dead* is probably the slickest of all Romero's zombie films. But because he was compelled to scale down his original vision of the film, it leaves substantial room for yet another sequel. Whether there will be one or not remains to be seen. After the "failure" of *Day of the Dead*, Romero parted amicably with longtime producer Rubinstein to pursue a number of different horror projects on his own for other companies. The first of these, *Monkey Shines* (1988), made for Orion Pictures, was a distinct disappointment. As of this writing, Menahem Golan's new 21st Century Pictures Company has persuaded Romero to update and remake his now 21-year-old *Night of the Living Dead* for a new generation of horror fans—in color this time and with a much bigger budget than he was able to muster for any of his previous zombie films. If this project (to be directed by Tom Savini) does indeed come about, I can't help but view the idea as an exercise in cinematic wheel-spinning—for not only has *Night of the Living Dead* been rereleased to television and the home video market in a fairly good computerized color version, but both *Dawn of the Dead* and *Day of the Dead* were made in color to begin with and succeed in updating Romero's zombie formula already. 21st Century might better give Romero the money to make the big budget epic conclusion to the series he'd wanted *Day of the Dead* to be.

Whatever happens, Romero's reputation will remain secure. His very influential (and vastly imitated) "zombie trilogy" stands out as a unique contribution to the evolution of the modern horror film. And *Dawn of the Dead* especially remains, for my money, one of the cleverest and most original horror films ever made.

THE DEVILS (1971)

A Warner Bros. Picture
Color /109 minutes

Credits

Director: Ken Russell; *Producers:* Robert H. Solo and
Ken Russell; *Screenplay:* Ken Russell based on *The
Devils* by John Whiting and *The Devils of Loudon* by
Aldous Huxley; *Cinematographer:* David Watkin; *Editor:* Michael Bradsell; *Music:* Peter Maxwell Davies; *Art
Director:* Robert Cartwright; *Videocassete source:*
Warner Home Video.

Cast

Father Grandier: Oliver Reed; *Sister Jeanne:* Vanessa
Redgrave; *Baron de Laubardemont:* Dudley Sutton;
Ibert: Max Adrian; *Mignon:* Murray Melvin; *Barré:*
Michael Gothard; *Madelyn de Brou:* Gemma Jones;
Philippe: Georgina Hale; *Richlieu:* Christopher Logue;
Louis XIII: Graham Armitage.

The deformed and sexually frustrated Sister Jeanne (Vanessa Redgrave),
whose longing for the attractive and powerful Father Grandier (Oliver
Reed) leads to the man's death.

The road to the plague-infested city of Loudon, which is soon to experience an outbreak of "demonic possession" as well.

Like a few other entries in this book, Ken Russell's *The Devils* is not a horror film in the traditional sense. Rather, it employs the generic trappings of the horror film both for impact and to make its points. The storyline deals extensively with witchcraft, demonic possession, exorcism and torture and is undeniably horrific. But Russell uses this material to show how religion can be abused and become twisted; to show how the state can manipulate events growing out of such abuse to destroy an honest and basically decent man; and to shock an audience benumbed by constant exposure to graphic, real-life horror on television news into a state of awareness. He succeeded so well that the abuse of religion aspect ended up being censored, while the excesses jolted a large number of critics into a denunciating frenzy. So infamous did the film become

that a reference to it popped up in Graham Greene's novel *The Honorary Consul*, in which the consul is called upon to deal with all the "fuss" surrounding "the British entry [at a South American Film Festival] by some fellow named Russell that is being called pornographic." Fortunately, *The Devils* has outlived most of its attacks to become an acknowledged—albeit controversial and unorthodox—classic of the modern horror film.

The film's demonic possession angle arises when unfounded accusations of sorcery are leveled at Father Urbain Grandier by a sexually frustrated (and hunchbacked) nun, Sister Jeanne. As it happens, Grandier also poses a threat to Cardinal Richlieu's plans to

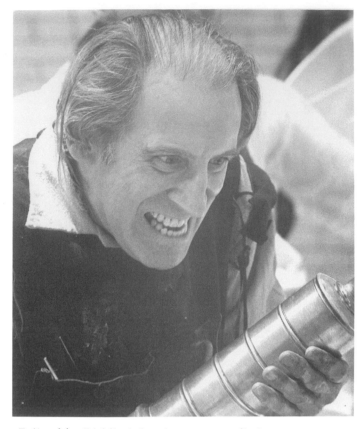

Enlisted by Richlieu's henchman as a medical expert on exorcising demons, the town apothecary (Max Adrian) prepares to use the clyster on Sister Jeanne (Vanessa Redgrave).

Still refusing to confess to the bogus crimes he's been charged with, Grandier (Oliver Reed) is dragged to the stake.

unify and control France. So, Sister Jeanne's wild accusations and hysterical ravings about Grandier—that he disguised himself as a demon and raped her—prove politically well-timed. The powers that be turn the underside of Grandier's own religion against him.

The notoriety of the film centers, rather unfairly, on the exorcism scenes, which involve the historically accurate use of the clyster (a barbaric device, rather like a giant turkey baster) to administer hot vaginal enemas as a way of purging the devil from the possessed nuns. In point of fact, this is neither the most horrific part of the film, nor is the process shown (as is often claimed) in any kind of detail. The mere *suggestion* of it, however, is quite sufficient to induce shudders in even the most jaded viewer.

In the late Sixties and early Seventies, the process of desensitizing a large portion of humanity through constant and unrelieved exposure to the Vietnam horrors unfolding nightly on the evening news was in full sway, and Russell was out to penetrate that rapidly forming shell. What he had not reckoned with was the very real difference between his film's scenes of horror and the real item. Brought forth with all the artistry at his command on the larger than life screen, Russell's filmic horrors in *The Devils* came across as more real than reality. They were so immediate, graphic and shocking that both casual filmgoers and serious critics alike were appalled to the point of *insisting* that the film contained scenes that had never been shot. In one

The process of humiliating and torturing Grandier (Oliver Reed) into a confession begins—as Laubardemont (Dudley Sutton) orders the vain priest's head shaved.

The wild-eyed Father Barré (Michael Gothard) in his John Lennon-style glasses applies the flame that will turn Grandier's (Oliver Reed) flesh to blisters.

113

The horrific execution of Father Grandier (Oliver Reed) in Ken Russell's *The Devils*.

Just as harrowing as the exorcism scenes are those of Grandier's torture at the hands of Father Barré (who is made up allegorically as a late Sixties long-haired hippy with John Lennon-style glasses) when it is decided that Grandier's confession is necessary in order to lend credibility to his trumped-up conviction. All the trappings of the torture chamber are brought into play, with particular emphasis on the systematic crushing of Grandier's legs by wedging them between pieces of wood and then driving additional slats into place from each side. Yet for all this nastiness (again, more suggested than shown), the point of the scene is Grandier's triumph over both his tormentors and his own ego. "You are no longer important," Richlieu's chief henchman, Baron de Laubardemont, tells him at one point. "I was never important," Grandier concedes, realizing at the same time, however, that by refusing to confess he is denying Richlieu final victory.

Despite the fact that Russell only uses these scenes of possession and torture to make a much larger point, he shrewdly develops the film so that the horror content continually increases, finally erupting into the most horrifying sequence of all—Grandier's execution by fire. In a genre noted for its numerous scenes of burning, this ranks as surely the most terrifying of all. Here, Russell eschews suggestion and graphically presents all the details with an unflinching eye so that we actually *do* see every appalling stage of the execution. Yet even here, it isn't so much the blistering, discoloring skin that remains in the memory as it is the hysteria surrounding the event. The real horror comes from the actions of the madly celebrating crowd, who view the execution as a theatrical event. Russell's point here is that because of the plague that has infected their city, the townsfolk have been exposed to so much suffering and death that they've become desensitized to them. Any contemporary viewer who feels superior to the populace of Loudon would do well to think back to his or her non-reaction to the latest tragedy witnessed on the nightly news.

legendary TV confrontation with British critic Alexander Walker, Russell became so frustrated over the critic's stern belief in a non-existent shot of Oliver Reed's testicles being crushed that he finally whacked Walker over the head with a rolled-up newspaper. Russell has since seen the error of his ways as concerns such outbursts and has promised that, should such an occasion present itself again, he will include an iron bar inside the paper.

MACBETH (1971)

A Playboy Production
A Columbia Pictures Release
Color /140 minutes

Lady Macbeth (Francesca Annis) confronts her brooding husband (Jon Finch) as he begins hatching his dastardly plans.

The three witches who will soon prophecy that Macbeth (Jon Finch) will become Thane of Cawdor and eventually King of Scotland.

Macbeth (Jon Finch) envisions his future in the witches' lair.

Credits

Director: Roman Polanski; *Producer:* Andrew Braunsberg; *Screenplay:* Roman Polanski and Kenneth Tynan, based on the play by William Shakespeare; *Cinematographer:* Gil Taylor; *Editor:* Alastair McIntyre; *Music:* The Third Ear Band; *Production Designer:* Wilfred Shingleton; *Videocassette source:* RCA/Columbia Home Video.

Cast

Macbeth: Jon Finch; *Lady Macbeth:* Francesca Annis; *Banquo:* Martin Shaw; *Duncan:* Nicholas Selby: *Ross:* John Stride; *Malcolm:* Stephen Chase; *Donalbain:* Paul Shelley; *Macduff:* Terence Bayler; *Lennox:* Andrew Laurence; *Mentieth:* Frank Wylie; *Angus:* Bernard Archard; *Three Witches:* Noelle Rimmington, Maisie MacFarquhard, Elsie Taylor.

Roman Polanski's overlooked and vastly underrated production of *Macbeth* had just about everything stacked against it when it debuted in 1971. Films based on Shakespeare's plays seldom performed well at the box office [Franco Zeffirelli's *The Taming of the Shrew* (1967) and *Romeo and Juliet* (1968) were recent exceptions] and Polanski's film conformed to this rule by recouping very little of its approximately $3 million cost. *Macbeth* was also the first venture into feature moviemaking by Hugh Hefner's *Playboy* magazine empire and this worked against the film as well. Though not always warmly embracing them, critics have always tended to treat films based on Shakespeare's plays with a certain degree of seriousness. *Playboy*'s "centerfold reputation" coupled with the excessive hype surrounding the film's several nude scenes (stills of which were published in the magazine) prejudiced many of these critics even before *Macbeth* was released. Polanski's own reputation as an innovative yet commercial director of a successful string of horror films didn't help much either.

Nor did the fact that *Macbeth* was the director's first film since the notorious Manson family slaughter of Polanski's wife, Sharon Tate, and several friends—an event that had catapulted Polanski's name into the headlines and made him one of the most recognized moviemakers in the world, though *not* for his films. Everybody, not just critics, seemed to be lying in wait for this film, wondering not only how Polanski would treat Shakespeare's macabre tale of witchcraft, ambition and murder, but how much of the director's recent personal tragedy would be reflected in the film. Polanski clearly recognized that the subject matter of his first film since the Tate tragedy would be subjected to greater scrutiny than any of his previous films. "A comedy, a [straight] horror film, or a thriller was out of the question," he wrote in his autobiography. Adapting the Bard seemed an ideal solution. A fan since his youth of Shakespeare's plays and, particularly, Laurence Oliver's 1948 *Hamlet*, Polanski decided that *Macbeth* was the one Shakespearean tragedy that had so far defied effective film translation (Orson Welles and Akira Kurosawa notwithstanding) and so, with the help of noted critic and Shakespearean scholar Kenneth Tynan, he determined to bring it to the screen.

Polanski's selection of *Macbeth* was really quite ingenious for it allowed him to have his cake and eat it too. While the play is by no means a conventional genre piece, it is, perhaps, the one Shakespeare play that clearly contains all the ingredients that are so traditional *to* the horror genre: madness, murder, black magic, the supernatural, apparitions, you name it. And so, rather than being an abrupt departure from the films he'd previously made, *Macbeth* was really a continuation of them.

At its roots, *Macbeth is* a horror story and Polanski treats it precisely that way. The film's dark, craggy landscapes and brooding castles—drenched with rain

Lady Macbeth (Francesca Annis) is told by Macbeth (Jon Finch) of the witches' prediction that power shall soon be within their grasp.

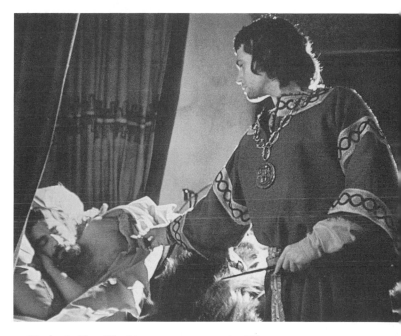

Macbeth (Jon Finch) prepares to murder King Duncan (Nicholas Selby).

The brutal murder of Banquo (Martin Shaw), who, the witches predict, will "beget kings though he be none" himself.

117

Warrior and expert swordsman Macbeth (Jon Finch) attempts to stave off the inevitable in a duel to the death with Macduff (Terence Bayler).

The downside of the witches' prophecy begins to come true as Birnam Wood "marches" on Dunsinane.

and illuminated by periodic bursts of lightning accompanied by ripples of thunder on the soundtrack—belong as much to the gothic world of Bram Stoker as to medieval world of Shakespeare's Macbeth. Polanski's evocation of the grotesque netherworld lair of the witches, who cavort in the nude on their unholy sabbat prophesying Macbeth's doom when "Birnham Wood shall come to Dunsinane," harkens back not only to the director's own *Rosemary's Baby* but Benjamin Christensen's silent horror classic *Witchcraft Through the Ages* (1920). And the film's numerous fantasy sequences—the appearance of Banquo's ghost; Macbeth's guilt-ridden nightmare in which he imagines Fleance (Banquo's son) and the murdered Banquo symbolically wrestling him for his crown; the drinking of the witches' potion, et al.—are all treated in the same soundless, surrealistic style as Carol and Rosemary's similar hallucinatory experiences in *Repulsion* and *Rosemary's Baby* respectively.

Polanski's descriptive approach to the play's violence makes his *Macbeth* even more of a horror film—particularly a *modern* (by cinema standards) horror film. And it was here that he ran afoul of most critics, who tended to view the film's abundant and graphically presented scenes of cruelty and carnage as being irrelevant to the story but not to Polanski's primary aim—which was to exorcise his private demons. Polanski has always rankled at this charge, but the fact is his *Macbeth* is an extremely bloody film—bloodier than all his other films put together—in which the world is portrayed as a barbarous place where savagery is not only all too commonplace but inescapable. Admittedly, the medieval world of the historic Macbeth was no less barbarous and cruel, but Polanski's approach here was analysed less in terms of its historical authenticity than its reflection upon his recent personal tragedy. And at the time, the film clearly seemed to support such an analysis—especially in light of such scenes as when the duplicitous Ross notifies MacDuff that, "Your castle is surprised, your wife and babe savagely slaughtered."

Though viewed as a shortcoming (by many Shakespearean purists, anyway), the personal viewpoint imposed on *Macbeth* by the director is, I feel, one of the films great strengths—and, perhaps, the source of the it's still considerable power to disturb.

HANDS OF THE RIPPER (1971)

A Hammer Film Production
A Universal Release
Color /85 minutes

Dr. Pritchard (Eric Porter) hastens the bloodstained Anna (Angharad Rees), the daughter of Jack the Ripper, away from the scene of one of her crimes.

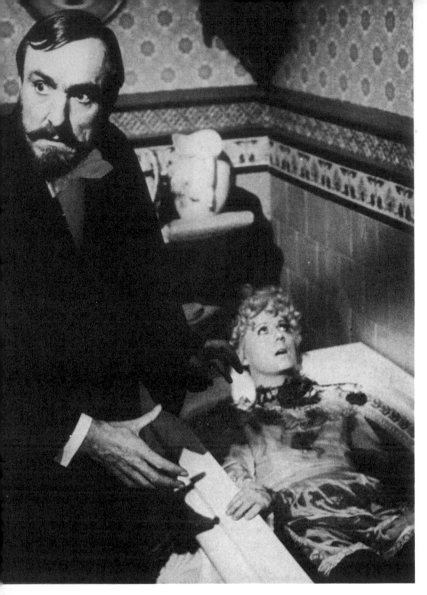

Dr. Pritchard (Eric Porter) discovers another victim of the daughter of Jack the Ripper.

Credits

Director: Peter Sasdy; *Producer:* Aida Young; *Screenplay:* L.W. Davidson, based on a short story by Edward Spencer Shew; *Cinematographer:* Kenneth Talbot; *Editor:* Christopher Barnes; *Music:* Christopher Gunning; *Art Director:* Roy Stannard; *Videocassette source:* VidAmerica.

Cast

Dr. John Pritchard: Eric Porter; *Anna:* Angharad Rees; *Laura:* Jane Merrow; *Michael Pritchard:* Keith Bell; *Dysart:* Derek Godfrey; *Mrs. Golding:* Dora Bryan; *Mrs. Bryant:* Marjorie Rhodes.

Hammer Films began toying with the legend of Jack the Ripper as early as 1950—well before the studio hit the big time with *Curse of Frankenstein*—with a little-seen thriller called *Room to Let.* Its premise was similar to that of Hitchcock's *The Lodger* (1926), but it lacked the Hitchcock film's technical precociousness. *Room to Let* was, in fact, a rather tepid affair, its strongest element being a very effective, low keyed performance by British character actor Valentine Dyall as the suspected "rooming house Ripper."

Much better was Hammer's *Dr. Jekyll and Sister Hyde* (1971). In it, the infamous Ripper murders are layed at the doorstep of Stevenson's fictional medical man, who must obtain female organs necessary for transforming into his distaff side. Just for good measure, the legendary body snatchers Burke and Hare were also thrown into the plot, despite the fact that their real-life crimes took place in Scotland, not Soho.

Hammer's second Ripper outing of 1971 was by far the best of the lot. It was called *Hands of the Ripper.* The film opens with a typical Hammer pre-credit sequence: a group of torch-wielding vigilantes is pursuing the Ripper through the streets of Whitechapel. The camera follows the familiar caped, top-hatted figure through the cobblestone streets to a tiny flat. The Ripper, it turns out, is a married man [we're never told who he is actually, but there are clues that he's a respected figure in the area]. Inside the flat, he stabs his wife to death in front of his little girl. After the gory Mary Kelly-like killing, he kisses his daughter and flees, beyond capture by the bobbies.

We next see his little girl, Anna, all grown up and working for a phony spiritualist. Concealed, she provides the spirit voices for the spiritualist's assembled suckers. One of the more reluctant and skeptical attendees, Dr. Pritchard, discovers Anna hiding behind a curtain and blows the spiritualist's scam. Later, the spiritualist sets up a liaison between a stuffy politician, Dysart, and Anna. It turns out to be a dangerous liaison indeed, ending with the gruesome death of the spiritualist, who is spiked to an oak door courtesy of a fireplace poker wielded by Anna herself. It seems that whenever certain circumstances arise that remind Anna of the traumatic scene of her mother's death, she falls into a murderous trance. These circumstances include a combination of reflecting light (reminding her of the gleam of the knife blade as it penetrated her mother), firelight (her mother had been stabbed in front of the family fireplace), and anyone attempting an affectionate kiss (her father had kissed her before he sped away).

When Dysart tells Pritchard, an early follower of Sigmund Freud, of the spiritualist's murder, which he (Dysart) witnessed, Pritchard becomes determined to cure the girl of her "insanity." Instead of curing her, however, he becomes so caught up in the girl's problems that he starts covering up her acts of violence instead, and so obsessed with her that he fails to see what triggers her murderous rages and eventually falls victim to her himself. The film concludes with a moving climax. Mortally wounded (Anna has run him through with a swordstick), Pritchard tracks the girl to St. Paul's Cathedral where she is about to murder his son's fiancée, Laura. The two women are high above the cathedral floor in the whispering gallery. Pritchard calls to Anna and she leaps from the balcony, falling upon him, uniting the two in death.

From a psycho-sexual standpoint, *Hands of the Ripper* is one of Hammer's most interesting character studies, for Pritchard, in fact, is just a sick as Anna. Adapted from a short story by Edward Spencer Shew, whose *A Companion to Murder* (1961) and *A Second Companion to Murder* (1962) are considered required references by true crime buffs, L.W. Davidson's script is full of intriguing complexities. Pritchard is a rather egocentric, tunnel-visioned rationalist. Blinded by some sort of perverse longing for the girl, he ignores the dangers in his layman's attempts to cure her, turning her into an even more lethal creature than she

Another lady of the night is about to fall victim to the *Hands of the Ripper*.

Dr. Pritchard (Eric Porter) uses truth serum and hypnosis on Anna (Angharad Rees) to get to the root of her problem.

initially was. His protective concern for the demented Anna is fascinatingly at odds with his attitude toward his own future daughter-in-law, whom he treats coldly and with undisguised distaste, even though the girl is blind. It's almost as if he scorns Laura's blindness as some kind of *false* affliction.

One question never answered by the film is whether Anna is insane or just possessed by the spirit of her father, Jack the Ripper. Though the film is quite forthright and graphic in most cases, it harks back to the psychological horror films of Val Lewton by leaving this question up to the viewer to decide. It seems clear in most respects that Anna is just reliving the trauma of her mother's death over and over, but it becomes equally obvious that Pritchard's attempts at Freudian psychoanalysis yield no medical solution to her condition. Dysart himself makes a strong case for possession, explaining that "no ordinary mortal" could have skewered a person so easily through a two-inch thick oak door, and yet Anna did just that. There are other hints along the way that what's at work here is more than just a mental disorder. The fact that Anna is working for a spiritualist, regardless of the spiritualist's being a fraud, is certainly more than coincidence.

Could she actually be *attracting* spirits to her without knowing it—including that of her father? Near the end of the film, when Anna menaces Laura in the whispering gallery, we briefly see her father's face superimposed over her own. But these are only hints. In the tradition not only of Lewton but of Henry James' *Turn of the Screw*, the conclusion is left to us.

Peter Sasdy's direction neatly recaptures the flavor of the earlier Hammer Horrors in the film's rich colors and Victorian elegance. But the grisly murder scenes are a lot more graphic than Hammer's earlier films. For U.S. release, much of this violence was trimmed in order to secure an "R" rating—a rather distinct departure from years past when the American versions of some of Hammer's films included an extra frame or two of explicit gore denied British release prints. The film was further bastardized when it aired on the ABC network in the early Eighties. The violence was cut still more and additional footage shot in Hollywood to pad out the running time. But the original British "X" certificate version of *Hands of the Ripper* has since been released on video, preserving, at least for the foreseeable future, one of the modern cinema's most intelligent and fascinating, if not definitive, Ripper films.

STRAW DOGS (1971)

Tom Hedden (Peter Vaughan), left, threatens the bartender (Robert Keegan) with violence for refusing to serve him another pint as Charlie Venner (Del Henney) and David Sumner (Dustin Hoffman) look on uneasily.

An ABC Pictures Presentation
Distributed by Cinerama Releasing Corporation
Color /113 minutes (118 minutes in the U.K.)

Dustin Hoffman discusses the complex character of David Sumner with director Sam Peckinpah on the set of *Straw Dogs*.

A quiet moment at home between the mismatched Sumners (Dustin Hoffman and Susan George.)

Credits

Director: Sam Peckinpah; *Producer:* Daniel Melnick; *Screenplay:* David Zelag Goodman and Sam Peckinpah, based on the novel *The Siege of Trencher's Farm* by Gorden M. Williams; *Cinematographer:* John Coquillon; *Editors:* Roger Spottiswoode, Paul Davies, Tony Lawson; *Music:* Jerry Fielding; *Production Designer:* Ray Simm; *Videocassette source:* CBS/Fox Video.

Cast

David Sumner: Dustin Hoffman; *Amy Sumner:* Susan George; *Tom Hedden:* Peter Vaughan; *Major Scott:* T.P. McKenna; *Charlie Venner:* Del Henney; *Norman Scutt:* Ken Hutchison; *Reverend Hood:* Colin Welland; *Chris Cawsey:* Jim Norton; *Janice Hedden:* Sally Thomsett; *Riddaway:* Conald Webster; *John Niles:* Peter Arne; *Henry Niles:* David Warner [uncredited].

Sam Peckinpah's *The Wild Bunch* (1969) was one of the great films of the turbulent Sixties, and, without a doubt, that controversial director's one sure masterpiece. It was an epic, vast in scope and subject matter, an attempt by Peckinpah to do for the Western what Akira Kurosawa, a major influence on him, had done for the samurai film in *Seven Samurai* (1954); that is, to create a "jidai-geki," a sprawling, authentic period piece within the framework of a tired and cliche-ridden genre.

Just as *Seven Samurai* had been, *The Wild Bunch* was cut by its distributor (Warner Bros.), who felt the film's box office appeal rested chiefly in its action sequences, not in its depth of characterization. Nevertheless, *The Wild Bunch* survived its surgery, as well as the barrage of criticism leveled at its graphic depiction of blood-letting and carnage, to become a bona fide American film classic.

In part a reply to those who criticized him of copping out by making a Western about mankind's violent instincts rather than a more contemporary film—about Vietnam, for example—Peckinpah's fifth feature, *Straw Dogs* (set in the present day), trained its sights on the theme of man's apparently insatiable appetite for violence with an even greater vengeance. In it, violence is from first frame to last the absolute concern of the film. Like *The Wild Bunch*, it too was

almost universally misunderstood—even by critics who came to its defense. David Denby of *The Atlantic Monthly*, for example, deemed the film as brilliant as *The Wild Bunch* but a lot harder to defend because "it speaks for the value of direct, instinctual fulfillment, physical courage and initiative, and the sexual rights of men over women." *Newsweek* praised it as "a flawless expression of a primitive vision of experience—a belief that home and hearth are inviolate and must be defended by blood, that a man must conquer other men to prove his courage and hold on to his woman." The film's horrified detractors were equally vocal. Judith Crist, for example, accused the director of having a "beast-in-man-fetish." If ever a movie succeeded in eluding the critics of its time, *Straw Dogs* was it.

Though based on a 1969 novel by Gordon M. Williams, *Straw Dogs* owes considerably greater debt to the work of anthropologist Robert Ardrey and his controversial studies on violence and territoriality in animals—drives which, Ardrey maintains, modern man has inherited. In writing the script with David Zelag Goodman, Peckinpah departed from the novel—though not nearly as much as his later interviews on the subject would lead one to believe—in order to pattern the film more closely on the theories of Ardrey, whose book *The Territorial Imperative* serves as the foundation upon which the central theme of *Straw Dogs* is built.

Peckinpah's modern wild bunch in *Straw Dogs*. From left to right: Jim Norton, Ken Hutchison, Peter Vaughan, Del Henney, Donald Webster, Michael Mundell.

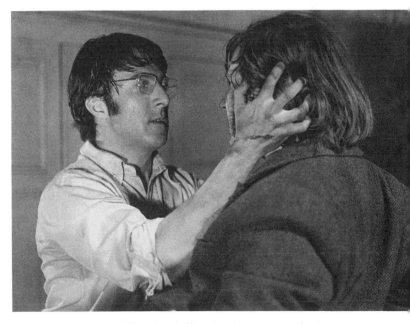

Sumner (Dustin Hoffman) tries to quiet down the hysterical Henry Niles (David Warner).

David Sumner (Dustin Hoffman) armed and ready for action.

A tense situation is forced on David Sumner (Dustin Hoffman) when Scutt (Ken Hutchison), Cawsey (Jim Norton) and Venner (Del Henney) demand that he turn Henry Niles over to them.

Shortly after the film begins, American expatriate David Sumner enters a pub and asks for "any American cigarettes," a subtle touch that reveals how tied he still is to his past, despite his protestations to the contrary. In the pub, he finds a drunk, Tom Hedden, who insists on being served another pint. When Harry the bartender refuses and places his hand over Hedden's empty glass, Hedden breaks the glass and cuts Harry's hand. Major Scott, the town magistrate, quickly intervenes and Sumner smiles at the man's ability to put down an unruly thug like Hedden so easily. This belief is ill-founded, however. Hedden stopped only because he wanted to. Hedden has no respect for Scott or his office. By offering to buy Scott a pint when both men know that the offer is totally insincere, Hedden demonstrates his total contempt for the law. His baiting of Scott, in fact, is simply a game by which he tests the frontiers of the magistrate's authority without reprisal. Later, during the climactic siege on Sumner's home, Scott's attempt to exercise his authority leads to his being murdered by Hedden.

Hedden is not alone in playing his baiting games; everyone in the film plays them—especially Sumner. Our first view of Sumner's kittenish wife, Amy, for instance, is not of her face, but of her breasts, undulating suggestively beneath her blouse as she walks along the village street, an open and conscious invitation for any nearby male to undress her with his eyes. When Amy buys Sumner a man-trap (or poacher trap), he says, "My wife's a collector, but I wind up with them." This is a veiled reference not just to Amy's penchant for picking up odd items, but her sexual appeal to other men. What Sumner fails to add (because he has chosen to deny it) is that this is probably the reason why he married her in the first place. The pair have little in common.

When Amy, first to be funny, then out of boredom and frustration, provokes her husband by altering the equations on his blackboard, then smearing the figures with gum, she fails to recognize in his anger with her ("Don't play games with me, Amy!") that by ridiculing his work, she ridicules him and his carefully constructed image of himself. And when Hedden and the others begin their assault on the house (to get at the child molester, Henry Niles), they provoke the same kind of response. Sumner's selection of sex-exuding Amy as a wife, his choice of profession, his home and the manner in which he chooses to live are all tied to his ego—and though he refuses to believe himself capable of it, he will even resort to violence to keep that ego intact. Incredibly, some critics (even those who liked the film) have termed Sumner's conversion from pacifist to killer as his "final acceptance of full manhood." Talk about missing the point. Sumner's actions don't make him a man. They force wisdom upon him. They make him realize—a bit late, unfortunately—that by denying his capacity for such actions, he has increased the inevitability of their occurrence. Clearly, the film shows that violence is a sexless instinct. Even Amy winds up killing a man (Riddaway) in order to protect what's hers—Sumner himself.

David Sumner is cold, dispassionate and smug—a Wise Man who views the folk as Straw Dogs. As a result, he provokes nearly everything that happens to him. He repudiates the notion that he carries with him the same aggressive instincts that have led to so much strife in his native land. And yet when Amy arouses his anger and frustration, he vents it irrationally by hurling apples at her pet cat until the animal cries out in pain and runs

Scutt (Ken Hutchison), left, threatens Venner (Del Henney), right, with a knife during the climactic siege; Sumner (Dustin Hoffman) and Amy (Susan George) are caught in the middle.

away. Later, he continues to take out his aggressions on the Reverend Hood by offering some barbed comments about how much bloodshed the Christian religion has visited upon mankind throughout the ages. Sumner's tragedy is that he refuses to acknowledge his real feelings and therefore precipitates the terrible siege that concludes the film. In effect, he pushes Amy and the villagers, however subtly, into making him prove that he has been right about himself only to discover that he has been disastrously wrong. By denying that he has the capacity to kill to ensure his own survival, Sumner helps to create a situation in which that conviction must be put to the test. One can't help but see in this a parallel to the dilemma facing the nuclear superpowers, who steadfastly maintain that they are morally incapable of triggering a nuclear war and yet, for years, have pushed, poked and prodded one another to the very brink of proving it.

A flawed—Dustin Hoffman is occasionally too much the milquetoast as Sumner—but powerful film, *Straw Dogs* offers a raw, horrific, but not cynical view of the human condition, one which seems to be born out time and time again in today's headlines. What is the violent gamesmanship inherent in political terrorism if not a vehicle through which certain disenfranchised (and gun-happy) groups pursue their own deadly territorial imperative? As *Straw Dogs* ends, David Sumner contemplates everything that's happened to him and he offers a chilling smile—one born of satisfaction ("I got 'em all!") yet awareness and bewilderment as well.

SISTERS (1973)

An American-International Release
Color /92 minutes

Philip Woode (Lisle Wilson) presents Danielle with a
surprise birthday cake.

Credits

Director: Brian De Palma; *Producer:* Edward R. Press-
man; *Screenplay:* Brian De Palma and Louisa Rose;
Cinematographer: Gregory Sandor; *Editor:* Paul Hirsch;
Music: Bernard Herrmann; *Production Designer:* Gary
Weist; *Videocassette source:* Warner Home Video.

Cast

Danielle Breton: Margot Kidder; *Grace Collier:* Jennifer
Salt; *Joseph Larch:* Charles Durning; *Emil Breton:* Bill
Finley; *Philip Woode:* Lisle Wilson; *Mr. McLennan:*
Barnard Huges; *Mrs. Collier:* Mary Davenport; *Detective
Kelley:* Dolph Sweet.

To fully appreciate (and enjoy) what Brian De Palma
achieved with *Sisters*, it's vital, I think, to turn a blind
eye to most of his output since then—for at the time of
its release, *Sisters* struck many critics, myself included,
as the most entertaining, insightful and deeply felt
homage to the art of Alfred Hitchcock that anyone had
yet produced. De Palma's endlessly repetitive and derivative work since then (*Obsession, Carrie, Dressed to
Kill, Blow Out, Body Double, Scarface, The Untouch-
ables*, et al., ad nauseum) has proven all of us wrong—
he is little more than a copycat stylist, and *Sisters* was
less an *homage* than a meticulously planned and
crafted pastiche. Nevertheless, the film remains De
Palma's best pastiche and a gripping and horrific suspense thriller to boot; in terms of audience impact, it
even surpassed Hitchcock's own *Frenzy*, released the
year before.

De Palma, whose previous features included the
anarchic, underground comedies *Greetings* and *Hi,
Mom!*, stated at the time of the release of *Sisters* that his
intention with the film was to "re-interpret Hitchcock's
plot elements in my own way, in a different form." He
only partially succeeded. Except for some split-screen
sequences (a form Hitchcock never used but which De
Palma employs with remarkable ingenuity and skill),
the technique is pure Hitchcock. As is the tightly
constructed plot, which is full of Hitchcockian red
herrings—one of which, however, is a shameless cheat
that involves a discussion between two shadowy figures on a wall where there could, in reality, only be one.

Danielle Breton is a Canadian model who meets a
young black man, Philip Woode, on a TV game show
called "Peeping Toms." She takes him home to spend

the night with her. The next morning, Woode wakes up to hear two women arguing in the adjacent room. Dominique, Danielle's twin sister, has come over to celebrate their birthday. Jealous that Danielle has a man with her, Dominique leaves in a huff. Sorry that he's messed up the party, Woode prepares to beat a hasty retreat, but Danielle persuades him to stay and celebrate her birthday with her. But first she asks him to pick up a prescription of painkillers for her at the local drug store. After he leaves, she goes into the bathroom and all but passes out on the floor in pain.

While Woode is getting the pills, he also picks up a birthday cake. When he returns to the apartment, he finds Danielle asleep in bed. He quietly lights the candles on the cake and takes it and a carving knife in to her. The figure that suddenly tosses away the bed-

But he gets the surprise instead when the jealous "Dominique" (Margot Kidder) scoops up the carving knife and stabs him repeatedly.

In an effectively staged split-screen sequence, Woode (Lisle Wilson) manages to crawl to the window and scrawl the word "Help" in his own blood on the glass.

The murder and Woode's scrawling of the message are overseen by Grace Collier (Jennifer Salt), an investigative reporter not well loved by the police.

Breton (Bill Finley) puts Grace (and the audience) under a bravura hallucination sequence.

sheets, however, is not Danielle, but Dominique, who snatches the knife and stabs Woode repeatedly. He manages to crawl to the window and write the word "Help" on the glass in his own blood before expiring from his wounds. The murder is observed from the

apartment building across the way by Grace Collier, an investigative reporter whose muckraking articles about the local police have not endeared her to the authorities. Grace calls the cops, but before they arrive, Danielle has cleaned up the murder she's convinced her sister committed while she herself was passed out in the bathroom. She is aided by her creepy ex-husband, Dr. Breton. Together, they stuff the dead man's body in a sofabed for shipment to parts unknown.

When the police refuse to believe Grace for lack of evidence, she sets out to solve the mystery on her own. She learns that the sisters were Canada's first pair of Siamese twins and that Dr. Breton was the surgeon who successfully separated them. Dominique, however, died during the operation, a complication that left Danielle emotionally as well as physically scarred. In fact, she's a murderous Jekyll and Hyde. It was she who killed Woode, not Dominique. Grace tracks Danielle and Breton to the latter's private sanitarium. Captured and put under hypnosis by Breton, she witnesses a bizarre love scene between the doctor and Danielle—who later slays Breton with a knife. The police arrive and take everyone away. But when they question Grace about the first murder she witnessed, she can recall nothing for, under hypnosis, Breton has erased her memory of the event.

There's no need to list the number of Hitchcock themes and films referred to by De Palma in *Sisters*. But perhaps because it was De Palma's first Hitchcock pastiche, there is a freshness to the film and its Hitchcockian hi-jinks that he has failed to duplicate since. The film is exciting, scary, suspenseful and amusing in a way that his subsequent "odes to Hitchcock" are not.

Much of the film's visceral impact can be attributed directly to its nightmarish music score—by longtime Hitchcock composer Bernard Herrmann. It's one of Herrmann's best and most unsettling—ranking right up there with his classic scores for Hitchcock's *Psycho* and *Vertigo*. De Palma was very lucky, in fact, to have secured Herrmann's services on the film—*Sisters* was, after all, a relatively low budget horror film being made by a young director for a minor studio. On the other hand, Herrmann, who had worked with giants like Hitchcock and Orson Welles, was not at all above offering his skills to the least likely bidder. He was very individualistic (or iconoclastic) in his choice of which films to score and which to decline. For example,

Danielle (Margot Kidder) and her ex-husband, Dr. Breton (Bill Finley), secret Woode's (Lisle Wilson) body in a sofabed.

Herrmann turned down what was probably a large financial offer from William Friedkin to score Warner Bros.' high profile horror movie *The Exorcist* in order to do Larry Cohen's low budget thriller *It's Alive!* Ironically, Lalo Schifrin, who went on to score *The Exorcist* instead, had his score thrown out—so, perhaps Herrmann knew what he was doing after all by turning the deal down.

Apparently, Herrmann and De Palma got on well together for Herrmann agreed to provide the score to De Palma's next Hitchcock pastiche, *Obsession* (1976), a ridiculous reworking of *Vertigo*. Herrmann's score, which is not at all like the one he composed for *Vertigo*, is the best part of the film. If Herrmann hadn't succombed to a sudden heart attack in 1975 (he was only 64), De Palma would very likely be using him still. In fact, Herrmann had been set to write the music for *Carrie* (1976). He was replaced by Pino Donaggio, whose score for *Carrie* and other De Palma thrillers in the Hitchcock mold unsuccessfully attempts to mimic the Herrmann style.

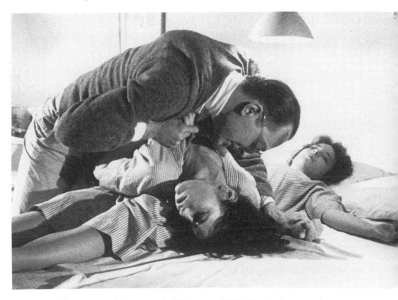

The mortally wounded Breton (Bill Finley) grapples with the murderous Danielle (Margot Kidder) as Grace (Jennifer Salt) languishes under hypnosis.

THE EXORCIST (1973)

A Hoya Production
A Warner Brothers Release
Color /121 minutes

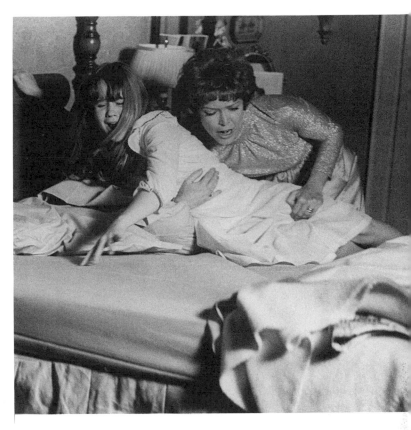

Credits

Director: William Friedkin; *Producer:* William Peter Blatty; *Screenplay:* William Peter Blatty, based on his novel; *Cinematographers:* Owen Roizman and Billy Williams; *Editor:* Evan Lottman and Norman Gay; *Music:* Tubular Bells and various classical composers; *Production Designer:* Bill Malley; *Videocassette source:* Warner Home Video.

Cast

Chris MacNeil: Ellen Burstyn; *Father Merrin:* Max von Sydow; *Lt. Kinderman:* Lee J. Cobb; *Sharon:* Kitty Winn; *Burke Dennings:* Jack MacGowran; *Father Karras:* Jason Miller; *Regan:* Linda Blair; *Father Dyer:* Rev. William O'Malley, S.J.; *Dr. Klein:* Barton Heyman; *Clinic Director:* Peter Masterson.

Chris (Ellen Burstyn) rescues the hysterical Regan (Linda Blair) from the "bouncing bed."

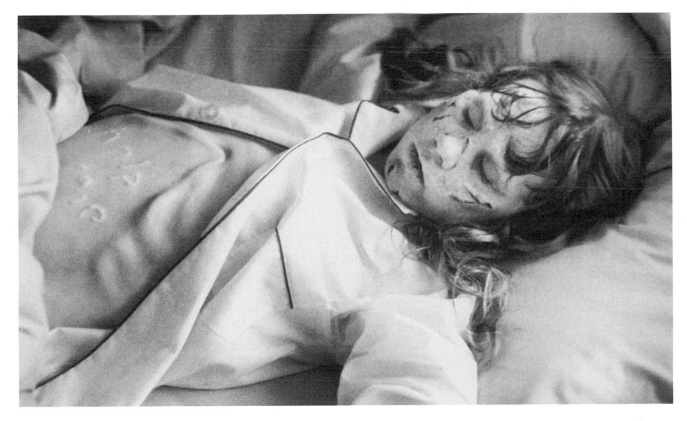

Regan's (Linda Blair) trapped spirit cries out to be rescued from demonic prossession by raising a series of welts forming the words "help me" on the girl's stomach—one of the many brilliantly executed effects orchestrated by makeup master Dick Smith.

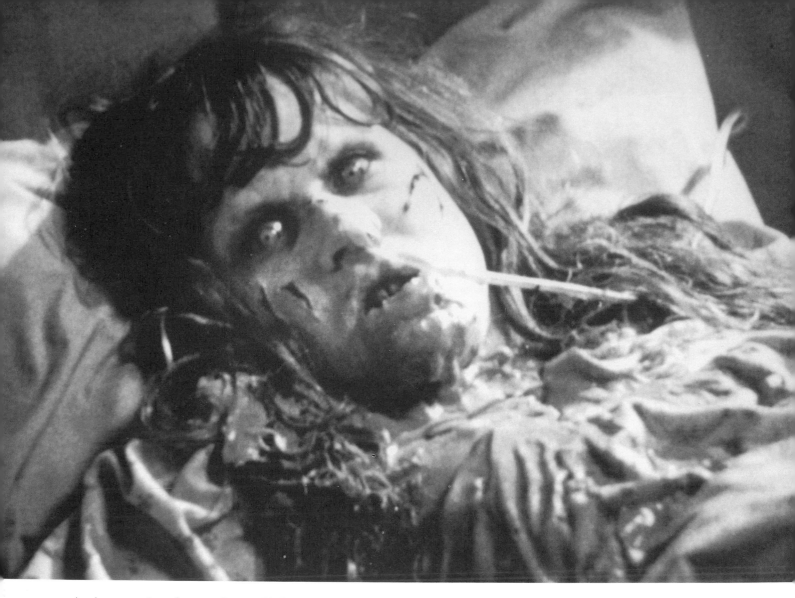

As the possession advances, Regan (Linda Blair) becomes a vomit-spewing little hellion.

Like it or dislike it, William Peter Blatty's *The Exorcist*, both as a book and as a movie, has had such an enormous influence on modern horror fiction and the modern horror film that its place in the modern horror hall of fame cannot be questioned.

Personally, while finding it to be as much of a page-turner as everyone else did, I didn't think the book was especially well written; in fact, I found its characters and various sub-plots to be both contrived and superficial and the dialogue to be either incredibly trite or downright unrealistic—which was surprising to me, as author Blatty enjoyed a considerable reputation as one of Hollywood's best and brightest screenwriters. But the power of the book's horror sequences could not be denied. This was no subtle Jamesian terror tale, but a balls-to-the-wall shocker whose stratospheric success paved the way for a whole new generation of bolder and even more graphic and disturbing horror writers, including Stephen King and the so-called "splatterpunk" novelists of the present day.

The film version, which producer Blatty adapted quite faithfully from his source novel, suffered from many of the novel's liabilities, I felt. But its power too could not be denied. It was a horror film like no other—one whose raw language and shockingly graphic scenes of demon-inspired horror and gore crumbled the walls of film censorship completely and changed the face not only of the modern horror film, but modern film as well.

Blatty based his story on one of the most widely publicized cases of demonic possession in 20th century American history. Blatty learned of the case through a series of *Washington Post* articles published in 1949 when he was a student at Georgetown University. The case involved a fourteen-year-old boy living in Mt. Rainier, Maryland. According to the articles, the boy's possession was first noticed by his parents due to a series of strange manifestations—scratching and marching sounds under his bed, furniture sliding across the room, the tilting of a chair on which he sat, the levitation of objects around him and so on. When red welts suddenly appeared on the boy's body as well, the parents consulted numerous medical authorities, but no explanations or cures could be found. Subsequently, a local priest was called in. After obtaining permission from church higher-ups, the priest conducted nearly thirty rites of exorcism over the next two months. While the rites were being carried out, the boy would curse, fight and lash out with his feet, kicking anyone near him. During some of these violent seizures, he even spoke in Latin, a language of which he had no knowledge.

After reading of a similar case seventy-five years earlier in Wisconsin, the priest forced the boy to wear a chain of religious medals and hold a crucifix during yet another rite of exorcism. The boy responded with even greater violence and five or more priests were called in to restrain him. At this point, the "demon" finally announced itself through the boy's lips and then departed—as mysteriously as it had come, leaving the boy with no recollection of his frightening experience. Whether the boy was, in fact, suffering from a strange physical or psychological malady, or was, indeed, demonically possessed remains open to question. But the priest's account, which is now lodged in official Roman Catholic archives, expresses no doubt that the boy was diabolically possessed. Blatty's novel and film, which follows the details of the boy's possession fairly, though it certainly elaborates upon them, and changes the lead character from a boy to a nine-year-old girl, take the same view.

Many people in Hollywood (and elsewhere) believed Blatty's novel to be unfilmable because of its profanity and graphic scenes of sacrilege—as when the demon child masturbates with a crucifix (certainly *that* couldn't be filmed!), elements which insiders felt would surely land the film with the dreaded "X" rating as well as the wrath of churches and churchgoers everywhere, thereby diminishing its box office potential. In addition, many of the book's most notable set pieces posed enormous technical problems. For example: even if the MPAA rating board would allow it, how could you possibly *bring off* the effect of Regan, the possessed child, spraying projectile vomit across the room and into the faces of her tormentors, Father Merrin and Karras? Writer-producer Blatty may have wondered about all of this as well, for in his first draft screenplay, he toned down a good deal of his novel and altered its structure considerably. When director William Friedkin saw how much Blatty's adaption departed from the novel, he urged him to do a second draft that followed the book more faithfully. This Blatty

did, and it was this second draft that was filmed. [Blatty subsequently published both drafts in book form.]

The job of realizing the screenplay's horrific scenes of possession and demonic mischief fell to veteran makeup artist Dick Smith, whose previous assignment had been *The Godfather*, a film noted—and often condemned—for its very realistic scenes of bloodshed. For Smith, the myriad of makeup and technical effects posed by *The Exorcist* proved even more challenging. Today, as a result of *The Exorcist* and Dick Smith, Hollywood's growing army of "special makeup effects technicians" enjoy greater prestige in and out of the industry than ever before. Their influence is now felt in almost every type of film; in some cases, they're even called in on a project before the director! The Academy of Motion Picture Arts and Sciences has even created a special Oscar award category for them.

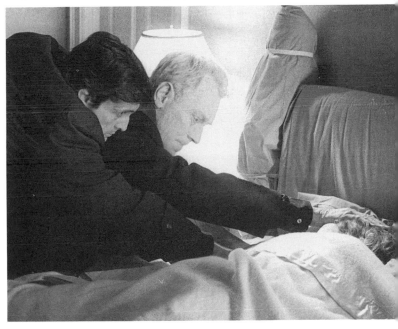

Father Karras (Jason Miller) and Father Merrin (Max von Sydow) try to drive out the evil spirit that has possessed Regan (Linda Blair).

Shivering from cold and fear, Karras (Jason Miller) performs the religious ritual aimed at exorcising the demon from the child's body.

The ailing Merrin (Max von Sydow) informs Karras (Jason Miller) that the younger priest will have to go it alone.

Despite the vulgar language and with all the novel's bizarre, "impossible-to-film" and potentially offensive images intact (yes, they did shoot the masturbation scene), *The Exorcist* was surprisingly released with an "R" rating rather than an "X." Controversy over the film did rage, but rather than hurting at the box office, it helped. Today, *The Exorcist* still reigns as one of the twenty most financially successful films in movie history and *the* highest grossing(!) horror film ever made, according to *Variety*. Few others before or since, in fact, have had quite the influence on the genre as *The Exorcist*.

How to account for its success? Well, for one thing, *The Exorcist* is that rare horror film to succeed in crossing all demographic boundaries. Everyone wanted to see it, not just kids. For another, it was a real shocker—though its shocks (like *Psycho*'s) have since been eclipsed by scores of ever more outrageous and technically ingenious modern horror films. [In fact, the film is now frequently shown on television *uncut*!] Among those *not* eclipsing it is its execrable sequel that John Boorman directed in 1977. And as this book goes to press, a second sequel—this one directed by author Blatty himself—is being filmed.

There are those who say the film also scored heavily because it tapped into human concerns about the "mysteries of faith"—a belief shared by both Blatty and Friedkin. But I think the best explanation as to why *The Exorcist* tapped such a nerve in people, especially adults, belongs to Stephen King, who wrote this of the phenomenon in his 1981 book *Danse Macabre*: "It [was] a film about explosive social change, a finely honed focusing point for that entire youth explosion that took place in the late Sixties and early Seventies. It was a movie for all those parents who felt, in a kind of agony and terror, that they were losing their children and could not understand why or how it was happening."

Regan (Linda Blair), the monstrous child-demon in *The Exorcist*.

BLOOD FOR DRACULA (1974)

(A.k.a. *Andy Warhol's Dracula*)
A Bryanston Pictures Release
Color /103 minutes

Udo Kier as Count Dracula in Paul Morrissey's sex
and splatter spoof, *Blood for Dracula*.

Credits

Director: Paul Morrissey; *Producer:* Andrew Braunsberg; *Screenplay:* Paul Morrissey; *Cinematographer:* Luigi Kuveiller; *Editor:* Franca Silvi and Jed Johnson; *Music:* Claudio Gizzi; *Production Designer:* Enrico Job; *Videocassette source:* Video Gems.

Cast

Count Dracula: Udo Kier; *Anton:* Arno Juerging; *Marquis:* Vittorio De Sica; *Mario:* Joe Dallesandro; *Marquisa:* Maxime McKendry; *Esmeralda:* Milena Vukotic; *Saphiria:* Dominique Darel; *Rubinia:* Stefania Casini; *Perla:* Silvia Dionisio; *Man in Pub:* Roman Polanski [uncredited].

When I attended the U.S. premiere of Paul Morrissey's *Blood for Dracula* at the 1974 Atlantic International Film Festival, I was expecting to be little impressed. Morrissey's previous horror film, *Andy Warhol's Frankenstein*, had struck me as an only moderately amusing freak show. I couldn't understand why Warhol/Morrissey had been given a half a million bucks by executive producer Carlo Ponti to make it. Perhaps, I thought, the film industry was just getting too jaded for me.

By Warhol/Morrissey standards, *Andy Warhol's Frankenstein* was a real movie with real production values—plus it was made in 3-D (or Spacevision as it was touted). All this made the film a distinctly commercial endeavor—though it was very much of a piece with past Warhol/Morrissey efforts; it was essentially a parody. In their earlier collaborations, Warhol/Morrissey took transvestites like Holly Woodlawn and pop art personalities like Viva and, in parody of the Hollywood star system, promoted them as "superstars." And in films like *Trash* and *Heat*, they poked fun at cinema vérité and underground filmmaking. *Heat*, released in 1972, brought them ever closer to the legitimate Hollywood scene, however, because it offered a bona fide actress (Sylvia Miles) playing a real role—that of an aging film personality who keeps a former child star-turned-unemployed adult actor on call for stud service. *Heat* was a commercial hit—*Sunset Boulevard* as reflected in the Warhol fun house mirror.

Andy Warhol's Frankenstein was an even more forthright commercial endeavor, a parody of the horror film, a genre of mass appeal. The film was a total send-

The ancestral car loaded down with his belongings, Dracula (Udo Kier) sets off for Italy in search of "where-gins."

up of all past *Frankenstein* movies in general and Hammer's *The Curse of Frankenstein* in particular. We always imagined that the obsessed Baron must have a sexual drive. Here, Warhol/Morrissey at last revealed what turned the Baron on. Mounting his gorgeous female creature, he feverishly slips his hand through an incision in her side and paws at her gall bladder until he climaxes. At last the truth: Baron Victor Frankenstein, the old lech, was an "intestinophile," a man who achieves sexual satisfaction by pawing every organ he can get his hands on, while his idiot assistant Otto looks on with tongue hanging out. The Baron is married to his own sister, with whom he has spawned two otherworldly children. The Baroness is a nymphomaniac who hires a farmer to fill the void in her life. And, of course, sex proves her undoing. Attempting to arouse the sole non-functioning part of her husband's male creature, she has her back broken in the embrace of her life. Searching for a head to cap off the torso of his male creature, Frankenstein mistakenly decapitates an aspiring monk (thus the creature's lack of ardor) and this proves *his* undoing—quite literally. He winds up with his liver dangling at the end of a spear a few feet from his nose and, thanks to Spacevision, a few inches from the audience's. Quoting Karloff, the creature confesses: "I belong dead." Then he rips open his stomach and spills his guts on the floor.

When Dracula (Udo Kier) meets his new neighbor, Vittorio de Sica (far left) and his four beautiful daughters, he thinks he's got it made.

Anton (Arno Juerging), Dracula's valet, plays a variation on the old shell game with Roman Polanski (in an uncredited cameo).

One critic wrote of *Andy Warhol's Frankenstein* that more spoofery and fewer buckets of gore might have improved it. That's debatable for the film's comic core lay precisely in its blood and gore. Nevertheless, Warhol/Morrissey's follow-up film, *Blood for Dracula*, does forego buckets of blood for more spoofery.

Back to the premier: when the tall, redheaded Morrissey stepped onstage to introduce *Blood for Dracula*, he was greeted by a thunderous round of applause—which surprised me. Then, when he spoke, I was completely taken aback. Totally devoid of pretense and more than a little nervous, Morrissey thanked the audience for being so nice in its approval of him. Then, a little embarrassed, he went on to thank the judges for inviting his "silly little movie" to the prestigious festival. By the end of the screening, I have to admit, the director won me over. And so had his film.

Blood for Dracula is indeed a "silly little movie" which laughs even harder than *Frankenstein* did at the conventions of the traditional horror movie, but does so with an elegance and sense of style only hinted at in the latter film. Dying from lack of virgin's (pronounced "where-gins") blood—due, unfortunately, to a lack of virgins—Dracula forsakes Transylvania for the purer

"If he's looking for virgins, what's he doing with you two whores [pronounced who-ers]?" The libidinous gardener (Joe Dallesandro) asks of his two playmates.

pastures of Roman Catholic Italy. Taking up residence in the house of a wealthy nobleman who has four beautiful daughters, the weak, wheelchair-bound Dracula quickly puts the bite on the first daughter only to discover that she's been lying to him about being a virgin. This sends him into a massive fit of vomiting in the bathroom. In this film, Dracula's nemesis isn't Van Helsing, but a libidinous gardener who always manages to be one daughter ahead of the starving vampire.

In the final reel, as Dracula chases the sole chaste daughter through the castle, the gardener rescues her by ripping off her dress and screwing her just in time against the living room wall. Then, for Grand Guignol fans who've been wondering what all this erotica is doing in a horror movie, Morrissey concludes the film with a spectacular Dracula demise (courtesy of special

Paul Morrissey (left), Joe Dallesandro and Udo Kier on the set of *Blood for Dracula*. "I play for absurdity, not shock," Morrissey says of his films.

Dracula (Udo Kier) puts the bite on one of the daughters, only to discover that she's not a "where-gin."

effects maestro Carlo Rambaldi) as the gardener pursues the hissing vampire with an axe, slowing him down by chopping off one limb at a time until there is very little left of the Count to impale with the requisite stake.

Perhaps because of its sumptuous period atmosphere and the presence in bit parts of two prestigious filmmakers (the late Vittorio de Sica and Roman Polanski, whose cameo is a gem), *Blood for Dracula* exudes a style and cinematic flair seen only in fleeting glimpses

142

The gardener (Joe Dallesandro) whittles Dracula (Udo Kier) down to size before staking him out.

in *Andy Warhol's Frankenstein*. Even Joe Dallesandro's terrible histrionics and absurdly out of place Brooklyn accent is used to greater comic effect. His announcement that Count Dracula is a "vampiyah" never fails to bring down the house.

The family that slays together, stays together. The Chainsaw gang: from
left to right: John Dugan, Jim Siedow, Gunnar Hansen, Edwin Neal
and the mummified remains of grandma.

THE TEXAS CHAINSAW MASSACRE (1974)

A Vortex/Henkel/Hooper Production
A Bryanston Pictures Release
Color /86 minutes

Credits

Director: Tobe Hooper; *Producer:* Tobe Hooper; *Screenplay:* Kim Henkel and Tobe Hooper; *Cinematographer:* Daniel Pearl; *Editor:* Sallye Richardson and Larry Carroll; *Music:* Tobe Hooper and Wayne Bell; *Art Director:* Robert A. Burns; *Videocassette source:* Media Home Entertainment.

Cast

Sally Hardesty: Marilyn Burns; *Franklin Hardesty:* Paul A. Partain; *Hitchhiker:* Edwin Neal; *Older Brother:* Jim Siedow; *Leatherface:* Gunnar Hansen; *Kirk:* William Vail; *Pam:* Terri McMinn; *Jerry:* Allen Danziger; *Grandpa:* John Dugan.

THE TEXAS CHAINSAW MASSACRE PART II (1986)

A Golan-Globus Production
A Cannon Films Release
Color/101 minutes

Credits

Director: Tobe Hooper; *Producer:* Menahem Golan and Yoram Globus; *Screenplay:* L.M. Kit Carson; *Cinematographer:* Richard Kooris; *Editor:* Alain Jakubowicz; *Music:* Tobe Hooper and Jerry Lambert; *Production Designer:* Cary White; *Videocassette source:* Media Home Entertainment.

Cast

Lt. "Lefty" Enright: Dennis Hopper; *Stretch:* Caroline Williams; *Cook:* Jim Siedow; *Leatherface:* Bill Johnson; *Chop-Top:* Bill Moseley; *Grandpa:* Ken Evert; *L.G. McPeters:* Lou Perry; *Detective:* Kirk Sisco.

Made by a group of amateurs hoping the film would propel them to Hollywood, *The Texas Chainsaw Massacre* delivered some very professional shocks at the time of its release—and continues to do so to this day despite scores of imitations, most of them a lot bloodier and even more sensational. When one of the characters wanders into an apparently empty house in search of someone to loan him gasoline and is suddenly hammered into a quivering pulp by an ape of a creature that rises out of nowhere dressed in a bloody butcher's apron and a mask made of human skin, viewers are reduced to a stunned silence. And, for the most part,

they stay that way throughout the remainder of the film, despite a storyline that is full of comic book excesses and absurdities and simplistic action. The heroine, Sally Hardesty, for example, in an effort to get away from the marauding crazies inside the house, twice plunges Douglas Fairbanks-style through windows, shattering the glass, then runs away a little cut up but otherwise undaunted. The fact that her first suc-

Pam (Terri McMinn) stumbles into the farmhouse chamber of horrors.

Leatherface (Gunnar Hansen) drags Pam (Terri McMinn) off to his workshop.

cessful plunge is through a *second story window* clearly shows that while *The Texas Chainsaw Massacre* aims for full-throttle horror, it does so with tongue firmly planted in cheek.

Chainsaw's ghoulish black humor tended to elude the few critics of the time who even bothered to review it, most of whom lambasted the film for scaling dangerous new heights (or lows, depending upon one's point of view) in cinematic mayhem and graphic violence. The irony is that the film is not, and never was, as graphically bloody as its detractors have made it out to be. What director Hooper, his cast and crew were really aiming at was the creation of an atmosphere and environment of unparalleled derangement and depravity—an EC comic book pushed to the limit. And they succeeded 100%. *Chainsaw* is a totally mad movie.

The house the film's young leads accidentally wander into is a chamber of horrors and sickness that makes the Bates motel look positively tame by comparison. The three brothers who live there with their blood-sucking, skeletal grandpa are so revoltingly twisted in body and mind and obsessed by blood, bones and raw meat that one wonders how they could have functioned for so long without local law officials getting suspicious—especially as the number of bones lying about the house and quantity of stolen cars in the back yard would indicate a missing persons file large enough to attract the action of the FBI.

Sally (Marilyn Burns) is bound, gagged and offered
up as victim to Grandpa (John Dugan).

According to an introductory title card, the movie
was based on an actual case. The names of the victims
are even mentioned, but all this is a ruse designed to
contribute a sense of reality to the absurdly mad
proceedings and send shivers up the spine. Actually, the
film, like *Psycho*, was suggested by the infamous Ed
Gein case of the 1950s, but bears little resemblance to
it except for the bone and flesh-littered farmhouse and
the cannibalism of the killers.

Sally and Franklin Hardesty, together with some
friends, are motoring through the Texas backwoods
looking for an old house that belongs to Franklin's
family. Along the way, they pick up a hitchhiker, who
eventually proves so deranged and dangerous (he slices
wheelchair-bound Franklin with a knife) that they toss
him out. Later, the vacationing party's van runs out of
gas, and Franklin stays behind while the others go off in
search of fuel. Two of the pair, Pam and Kirk, come

upon a ramshackle farmhouse where they encounter
and are killed by the portly Leatherface, a chainsaw-
wielding maniac with the mental age of an infant, who
lives in the farmhouse with his two brothers—one of
whom turns out to be the crazy hitchhiker.

The remaining young people are eventually drawn
into the vortex of horror and carnage as well until only
Sally remains alive. She is captured, tied up and presented to the brothers' aging grandpa as a sacrificial
offering. Grandpa is too infirm to carry out the murder,
however, and she manages to escape—pursued by
Leatherface and the hitchhiker, who is summarily run
over by a passing truck. Covered with blood and
mentally unhinged by her ordeal, Sally succeeds in
flagging down a pick-up truck and gets away, leaving
the demented Leatherface whirling about on the road,
buzzing his chainsaw in frustration.

A friend of mine accurately described the film as "a
trip through hell." And that indeed it is. It remains to
this day one of the scariest horror movies ever made—
exceedingly well crafted on its low budget and, for
most part, very well acted by its primarily all-amateur

148

cast, most of whom were recruited from the drama department of the University of Texas at Austin (Jim Siedow was the only professional in the group.) Though the film was a huge cult hit worldwide, it did not succeed in making its creators much money, nor did it propel anyone to Hollywood—except for director Tobe Hooper, whose body of work since has been decidedly mixed.

Eaten Alive (1976), another ghoulish *Chainsaw*—like thriller about a depraved motel owner who feeds his guests to his pet gator, got a spotty release, then fell into a distribution black hole, reemerging over the years under several different titles, including *Starlight Slaughter, Horror Hotel* and *Death Trap*. Hooper's *The Funhouse*, made in 1981, fared somewhat better at the box office mainly because its distributor, Universal, managed to give it a major studio release. *The Funhouse* is about a group of teenagers who test their nerves by staying after hours in a carnival funhouse, where one of the "attractions," a deranged and hideous mutant, is running around killing people. Like *Eaten Alive*, its stylistic ties to *Chainsaw*—outrageous horror mixed with bizarre black comedy—are clear.

Then came the big time. Busy with *E.T.*, producer-director-mogul Steven Spielberg hired Hooper to direct *Poltergeist*, a megabuck special effects extravaganza about unquiet spirits from "the other side" who terrorize an average suburban family because some greedy real estate developer erected their home over an Indian burial ground. A box office smash (*Chainsaw* was a substantial hit too, but took a few years to rack up its impressive earnings), *Poltergeist* proved that Hooper could make a mainstream Hollywood-style horror film with the best of them—although rumors flew thick and fast that Spielberg was less than satisfied with Hooper's work on the film and had usurped directorial control. *Variety* fueled the speculation with its headline "Tobe or Not Tobe." Hooper denied this, maintaining that the film was *his* work. At any case, the fact remains that *Poltergeist* looks and sounds more like a Spielberg film than a Hooper one. [The same can be said, however, about most other films Spielberg has produced but did not direct.] Regardless of the surrounding controversy, *Poltergeist* did succeed in giving Hooper's career a decided shot in the arm. Two more big budget (though not as big as *Poltergeist*) special effects films followed: *Lifeforce* (1985), a lifeless (and very loose)—adaptation of Colin Wilson's intriguing novel about the origins of

Leatherface (Gunnar Hansen) offers Grandpa (John Dugan) a helping hand—in this case Sally's hand. The blood the old geezer is licking from her fingertips is meant as an appetizer.

Screaming like Fay Wray, Sally (Marilyn Burns) manages to get away yet again with Leatherface (Gunnar Hansen) in hot pursuit.

the vampire myth, *The Space Vampires*, and *Invaders from Mars* (1986), an update of William Cameron Menzies' cult 1953 thriller. The less said about these two derivative and completely uninspired potboilers the better. The same goes for *Salem's Lot* (1979), Hooper's brief foray into the timid land of network television, a medium not at all conducive to bringing out the best in Hooper, but ideal for bringing out the worst.

I think most modern horror film fans will agree that when Hooper "went Hollywood," his work lost much of the outrageous, horrific and blackly humorous power that made *Chainsaw* so distinctive. Horror movies, by their very nature, are confrontational. *Chainsaw*, like *Psycho*, was even more than that. It was a full scale assault on the audience's sensibilities and nerve ends. *Eaten Alive* and *Funhouse*, despite their failings, were clearly the work of the same man who made *Chainsaw*—whereas Hooper's subsequent features could have been made by anyone. It's quite possible that Hooper sensed this too, for with his next film, he traveled back to his roots: *The Texas Chainsaw Massacre Part II*.

Part of the decision was probably commercial as well, considering the involvement of the new film's financial backer, the exploitatively savvy Cannon Films. *Chainsaw* was, after all, a cult film with a proven reputation, box office track record and a well known and highly exploitable title behind it. Everyone was making sequels to successful—and even only moderately successful—films these days, so why not a *Chainsaw II* ? Actually, Hooper had been trying to get a *Chainsaw* sequel off the ground for years, but the rights to the first film had been mired in a morass of litigation almost from its conception. By 1986 apparently, the way had cleared, however.

While making *Invaders From Mars*, Hooper discussed the idea of a *Chainsaw* sequel with maverick writer, independent filmmaker and fellow Texan L.M. Kit Carson (Carson's wife, Karen Black, was then working for Hooper on *Invaders*), whose past work included the cult film *David Holzman's Diary* (1968) and the remake of *Breathless* (1983), both in collaboration with Jim McBride.

Carson proved to be an ideal collaborative choice. His script for *Chainsaw II*, like his work with Jim McBride, is subversive, wildly satiric and quite funny in

The old *Chainsaw* family, still staying together and slaying together 12 years later in *The Texas Chainsaw Massacre Part II*. From left to right: Grandpa (Ken Evert); Leatherface (Bill Johnson); Chop-Top (Bill Moseley); Cook (Jim Siedow); plus the unidentified corpse of one of the many, *many* victims.

spots. It is also extremely horrific—too much so even according to many fans of the genre, not a few of whom were as repelled by the film's grotesqueries as those critics who denounce such fare. I frankly admit that I too was "appalled" by the film's brutal excesses when I saw it for the first time. In the graphic bloodletting department, *Chainsaw II* is everything that *Chainsaw I* was accused of being but was not. In fact, by comparison *Chainsaw I* was a model of restraint. I thus dismissed the sequel for grossly pandering to the *Friday the 13th* crowd. A friend, however, persuaded me to take a second look. He felt, as I do now as well, that in my disappointment with Hooper and Carson for having "gone for the gore" I had overlooked, or ignored, the film's primary focus, which was satire. He was right.

Chainsaw II is primarily a satire—and a vicious one—that literally skewers its victims. And they are legion.

Even its graphic excesses, I realized on viewing the film a second time, were laced with satiric poison. "You like to be entertained by ultra-violent movies, folks?" Hooper and Carson seemed to be saying. "Okay, here's one that'll make you review your concept of entertainment. *Take that!*"

151

Stretch (Caroline Williams) stumbles upon the mummified remains of Grandma within the hellish caverns beneath the Texas Battleland Amusement Park.

Chainsaw II also takes on the modern American landscape—particularly the landscape of the South (the film is surely no "I love Texas" bumper sticker). It is a cry of outrage at America's gun culture, which seems to have reached epidemic proportions, though the film absurdly replaces guns with chainsaws. The satiric point is eminently clear though—especially when you see Dennis Hopper, all decked out with his specially-made chainsaw holsters strapped to his side, practicing his quick draw in preparation for the final *buzz-out* with Leatherface and the boys. A spectacular event that will take place not at the O.K. Corral, but the '80s equivalent: The Texas Battleland Amusement Park, a surrealistic landscape of bluffs and blinds where regular folks can stalk and "kill" each other for fun and frolic. "It's what everybody wants," the entrepreneurial Chop-Top says of the Park. *"Namland!"*

The demented spirit of modern day entrepeneurship—insider trading, hostile takeovers, influence peddling, get-rich-quick, me, me, me—is one of the real keys to *Chainsaw II*. Headed by the "success platitude" spouting Jim Siedow (the J.R. Ewing of his clan), the chainsaw boys have closed up their backwater barbecue stand and headed for where the real action is—the big city big time—where they've turned their special recipe for barbecue and chile ("The secret's in the meat!") into a rolling success. Rather than wait for their secret ingredients to stop by the farmhouse, they pick them off on lonely bridges and wherever else they find them. (So what's another missing persons case or twenty? The police files are loaded with them.) The walls come crashing in, however, when Hopper, as a Texas Ranger relative of Sally and Franklin Hardesty (who have mysteriously gained the additional name of Enright), tracks the slicers to their lair with the help of a female deejay and sets out to give them a taste of their own recipe for success. Make no mistake, Hopper proves to be as crazy as they are. In fact, *everybody* in this film is crazy—even the gal deejay, who had hoped cracking the case would propel her into big time broadcasting (success again), but goes bonkers in the end like everyone else. This is truly a chronicle of the American Dream gone sour.

The Texas Chainsaw Massacre and its even more outrageous, horrific and darkly humorous sequel remain, in my opinion, not only Tobe Hooper's best work, but two of the most accomplished and effective modern horror films to date.

Leatherface (Bill Johnson) and Chop-Top (Bill Moseley) run riot inside the radio station.

CAPTAIN KRONOS: VAMPIRE HUNTER (1974)

A Hammer Production
A Paramount Pictures Release
Color /91 minutes

German-born Horst Janson portrays the heroic and swashbuckling hero, Captain Kronos (his name is Greek for *time*), who tries to destroy the evil that has possessed a small village.

Dr. Marcus (John Carson) stares in horror at the body of a young girl who has fallen victim to a vampire.

Credits

Director: Brian Clemens; *Producers:* Albert Fennell and Brian Clemens; *Screenplay:* Brian Clemens; *Cinematographer:* Ian Wilson; *Editor:* James Needs; *Music:* Laurie Johnson; *Production Designer:* Robert Jones; *Videocassette source:* Gateway [Paramount] Home Video.

Cast

Captain Kronos: Horst Janson; *Dr. Marcus:* John Carson; *Paul Durward:* Shane Briant; *Professor Grost:* John Cater; *Carla:* Caroline Munro; *Kerro:* Ian Hendry; *Lady Durward:* Wanda Ventham; *Hagen:* William Hobbs; *Sara Durward:* Lois Dane.

By stretching the boundaries of the cliche-worn vampire subgenre and treating his tale as if it were a Clint Eastwood Western transposed to middle Europe, writer-director Brian Clemens fashioned *Captain Kronos: Vampire Hunter* into one of the freshest, most entertaining vampire movies since Polanski's *The Fearless Vampire Killers*.

Kronos retired Dracula to a well-deserved grave. Its vampire, whose identity is concealed from the audience until the final reel to add a dimension of mystery to the story as well, wanders about in the daylight and drinks blood only as an appetizer, spilling just a tiny drop, about the size of a tear, on his victims' lips. His main course is youth itself.

Clemens' larger-than-life Aryan hero (a former Captain in some "Imperial Guard") is Van Helsing in uniform, but just as determined to track down and kill vampires in whatever form they exist. His crusade is no

155

Captain Kronos (Horst Janson), prepares to fight off
the villagers who believe he is the cause of the
vampiric plague that has infected their community.

less neurotic than Van Helsing's but simpler to understand. It seems that when he returned home from "the
wars" some years ago, he found his mother and sister
had been turned into a pair of shrieking vampires,
whose lethal embrace left him with an ugly set of scars
on the back of his neck.

Accompanied by the hunchbacked Professor Grost,
the brains to Kronos' brawn, he arrives in town to assist
his friend, Dr. Marcus, in tracking down the villain who
has literally been sapping the youth of the village.
Numerous suspects present themselves—including
Marcus himself.

What gives *Kronos* its special panache is *The
Avengers*-style wit which Clemens, who created that
popular TV series, brings to the film, his directorial
debut. He turns the film upside down, infusing it with
elements from other genres (science-fiction, the Western, the mystery) then stirring the pot with unders-
tated relish. He has his vampire pass by a cluster of fresh
flowers, causing them to wilt. And he stages many of
the film's key set pieces in broad daylight—a nod,

perhaps, to Alfred Hitchcock. Established as a legendary swordsman, Kronos' first duel in a local pub is an
amusing parody of the cliched barroom brawl scene
from scores of Westerns in which the quiet stranger in
town is suddenly put upon by a gang of rowdies, whom
he proceeds to decimate without so much as mussing a
hair. Clemens pokes fun at the cliché by allowing us to
see Kronos do nothing more than draw his sword and
return it to its sheath. Then he cuts to a wide shot and
we see each of the bad guys crumble slowly to the floor,
the walls covered with drops of their blood.

Perhaps best summing up the combined elements of
humor and horror that make the film such an enjoyable
romp is the scene where the good Dr. Marcus discovers
that he has become a vampire himself. He turns to
Kronos and Grost for help, and Kronos ties him to a
chair, forcing Marcus to ward the affliction off cold
turkey. Knowing this will be fruitless, Marcus begs to
be killed. Kronos and Grost try to comply, first by
driving a spear into the man's chest, then by hanging
him (chair and all), finally by threatening him with
flames. Nothing works until a small crucifix is acci-
dently embedded in the Marcus' chest. In most vampire
movies, it is the vampire who always seems to be at a

disadvantage. He (or she) is susceptible to crosses, garlic, running water, sunlight, mirrors, stakes, you name it. Here, Clemens turns the tables and gives the vampires the upper hand (which is as it should be in order to create a reasonable sense of menace), forcing his protagonists to work hard to save their own and everyone else's skins. It's an inspired twist which—especially in this scene—succeeds in eliciting from viewers as many smiles as it does gasps.

The film's climactic swordfight staged by William

Kronos (Horst Janson) and Grost (John Cater) take a cross from a graveyard to prepare for their battle against the mysterious vampire.

Grost (John Cater, left), Dr. Marcus (John Carson, center), Carla (Caroline Munro) and Kronos (Horst Janson) plan how to set a trap for a vampire using bells and ribbons.

The climatic duel between the unmasked vampire, Hagen (William Hobbs), and Kronos (Horst Janson), here striking a very Errol Flynn-like pose.

Grost (John Cater) realizes he must kill his friend Dr. Marcus (John Carson) to destroy the evil spell that has possessed him.

Hobbs (who plays the chief villain: Kronos' opponent in the duel) is also an exciting piece of work. Hobbs, a fencing master and former fight arranger with Britain's National Theatre and the Royal Shakespeare Company, choreographed all the sword play in the film—a duty he also performed for Roman Polanski's *Macbeth*, where he staged the spectacular duel between Macbeth and Macduff that climaxes with Macbeth's decapitation.

Pleased by the success of its *Dr. Jekyll and Sister Hyde* (1972), which Clemens wrote but did not direct, Hammer purchased Clemens' *Kronos* script with the hope of launching it as a series to replace its ailing Dracula films. Even before shooting began, Clemens already had three or four more adventures for Kronos in various stages of development. Spottily released in the U.S. as a companion feature to Hammer's *Frankenstein and the Monster From Hell*, Clemens' *Kronos* failed at the box-office and the series idea was scrapped—even though the film scored many favorable reviews and had since become a cult favorite among horror buffs. Clemens then returned to television, resurrecting his earlier cult TV series as *The New Avengers*. It debuted on American television September 15, 1978—but was cancelled the following March.

JAWS (1975)

A Zanuck/Brown Production
A Universal Release
Color /124 minutes

Icthyologist Matt Hooper (Richard Dreyfuss) and Sheriff Brody (Roy Scheider) prepare to cut open the corpse of a captured shark to look for traces of human victims.

Still on the loose, the great white shark attacks some swimmers.

Credits

Director: Steven Spielberg; *Producers:* Richard Zanuck and David Brown; *Screenplay:* Peter Benchley and Carl Gottlieb, based on Benchley's novel; *Cinematographer:* Bill Butler; *Editor:* Verna Fields; *Music:* John Williams; *Production Designer:* Jospeh Alves, Jr.; *Videocassette source:* MCA Home Video.

Cast

Chief Martin Brody: Roy Scheider; *Quint:* Robert Shaw; *Matt Hooper:* Richard Dreyfuss; *Ellen Brody:* Lorraine Gary; *Mayor Larry Vaughn:* Murray Hamilton; *Harry Meadows:* Carl Gottlieb; *Chrissie:* Susan Backlinie; *TV Reporter:* Peter Benchley.

Steven Spielberg has described *Jaws* as "a great episode of *Sea Hunt* mixed with a little *Moby Dick.*" Add Jack Arnold's *The Creature From the Black Lagoon* and Disney's *20,000 Leagues Under the Sea* (both 1954) and you have a fairly accurate description of the film's major sources. Oh yes, I almost forgot one other major source: the source novel for the movie.

Peter Benchley's book was fundamentally a concoction—a well-oiled thrill machine crafted by the author (with substantial input from his publisher, it has been reported) to make the most of its commercial potential. And that it did. The "most-read" novel since Mario Puzo's *The Godfather*, the book hit the best-seller list in a spectacular way, catapulting Benchley into the literary major leagues (earnings-wise, that is) and adding a brand new monster to the horror hall of fame. It was inevitable that such a hot property would be picked up for the movies (actually, the rights had been sold *before* the book became a megahit). Not so inevitable was the prospect of the screen version's turning out to be a considerable improvement over the book and an even bigger hit to boot. In fact, all through shooting (a technical and logistical nightmare that stretched on for almost a year), the consensus of most involved with the project was that *Jaws* the movie might very well prove to be a bust. An almost sure sign that disaster was in store was the fact that the script was continually being rewritten even as shooting progressed. In addition to the author's own draft was the contribution—a major rewrite—of Carl Gottlieb, who would share screen credit with Benchley. Playwright Howard Sackler and writer-director John Milius were called in to supply extra scenes as well. The irony is that the script—written in patchwork style though it may have been—succeeded in adding some emotional resonance to the tale that had woefully been missing. [The novel keeps you turning the pages to be sure, but you don't give a damn what happens to anybody.]

In adapting the book to the screen, Spielberg and his various collaborators threw out a good deal of Benchley's more melodramatic contrivances (the Mafia's fingers in town politics and the lucrative tourist trade; the adulterous affair between ichthyologist Matt Hooper and Sheriff Brody's wife), transformed all the major characters into something more than potential shark meat, and, most importantly, revised the ending in order to give the story something it didn't have before—a hero.

Portrayed in the novel as a bit of wimp for whom the reader can muster little empathy, Roy Scheider's Sheriff Brody is transformed by the film into a believable everyman hero with whom the viewer continually identifies. Pressured into inaction by the seaside town's greedy officials, Brody is challenged with overcoming his guilt over the lives that have been lost as well his own deep-seated fear of the water in order to carry out what he clearly sees as his duty. Though he appears the least likely of the shark-hunting trio to actually bring about the monster's destruction, he is, in fact, the one who accomplishes the job. With the massive great white shark bearing down on him, Brody fires a bullet into a canister of oxygen lodged in the beast's mouth and blows the creature to bits.

The other two members of the shark hunting expedition are equally well drawn in the film. Richard Dreyfuss' Matt Hooper (in the book an adulterous, well-heeled and pampered egomaniac who gets a well-deserved comeuppance when he's eaten by the shark) becomes a source of strength to Brody by acting as his dedicated aide and loyal confidant. When Hooper tremulously descends into the water inside the flimsy shark cage and can't summon the spit to moisten his goggles, we're right there with him and genuinely hoping that he will survive. It is to the filmmaker's credit that after developing Hooper into such a winning character, they didn't alienate the viewer's feelings by having him perish.

Quint (Robert Shaw), Brody (Roy Scheider) and Hooper (Richard Dreyfuss) set out to kill the beast.

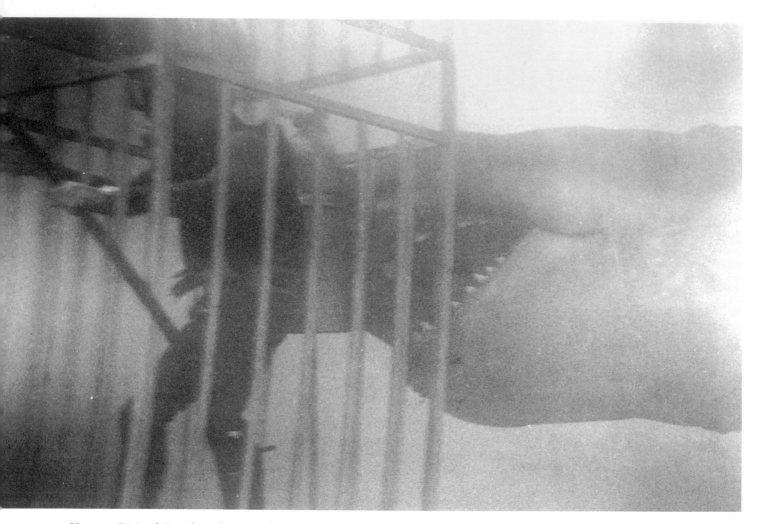

Hooper (Richard Dreyfuss) discovers that the flimsy shark cage is no match for *Jaws*.

Robert Shaw's Irish-brogued Quint (sort of a junior league Captain Ahab in the book) also becomes more multi-dimensional in the film. The motives behind his escalating obsession to destroy the shark—even if he has to kill himself and everyone else to do it—are frighteningly revealed in one of the film's best and creepiest scenes (written expressly for the film by John Milius) in which Quint tells of his nightmarish World War II experiences aboard the USS *Indianapolis*, the ship that delivered the Hiroshima bomb and was later sunk by the Japanese in shark-infested waters, resulting in the loss of almost a thousand men. Having survived that horrific experience, it's almost as if Quint (like some of the Nazi death camp survivors) harbors a secret guilt over having been spared and is determined not to let that happen again. The scene provides a terrifying edge to his character that not only makes his mad destruction of the boat (his surrogate self) more credible, but contributes to Hooper and Brody's (as well as our own) growing sense of panic—for Quint is clearly as much of a danger as the shark itself.

Spielberg's direction of *Jaws* lacks the cloying, manipulative sentimentality and emphasis on empty (albeit exciting) wall-to-wall action that has become characteristic of his later (yet even more financial successful) work. The film's plentiful tension and suspense grow as much out of our involvement with and concern for the characters as from our fear of the "monster" itself. Quite wisely, Spielberg also avoids showing us too much of that monster—until the spectacular finale, of course, when the requirements of the story demand that it make a prolonged appearance. One of the reasons why this decision was so wise is due to the mechanical shark itself, which, ingeniously constructed though it is, does tend to look obviously fake if the camera lingers upon it too much. Fortunately, Spielberg's doesn't—not even at the end, where he counteracts the problem of over exposure by offering only quick shots of the beast, thereby keeping our suspension of disbelief intact. Regardless of the box office returns of his subsequent films, *Jaws* (along with his 1971 telefilm *Duel*) remains to me Spielberg's best work.

THE TENANT (1976)

A Paramount Pictures Release
Color /125 minutes

The apartment concierge (Shelly Winters) points out to Trelkovsky (Roman Polanski) the courtyard where the previous occupant had plunged to her death.

163

Trelkovsky (Roman Polanski) imagines that he is being attacked by a tramp hiding in the entrance way to the apartment building.

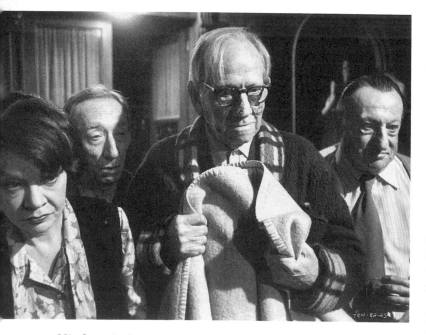

His fantasized "prosecutors" descend upon the ailing Trelkovsky (Roman Polanski).

Credits

Director: Roman Polanski; *Producer:* Andrew Braunsberg; *Screenplay:* Roman Polanski and Gerald Brach, based on the novel by Roland Toper; *Cinematographer:* Sven Nykvist; *Editor:* Francoise Bonnot; *Music:* Philippe Sarde; *Production Designer:* Pierre Guffroy; *Videocassette source:* Gateway Home Video.

Cast

Trelkovsky: Roman Polanski; *Stella:* Isabelle Adjani; *The Concierge:* Shelley Winters; *Monsieur Zy:* Melvyn Douglas; *Madame Dioz:* Jo Van Fleet; *Scope:* Bernard Fresson; *Madame Gaderian:* Lila Kedrova.

The Tenant completed the trilogy of surrealistic, psychological case study films Roman Polanski had begun with *Repulsion* (1965), his fist commercial success, and then continued with the even more accessible *Rosemary's Baby* (1968). The film is based on a short, Kafkaesque novel by French cartoonist Roland Topor that was published in 1964. Originally, Polanski had intended to adapt Topor's novel to the screen following the success of *Repulsion*. But because the two works were so similar, he felt he would be accused of repeating himself and decided to put *The Tenant* temporarily on the back burner.

In the wake of the critical and box office failures of *Macbeth* (1971) and the outrageous sex comedy *What* (a.k.a. *Diary of Forbidden Dreams*, 1973), which scarcely got any release at all, the director's career was at a critical and commercial low point. The smash hit success of *Chinatown* (1974) shot him back to the top again, however. Bankable once more, Polanski attempted to get his long delayed, multi-million dollar swashbuckler-comedy *Pirates* off the ground with Paramount. But when another big budget pirate film, Universal's *Swashbuckler* (1976), ran into trouble (and eventually nose-dived at the box office), Paramount got cold feet. The studio asked Polanski if he had another, less expensive project in mind and he immediately thought of *The Tenant*—to which, ironically, Paramount owned the rights.

Working with his long time collaborator Gerald Brach, Polanski quickly adapted the novel, shot the film (with himself in the lead) and premiered *The Tenant* in a fast eight months. The completed movie and Polanski's performance as the central character, a timid office clerk whose personality problems and alienation push over into schizophrenia, received as many brickbats as accolades. Audiences stayed away and the film disappeared from release almost overnight.

Over the years, however, its status has grown and it is now viewed as a cult classic—a chilling topper to Polanski's "nightmare trilogy" and, perhaps, the most personal film of the three. [It does seem that the more personal Polanski gets, the more his box office chances diminish; *Tess* (1979) is a rare exception.]

Trelkovsky, the film's main character is—like Polanski himself—a naturalized French citizen of Polish extraction, an outsider struggling to make ends meet in the cosmopolitan city of Paris (exactly as Polanski himself had been struggling to carve a career for himself as a filmmaker in the West at the time of the novel's publication). Apartments are expensive and hard to come by, but Trelkovsky manages to locate one in a run-down quarter of the city. The concierge tells him that the previous tenant, a woman, threw herself out of the window and is in the hospital. The landlord, Monsieur Zy, is willing to rent the apartment to Trelkovsky for a premium, provided the former tenant fails to recover.

Posing as a friend of the tenant, Trelkovsky goes to the hospital to check out her condition and finds the woman swathed in bandages like an Egyptian mummy. There, he also meets a friend of the woman, an attractive brunette named Stella. When the bandaged woman looks up at them, she lets out an unholy scream. Trelkovsky overcomes his basic shyness and takes Stella to a nearby cafe for a glass of wine, then to a movie. The rest of the evening goes nowhere, however, and the two go their separate ways. The next day, Trelkovsky learns that the former tenant has died.

He hurries back to the apartment to make a deal with Zy, assuring him that he is a bachelor, lives quietly, and will not make any noise. Trelkovsky moves his meager belongings into the drab apartment and invites some of his co-workers over for a housewarming. The noise they make outrages the neighbors and the next day, Zy warns Trelkovsky that he will be evicted if he causes any more disturbances. Obsessed with keeping quiet, Trelkovsky takes to tiptoeing about the apartment and watching his TV without sound. Soon he begins to hear noises he cannot identify, knocks at the door when

Another of Trelkovsky's paranoid visions: in this one, he imagines Jo Van Fleet threatening another of the apartment's tenants (Lila Kedrova) with a crowbar.

Resting at Stella's apartment, Trelkovsky (Roman Polanski) becomes convinced that she is in on the "conspiracy" to drive him to suicide and trashes her place.

there is no one there, and imagines his neighbors spying on him from the communal bathroom across the way. Eventually, he comes to believe that Zy and others in the building drove the former tenant to suicide and are trying to turn him into a reincarnation of the woman and drive him to a similar fate.

Trelkovsky comes to identify with the dead woman so strongly that he starts wearing some of the clothes she left behind, using her makeup and smoking her brand of cigarettes. Feeling that his neighbors are closing in, he turns to Stella, but his paranoia has zoomed so far out of control that he becomes convinced she's part of the conspiracy and wrecks her apartment. Desperate to protect himself, he attempts to

Trelkovsky (Roman Polanski) is attended to by a concerned man and woman (Claude Dauphin and Louba Chazel) who have accidentally hit him with their car.

buy a gun from a bartender, but the man chases him from the place and Trelkovsky is struck by a car. As the solicitous motorist and his wife try to attend to him, Trelkovsky sees them transformed into his persecutors back at the apartment. Taken there to recuperate, he escapes from them, runs up to his apartment and jumps from the window—not once, but, as if crying out one last time to establish his *own* identity, *twice.*

Like *Repulsion* and *Rosemary's Baby*—and, indeed, most of Polanski's films (even *Macbeth*, which closes with the very Polanskian twist of having Donalbain, the next in line for the throne, stumble upon the witches' lair just as the ambitious Macbeth had), *The Tenant* concludes essentially where it began. Flat on his back in the hospital and, except for one exposed eye, covered from head to foot in bandages just as the previous tenant was, Trelkovsky looks up to see Stella and *himself* standing by the bed and lets out the same, bloodcurdling cry of dispair—and recognition.

A potent psychological chiller—perhaps the most potent and disturbing ever made, *The Tenant* remains (as of this writing) Polanski's swan-song to the horror genre. Hopefully, he will return to it, for the man has a genuine gift for illuminating that most frightening of all genre landscapes on the big screen—the dark and sometimes twisted corners that exist within the human mind.

THE HILLS HAVE EYES (1977)

Vanguard Releasing
Color /89 minutes

The cannibalistic hill folks kidnap Doug and Lynne's (Martin Speer, Dee Wallace) baby and take it back to their cave, announcing, "We caught us a young Thanksgiving turkey!"

Credits

Director: Wes Craven; *Producer:* Peter Locke; *Screenplay:* Wes Caven; *Cinematographer:* Eric Saarinen; *Editor:* Wes Craven; *Music:* Don Peake; *Art Director:* Robert Burns; *Videocassette source:* Vestron Video

Cast

Brenda Carter: Susan Lanier; *Bobby Carter:* Robert Houston; *Ethel Carter:* Virginia Vincent; *Bob Carter:* Russ Grieve; *Lynne Wood:* Dee Wallace; *Doug Wood:* Martin Speer; *Katie Wood:* Brenda Marinoff; *Jupiter:* James Whitworth; *Mama:* Cordy Clark; *Ruby:* Janus Blythe; *Pluto:* Michael Berryman; *Mars:* Lance Gordon; *Mercury:* Authur King; *Fred:* John Steadman.

Writer-director Wes Craven (left) and cinematographer
Eric Saarinen relax between takes inside the camper
set of *The Hills Have Eyes.*

Wes Craven, a one-time high school teacher of
English, burst onto the horror scene in 1972 with *Last
House on the Left*, a cheap, ultra-violent and thoroughly
amateurish revenge thriller that became a considerable
hit on the exploitation film circuit. Though *Last House*
does have its advocates (critic Roger Ebert, among
them), it received mostly scathing reviews and stirred
up a fair amount of protest because of its shocking
depiction of such previously taboo screen subjects as
mutilation, necrophilia and castration. To counter these
blasts and give the film an air of legitimacy, its distributor, Hallmark Releasing (who often gave their films a
fictitious "V for Violence" rating and dispensed free
vomit bags to customers as a come-on), reminded
critics that writer-director-editor Craven had based the
film (however loosely) on Ingmar Bergman's classic
morality tale, *The Virgin Spring* (1960). I doubt that
this advertising ploy changed many people's minds, but
it kept the flames of controversy burning, and, as a
result, Craven's career was launched, as well as that of
his partner, Sean S. Cunningham, who would go on to
make *Friday the 13th.*

Despite its solid box office performance and its
admitted power to disturb (the atmosphere of the film
is so relentlessly sleazy that, unlike *Psycho*, the film
makes you want to run for the shower after seeing it),
Last House gives little evidence of being the work of a
potentially major genre film talent. [The films of
goremeister Herschel Gordon Lewis boast many of the
same "qualities" as *Last House.*] It is atrociously acted
and shoddily made—something that cannot be said of
Craven's immediate follow-up, *The Hills Have Eyes*, a
film which, due mostly to poor distribution, fared far
less well at the box office, but which has since achieved
a well deserved reputation as a modern classic on a par
with George Romero's *Night of the Living Dead* and
Tobe Hooper's *The Texas Chainsaw Massacre.*

Like many modern horror filmmakers, Craven sub-
scribes to the view that the screen's traditional movie
monsters have long since lost their power to scare
audiences. His shockers belong very much to the
post-*Psycho* school of horror in that Craven's centerpiece horror characters—even if given a supernatural
presence like Freddy Krueger—stem more from real
life than folklore. Very often, they have a basis in fact
that makes them all the more unsettling. This was

certainly true of *Last House on the Left* with its resonances of the Charles Manson cult murder case, which was then in the headlines, and is doubly so of *The Hills Have Eyes*, which not only recalled Manson again but was directly inspired by the real-life tale of cannibal-killer Sawney Bean.

Legendary in the annals of Scottish crime, Sawney Bean was a 15th century highwayman and murderer who lived in a cave with his common law wife, spawning several children and, through incest, more than a dozen grandchildren over a twenty-five year period. To survive, the atavistic Beans kidnapped and murdered scores of travelers for their valuables, then ate the corpses of their victims. When they were finally caught, the remorseless Beans were dispatched without a trial, their method of execution just as hideous as the crimes they had committed. The male members of the clan slowly bled to death after having their arms and legs chopped off, while the females were slowly burned alive. These horrific methods of retribution left many legal and moral scholars wondering which was more brutal, the crime or the punishment? Craven's updated retelling of the Bean case raises this same question. [*Last House* poses a similar question, but in a much more exploitative and far less satisfying manner.]

The Beans of the film are a pack of inbreeding desert rats (shades of the Manson family) headed by the brutish Jupiter. They live in the mountains near a nuclear test site, breaking into the local PX for supplies and feeding off animals and errant travelers to survive. On their way to California, the family of a retired cop cracks up its car and camper under the watchful eyes of the hill tribe, and as the cop and his son-in-law set out on foot to get help, the hill folks launch a campaign of terror that rapidly escalates into an all-out war which claims the lives of several members of both families.

Except for Ruby, the young female member of the hill clan who wishes to escape from her uncivilized environment, the film makes no effort to generate sympathy for the brutish hill folks. But it doesn't portray them as stereotypical psychos either. Like other creatures of the desert, they're just animals, who, being human as well, act with a superior animal cunning to achieve their atavistic desires. Instead, our sympathies rest entirely with the beleaguered travelers, who wound up in this ordeal in the first place when they swerved their car to avoid killing a rabbit. Unable to

Ruby (Janus Blythe), who wishes to escape from her uncivilized environment, helps the travelers by killing one of her brothers with a rattlesnake.

Michael Berryman as Pluto, one of the degenerate members of the hill tribe.

169

His wife (Dee Wallace) murdered and his daughter kidnapped, the vengeful Doug (Martin Speer) uses the family dog, Beast, to track the deadly hill folks to their lair.

believe what's happening to them—or that such creatures could even exist in the modern world—they are at first no match for the hill folks, and, as a result, their forces are (in some cases quite needlessly) decimated. The tide begins to turn, however, when the survivors descend to the hill folks' level, albeit in a much more calculatingly brutal manner, their new-found purpose no longer just to survive the ordeal by escaping from or defeating their attackers, but to vengefully wipe them off the face of the earth.

The real success or failure of a film of this kind rises or falls with its ability to keep an audience on the edge of its collective seat. Better than any film Craven has made since (certainly moreso than the lame sequel to *Hills* he made eight years later, the less said about which the better), *The Hills Have Eyes* eminently achieves this goal. By confining most of the film's action to the area in and around the crippled camper—and having most of that action take place at night—*The Hills Have Eyes*, like all the best horror films, generates an atmosphere of claustrophobia and tension that is almost palpable. Craven maintains such a high level of suspense in these scenes that when the morning light begins to break, the viewer breathes almost as much of a sigh of relief as the beleaguered folks in the camper.

MURDER BY DECREE (1979)

Ambassador Films
An Avco-Embassy Release
Color /121 minutes

James Mason as Dr. Watson and Christopher Plummer as Sherlock
Holmes in Bob Clark's fictional solution to the Jack the Ripper saga,
Murder By Decree.

Credits

Director: Bob Clark; *Producers:* Rene Dupont and Bob
Clark; *Screenplay:* John Hopkins, based on *The Ripper
File* by John Lloyd and Elwyn Jones; *Cinematographer:*
Reginald Morris; *Editor:* Stan Cole; *Music:* Carl Zittrer
and Paul Zaza; *Production Designer:* Harry Pottle;
Videocassette source: Nelson Home Video.

Cast

Sherlock Holmes: Christopher Plummer; *Dr. Watson:*
James Mason; *Inspector Foxborough:* David Hemmings;
Inspector Lestrade: Frank Finlay; *Sir Charles Warren:*
Anthony Quayle; *Annie Crook:* Genevieve Bujold; *Lord
Salisbury:* Sir John Gielgud; *Mary Kelly:* Susan Clark;
Robert Lees: Donald Sutherland.

Watson (James Mason) and Holmes (Christopher Plummer) come to the conclusion that all the Ripper's victims knew each other and that the motive for the murders may stem from their acquaintance.

Holmes (Christopher Plummer) tries to get Mary Kelly (Susan Clark) to reveal the truth of why she's in fear for her life.

Of the many, *many* films spawned by the legendary saga of Jack the Ripper, *Murder by Decree* stands at the top—not only because of its precise attention to period and historical detail, but because it actually attempts to pose a solution to the mystery. The theory it puts forth, which was widely disputed at the time, has since been disproven (at least part of it has), but then it seemed very compelling indeed.

The theory goes this way. Sometime in the late 1880s, Prince Edward (the Duke of Clarence), grandson of Queen Victoria and heir presumptive to the throne of England, met and married a Catholic shop girl named Annie Elizabeth Crook. The unsanctioned union produced a child which they named Alice Margaret. When Eddie's indiscretion was discovered by certain government officials, it sent shockwaves through the monarchy, which was then being assaulted on a number of fronts by a variety of political factions bent on bringing the monarchy down. Eddie's crime (that he, Protestant heir to the throne, had married a Catholic of the lower classes) was precisely the kind of scandalous political ammunition these factions needed, the government officials thought. And so, all trace of the "illegal" union had to be eradicated.

Eddie was given a good dressing down (possibly by his very intimidating grandmother, the Queen) and his "bride" was spirited away to an insane asylum and incarcerated there until she died. The child could not be found, but as she was only a toddler, she proved less of an immediate threat than did her guardian, a prostitute friend of Annie Crook's named Mary Kelly, who had actually witnessed the marriage ceremony. To find and silence her forever, the Queen's physician, Sir William Gull, and Eddie's personal coachman, John Netley, launched a search for Mary Kelly—and anyone she may have told of the affair—among the prostitutes of Whitechapel.

The subsequent murders Gull and Netley were later said to have committed to cover up the affair were made to look the work of a maniac striking at random—a maniac who was quickly dubbed Jack the Ripper. In total, five women were killed to keep the secret quiet, the last being Mary Kelly herself, who was savagely mutilated in an attempt to drag from her the whereabouts of the missing child. She died without telling, but the cover-up, it was felt, was secure. And so, with Kelly's death, the Ripper murders stopped and the elusive Jack (Gull and Netley) disappeared forever into the London fog.

This theory, which as I said has since been disproven by a number of researchers into the Ripper case, nevertheless caused quite a stir when it first was made known. It did not originate with *Murder by Decree*. It was initially uncovered by writers Elwyn Jones and John Lloyd for a television mini-series they were developing for the BBC. Called *The Ripper File*, it aired in six parts in 1973 and has since been syndicated throughout the world. [Jones and Lloyd published their findings in book form in 1975.] Their conclusions were picked up on and explored in elaborate detail by another writer, Stephen Knight, who published his own

Following an attempt on Holmes' life, Watson, (James Mason) nurses his friend back to health as the devious Inspector Foxborough (David Hemmings) looks on.

On the trail of Jack the Ripper in the slums of Whitechapel, Watson (James Mason) is accosted by a prostitute (Christine Kessler) who says she has some important information.

Holmes (Christopher Plummer) and Watson (James Mason) take the train to an asylum where the key to the Ripper murders is incarcerated.

book posing this same theory, *Jack the Ripper: The Final Solution*, in 1976. Knight's exhaustively researched book had an even greater impact than the television series and became an immediate best-seller. It is still in print and widely read today.

The source of the theory posed by Jones, Lloyd and Knight was a man named Joseph Sickert, son of the artist Walter Sickert. According to Joseph, his father was a contemporary and close friend of the Duke of Clar-

As he closes in on Jack the Ripper, Holmes (Christopher Plummer) discovers the truth of the dying Foxborough's (David Hemmings) complicity in the affair.

ence who had intimate knowledge of the whole affair—knowledge which he subsequently passed on to his son. Joseph said that after the murder of Mary Kelly, Walter Sickert had taken the child of Eddie and Annie Elizabeth's union under his wing and when the child, Alice Margaret, grew up, Walter married her. It was this marriage that had produced Joseph himself. At the conclusion of the BBC series, Joseph Sickert revealed this long kept secret on camera, then—again based on what his father had told him—embellished the tale by tying it into the Ripper business. The sensation caused by the story boomeranged on Joseph Sickert, however, when in Knight's book, the author made a case that Sickert's father, Walter, had participated in the Ripper murders as well. To clear the air, Joseph Sickert again went on record—in 1978—with the even more astonishing revelation that he had made the story up—or part of it anyway. He still insisted that the story of his mother's parentage was true, but that the conspiracy angle and its connection to the Ripper murders had been a total fabrication on his part. Nevertheless, it still made for a "ripping good" tale—sort of a Profumo Affair and Watergate all wrapped into one—and by that time, plans were already underway to make the theory the basis of a feature film, *Murder by Decree*.

Strictly speaking, *Murder by Decree* is not a remake of the BBC's *The Ripper File* series, but it does use the program's "findings" as well as the conceit of having the mystery unraveled and the "truth" revealed by two famous, though fictional, sleuths. In *The Ripper File*, the challenge of tracking down the Ripper was taken up, almost a century after the fact, by Detectives Barlow and Watt, characters in a then-popular BBC police series called *Z Cars*. In *Murder by Decree*, the case is taken on by the much more famous Sherlock Holmes and Dr. Watson during the year 1888 as the events themselves were unfolding. This was not the first time that Holmes and Watson had pursued the Ripper on the big screen. The 1965 *A Study in Terror* (starring John Neville as Holmes and Donald Houston as Watson) did as well, but the stellar *Murder by Decree* is a far more authentic and complex film which adheres more closely not only to the lore surrounding the Ripper case, but most of the facts as well.

Holmes and Watson are called in on the case by the Whitechapel Vigilance Committee (which did exist) because Scotland Yard—in the form of the likable and ineffective Lestrade—doesn't appear to be getting anywhere. Holmes and Watson, like Barlow and Watt,

Holmes (Christopher Plummer) and Watson (James Mason) get the story behind the Ripper murders from the pathetic Annie Crook (Genevieve Bujold).

methodically explore the many details of the case (which are all quite accurately described in the film) and uncover the conspiracy. They track the pathetic Annie Crook to the asylum where she has been unjustly consigned by the Queen's physician (and one of the pseudo-Rippers), Sir William Gull, who is called Sir Thomas Spivey in the film. Holmes learns the whereabouts of the missing child and uses this knowledge to blackmail the government into ceasing its murderous cover-up. He agrees to keep silent about the affair so long as no harm comes to the innocent child of Eddie and Annie's scandalous union. The Prime Minister, Lord Salisbury, agrees and Holmes, still stunned by all that he has learned, goes back to Baker Street to unwind with his violin.

In addition to the very fine performances of all concerned, its exceedingly high production values and scarifying atmosphere and set pieces (the murder of Mary Kelly, though subtly photographed, is particularly ghoulish, as it was in real life), what sets *Murder by Decree* apart from other Ripper films is its absolute conviction that the story it is telling is *the truth*. That it is indeed the *final solution* to the century-old mystery. We now know that it is not, but that knowledge does not diminish the film's many authentic qualities, general persuasiveness and impact in any way. It is still the best Jack the Ripper movie ever made. Even the multi-million dollar television film, *Jack the Ripper*, starring Michael Caine that was made and aired during the centennial of the Ripper's reign of terror, doesn't come close to it—although it too fingers Gull and Netley as the guilty ones, albeit for a very different (and far less compelling) reason.

THE BROOD (1979)

A New World Pictures Release
Color /91 minutes

Frank Carveth (Art Hindle) confronts Dr. Raglan (Oliver Reed) at the Somafree Institute.

Credits

Director: David Cronenberg; *Producer:* Claude Heroux; *Screenplay:* David Cronenberg; *Cinematographer:* Mark Irwin; *Editor:* Alan Collins; *Music:* Howard Shore; *Art Director:* Carol Spier; *Videocassette source:* Embassy Home Video.

Cast

Dr. Hal Raglan: Oliver Reed; *Nola Carveth:* Samantha Eggar; *Frank Carveth:* Art Hindle; *Candy Carveth:* Cindy Hinds; *Barton Kelly:* Henry Beckman; *Juliana Kelly:* Nuala Fitzgerald; *Ruth Mayer:* Susan Hogan; *Inspector Mrazek:* Michael Magee; *Jan Hartog:* Robert Silverman.

With *The Dead Zone*, his 1983 box office winner based on the best-selling novel by Stephen King, Canadian shockmaster David Cronenberg not only began reaching larger audiences than ever before, but also started getting better reviews. Prior to *The Dead Zone*, Cronenberg had been considered—by most mainstream critics certainly, and even by some genre aficionados as well—as a director of over-the-top gore epics perversely designed to "disgust the mind and repel the senses." Cronenberg's subsequent films, the superb remake of *The Fly* (1986) and the low in gore but compelling *Dead Ringers* (1988), further cemented his improved critical and box office standing—to such an extent that he is now considered a "hot property" at studios that previously wouldn't have let him through their gates and an "important director" by most of the mainstream and genre press as well.

What sparked this impressive turnaround was not so much a change in Cronenberg's choice of material or approach to that material (both remain as perverse and grisly as ever), but a significant growth in the director's attitude toward the *characters* in his films. Putting it simply: there is an empathy for those characters and a determination to make the viewer care for them that was substantively missing before.

It has been argued that the emotional highs reached by his three most recent (as of this writing) films are due less to Cronenberg than to his access to bigger budgets and resulting ability to attract actors of greater skill and range—Christopher Walken in *The Dead Zone*, Jeff Goldblum in *The Fly* and Jeremy Irons in *Dead Ringers*. I believe this argument to be erroneous. While it is certainly true that these men are superlative actors and that a good actor can strike emotional chords in an audience that are beyond the reach of a mediocre actor, the fact is that some of Cronenberg's earlier films boasted many equally fine performers in lead roles: Oliver Reed, Samantha Eggar, Patrick McGoohan, James Woods. I believe the difference between Cronenberg's work today and his work of yesterday rests chiefly with Cronenberg himself.

Despite his continuing preference to shoot his films in chill and frosty fall and winter weather, Cronenberg himself seems to have warmed up. Though just as absorbed in visualizing horrifying and often disgusting images, he no longer lets that absorption dominate or overwhelm his equally important thematic concerns—

Nola Carveth (Samantha Eggar) has been undergoing a strange metamorphosis at the Somafree Institute.

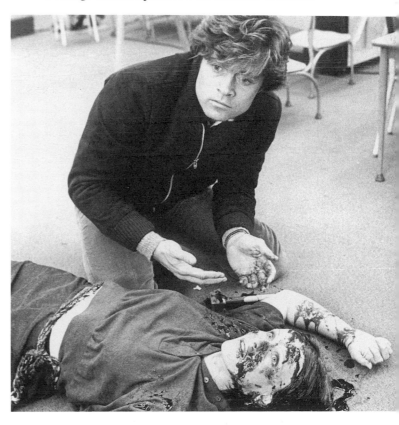

Frank (Art Hindle) discovers the body of his daughter's teacher, Ruth (Susan Hogan), who has been brutally murdered in a jealous rage by Nola's "id creatures," known as *The Brood*.

177

or the characters he creates to explore those concerns. Cronenberg's grisly images have always been tied to his themes and seldom indulged in for their own sake alone, but in the work of "the new Cronenberg," theme and character now share *equal* billing—which is why his work now packs so much more emotional wallop. As a filmmaker, Cronenberg has at last found his voice. But to say—as many once-damning but now approving critics have—that that voice was never the least bit evident before is patently wrong. For it was clearly there, struggling to make a sound, in Cronenberg's critically drubbed *The Brood*.

Frank Carveth has separated from his psychologically disturbed wife, Nola, who has voluntarily placed herself under the care of the mysterious Dr. Hal Raglan at Raglan's Somafree Institute, where she remains incommunicado undergoing some kind of unorthodox therapy. Raglan refuses to discuss Nola's treatment with Frank, though he has published a book about his unorthodox theories called *The Shape of Rage*, the cover of which is prominently displayed in the doctor's office.

Frank's five-year-old daughter Candy, who was abused by the disturbed Nola, has had a tough time coping with her parents' separation and is experiencing some psychological changes of her own, becoming distant and remote. At his wit's end, Frank, who feels that Raglan is somehow responsible, decides to investigate, but his efforts are thwarted at every turn. Raglan remains as tight-lipped as ever; the police cannot or will not help him; and ex-patients of Raglan's become terrified at the mention of the doctor's name—though one of them does give Frank an important clue as to what's going on. Before he can learn more, however, a series of

The Brood attacks Candy (Cindy Hinds).

bizarre murders rocks the city. Nola's mother, Juliana, her father, Barton, and her daughter's school teacher, Ruth, are beaten to death by some vengeful, murderous creatures the height of small children, who seem bent on destroying anyone who gets in their way.

Frank traces the source of the murders to the Institute—and to Nola herself, whose therapy involves externalizing her inner rage in physical form. These physical manifestations, the brood of small creatures, carry out her murderous revenge against those who've hurt, angered or threatened her in any way—including her parents, who abused *her* as a child, and the teacher, who has begun to replace Nola in Frank and Candy's affections.

The creatures kidnap Candy and take her to the Institute. Frank breaks in and Raglan, who realizes his techniques have succeeded beyond his worst imaginings, agrees to help by snatching the child away from the murderous brood. All Frank has to do is keep Nola mollified during the rescue attempt, for any abrupt change in her emotions is liable to spur the dangerous brood into action. As he attempts to keep Nola calm, Frank is witness to the disgusting birth of one of her id creatures and his horrified reaction rouses her to anger. The brood kill Raglan and turn on Candy, but Frank succeeds in rescuing the terrified child and spiriting her away from the nightmarish institute. As Frank drives the now even more subdued child home, he studies her with grave concern. He has good reason, for as the camera offers us a close-up glimpse of her arm, we see that a series of mysterious lumps have begun to form on her flesh—indications of another deadly brood yet to come.

This chilling conclusion is more than just a set up for a possible sequel; it's an unsettling summation of the theme *The Brood* is metaphorically dealing with: the problem of child abuse. Nola's inner rage stems from her having been an abused child, an experience that has prompted her to become an abusive parent. Like her, the conclusion says, the abused Candy will probably grow into an abusive parent as well. The grisly sequence showing the birth of one of Nola's id creatures (a grotesque perversion of the act of becoming a parent, just as child abuse is a grotesque perversion of the act of *being* a parent) and the lumps on Candy's arm are symbolic representations of this deadly psychological chain reaction. Though this theme couldn't be stated more clearly by the film, most critics at the time

Candy (Cindy Hinds) is kidnapped and taken to the Somafree Institute by *The Brood*.

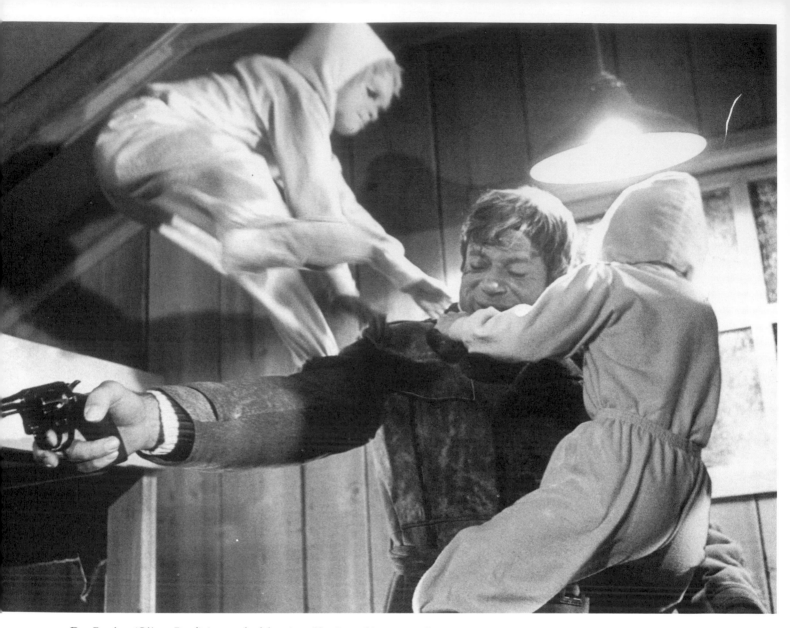

Dr. Raglan (Oliver Reed) is attacked by the offspring of his scientific
experiment gone awry, *The Brood*.

failed to see it and dismissed *The Brood* as nothing
more than a revoltingly exploitative gorefest.

The coolness of Cronenberg's approach may have
prompted this reaction, for it poses one major problem:
the film fails to elicit much sympathy for most of the
characters involved. This results in the film's closing
shot being less emotionally charged than it might
otherwise have been—though it *is* disturbing and does
leave most critics today pondering the right questions.
Oddly, the one character who does capture a certain
amount of audience sympathy—particularly towards
the end—is Raglan himself. The sequence in which he
attempts to rescue Candy from the brood is genuinely
nerve-wracking, not only because Cronenberg's direction is so suspenseful, but also because we don't want
any harm to come to Raglan, whom we no longer see as
the villain, but as the film's only hero. Frank Carveth is

certainly no hero. In fact, he constantly proves himself
incapable of helping anyone—not himself, not Candy,
not Nola and not Raglan, whose death directly results
from Frank's inability to do what the doctor ordered:
keep Nola calm.

One explanation as to why we come to care about
Raglan rests with Oliver Reed, who pulled off a similar
trick in Ken Russell's *Tommy* (1975), where he played
an even more disagreeable character, yet remained
completely likable throughout the entire film. But the
main explanation is that in *The Brood*, we were beginning to see signs of the emerging "new Cronenberg."
This becomes very clear, I think, if one takes a close
look at the director's remake of *The Fly*, where all the
characters are extremely sympathetic—even the arguable villain, Stathis Borans (John Getz), who, like Hal
Raglan, also turns hero in the end.

ALIEN (1979)

A Brandywine-Shusett Production
A Twentieth-Century Fox Release
Color /124 minutes

The embryonic alien bursts through
the stomach of its host, Kane (John
Hurt).

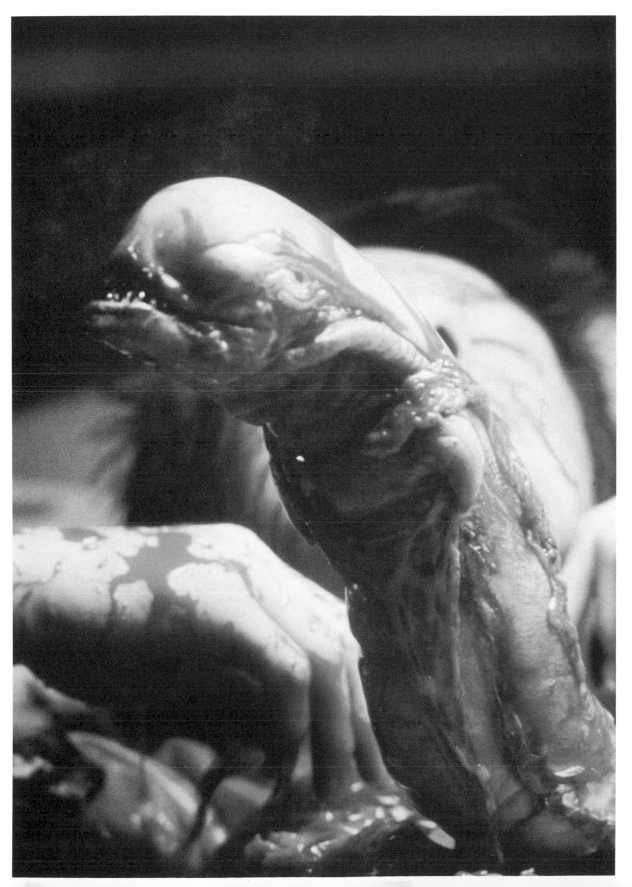

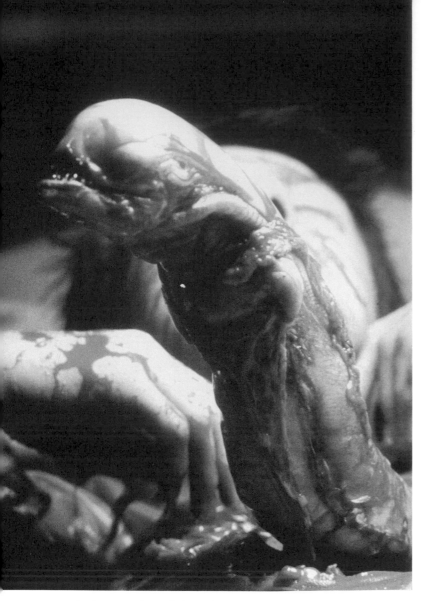

A close-up view of the embryonic alien that has just killed Kane.

The embryonic alien surveys the situation before screeching off to hide in the bowels of the ship Nostromo.

Credits

Director: Ridley Scott; *Producers:* Gordon Carroll, David Giler and Walter Hill; *Screenplay:* Dan O'Bannon; *Cinematographer:* Derek Van Lint; *Editors:* Jerry Rawlings and Peter Weatherley; *Music:* Jerry Goldsmith; *Production Designer:* Michael Seymour; *Videocassette source:* CBS/Fox Home Video.

Cast

Dallas: Tom Skerritt; *Ripley:* Sigourney Weaver; *Lambert:* Veronica Cartwright; *Brett:* Harry Dean Stanton; *Kane:* John Hurt; *Ash:* Ian Holm; *Parker:* Yaphet Kotto.

More than one critic correctly described *Alien* as being less a science-fiction movie than a "haunted house" movie—with the film's bedevilled spaceship, the Nostromo, taking the place of the traditional haunted house so beloved of past genre filmmakers. *Alien* makes no pretense otherwise—for, like all the best modern horror films, it doesn't deny that the genre *has* a past and, in fact, is quite upfront about the specific films it draws upon and makes reference to.

One doesn't have to look very far into the past to find what some of those films are, either. Howard Hawks' 1951 classic *The Thing* is certainly one of them—as is Edward L. Cahn's less well known *It! The Terror From Beyond Space*, a very low budget, but quite effective, monster-on-the-loose potboiler made in 1958. Haunted house movies themselves, both *The Thing* and *It!* each dealt with the struggle for survival of a small group of people whose isolated outpost is suddenly intruded upon by a malevolent alien creature from outer space. In the case of *It!*, the claustrophobic setting in which the alien creature goes about its murderous deeds is not an Arctic research station, but a *spaceship*, thus forming an even stronger link with *Alien*.

Written by noted science-fiction novelist and short story writer Jerome Bixby, *It!* begins like *Aliens* (1986), the hugely successful sequel to *Alien* (more about which later on), as the sole survivor (Marshall Thompson) of a space expedition gone mysteriously and terribly awry is picked up by a rescue ship bound for earth. Arrested on suspicion of having murdered his crew when food supplies started running low, Thompson insists that his shipmates were murdered by an alien being that invaded their Martian camp. No one believes him until, one by one, the crew members of the rescue ship start getting slaughtered by a similar creature that slipped unseen onto the ship prior to its take-off from Mars. More humanoid in appearance than the insect-like leviathan H.R. Giger designed for *Alien*, "It" is equally fleet-footed and phantom-like in its ability to move about the ship undetected, then popping up when least expected, bursting through steel bulkheads to maul people with its deadly claws. Like the beast in *Alien*, "It" uses the ship's ventilation shaft system to move about in. This gives the beleaguered crew an idea. Donning protective space suits (just as sole survivor Sigourney Weaver does at the climax of *Alien*), they open the air locks to rob the creature of oxygen. As the air, rather than the beast itself, is sucked from the ship, "It" slowly perishes.

Though it contains a number of similar elements, *Alien* is by no means a remake of *It! The Terror From Beyond Space*—and wasn't meant to be. What it was meant to be, at least initially, was a low budget outer space monster movie, a loving salute to all the outer space invader flicks of the Fifties, both good and bad, including *It!*. But as Dan O'Bannon and Ronald Shusett's script passed through various studios and various hands, the concept grew and grew until it became very much a summation of the alien invader sub-genre. Several directors were approached to tackle the project, including Walter Hill, who worked [uncredited] on the script and eventually shared a producer's credit. The job finally fell, however, to the British-born Ridley Scott, a highly successful director of television commercials with only one other feature film to his credit, the visually breathtaking but dramatically flat *The Duellists* (1977), based on a story by Joseph Conrad. For *Alien*, Scott insisted on yet more script stages before the approximately $9 million production was scheduled to roll.

Like *The Duellists*—and, indeed, all of Scott's subsequent efforts—*Alien* depends mainly on atmosphere and imagery rather than character or audience identification with the characters for its impact. But impact it certainly had—and still has. As with that other mainstream monster hit before it, *The Exorcist* (1973), *Alien*'s influence on the modern horror film (and modern science-fiction film as well) remains profound. Its nightmarishly dark, other worldly *film noir* atmosphere, its distinctive set designs, its gruesome

Ripley (Sigourney Weaver), Parker (Yaphet Kotto) and Brett (Harry Dean Stanton) search for the murderous creature that has invaded their ship.

shock sequences (most notably John Hurt's demise at the dinner table when the alien parasite that is using his body as a host bursts through his chest and screeches off to grow and play hide and seek for the remainder of the movie)—even Giger's alien design itself—have been imitated, cloned or parodied by countless other, and mostly lesser, films since. For some reason, however, the film was slightly cut for its American release. Shorn from all American prints of the film is a brief sequence in which Officer Ripley [a role originally intended for a male actor, but given a gender change and filled by Sigourney Weaver at the last minute] discovers the remains of Dallas, the Nostromo's commanding officer, stored inside a cocoon which the alien returns to for periodic snacks. Knowing he's a goner, Dallas gives his last order, instructing Ripley to get away and save herself—which she tearfully does. The scene is carefully described in Alan Dean Foster's novelization of O'Bannon's screenplay and appears intact in all European release prints and European videocassettes of the film. While the scene's absence from American prints doesn't damage the film, its removal seems quite arbitrary—for not only is it quite eerie (and appropriately shocking and disgusting), but the emotional interplay between the self-sacrificing Dallas and the horrified and guilt-ridden Ripley suggests that their relationship might have had its intimate side as well.

The deadly alien, now grown to gargantuan proportions.

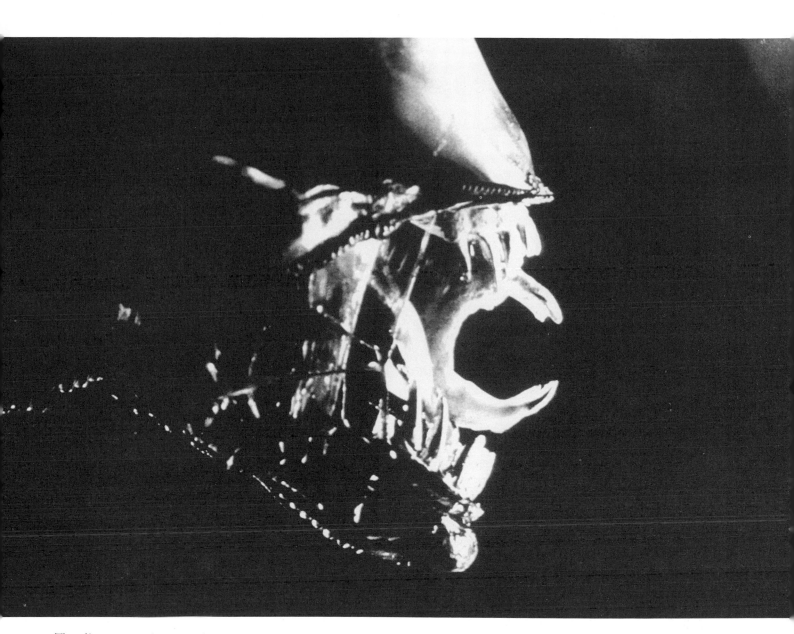

The alien exposes its razor sharp teeth as it prepares to kill Parker (Yaphet Kotto).

Alien was such a huge hit commercially (and, for the most part, critically as well) that a sequel was inevitable—though it took Twentieth Century-Fox seven years to get around to it. The assignment of rescuing sole survivor Ripley from her space sleep and concocting a legitimate rationale for her returning to the demon planet from which she miraculously escaped with little more than her underwear fell this time to James Cameron, whose previous science-fiction/horror thriller, *The Terminator* (1984) with Arnold Schwarzeneggar as a cybernaut killing machine from the future, had been very obviously patterned after *Alien*. Whereas Ridley Scott's progenitor aimed for a somber but tension-filled atmosphere that was periodically ruptured by nerve-jangling shock sequences, Cameron's

sequel, called *Aliens*, sought to give audiences a thrilling roller coaster ride in which the film's relentless pace never slackened. This time around, the undaunted Ripley and a gradually diminishing company of space age marines take on not one acid-bleeding alien, but scores of them, including a gigantic Queen Bee alien and her revolting larvae. Obviously Cameron knew what he was doing because *Aliens* turned out to be a bigger critical and box office success than its predecessor; it even earned Sigourney Weaver an Oscar nomination as Best Actress.

While I don't deny the skill and ingenuity with which writer-director Cameron went about his task, I have to admit that I personally find the first film eerier, more full of surprises and generally more shocking and disquieting than its elaborate, bigger budgeted sequel. But then, I've always been a real sucker for "haunted house" movies. And *Alien* is one of the best.

ALTERED STATES (1980)

A Warner Bros. Picture
Color /102 minutes

Loner scientist Eddie Jessup (William Hurt) experiments with sensory deprivation in the opening scene of *Altered States*.

Credits

Director: Ken Russell; *Producer:* Howard Gottfried; *Screenplay:* Sidney Aaron [Paddy Chayefsky] based on the novel by Paddy Chayefsky; *Cinematographer:* Jordan Cronenweth; *Editor:* Eric Jenkins; *Music:* John Corigliano; *Production Designer:* Richard McDonald; *Videocassette source:* Warner Home Video.

Cast

Eddie Jessup: William Hurt; *Emily Jessup:* Blair Brown; *Arthur Rosenberg:* Bob Balaban; *Mason Parrish:* Charles Haid; *Eccheverria:* Thaoo Penghlis; *Primal Man:* Miguel Godreau; *Sylvia Rosenberg:* Dori Brenner; *Hobart:* Peter Brandon; *The Brujo:* Charles White Eagle; *Margaret Jessup:* Drew Barrymore; *Grace Jessup:* Megan Jeffers; *Hector Ortego:* Jack Murdoch; *X-Ray Technician:* John Larroquette.

As a rule, big budgets and horror films don't mix well. *Altered States* pretty much adheres to that rule since its greatness emerges more in spite of than because of the money that was lavished upon it.

The project was a beleaguered one inherited by Ken Russell when the film's original director, Arthur Penn, walked away from it. At the time, Russell's professional stock was at an all-time low. His 1975 success with *Tommy* had long been overshadowed by the box office failures of *Lisztomania* (1975) and the even more expensive *Valentino* (1977). The flamboyant genius, who in the early 1970s had been on a seemingly non-stop roll, found himself for the first time in over ten years a hired hand, helming a troubled and troublesome production not of his own making.

The package Russell was handed included a ready-made set of special effects by John Dykstra, which he immediately scrapped—a concession that was easily granted him since Russell was hired in large part to boost the visual impact of the film's numerous fantasy sequences. A far thornier problem was Paddy Chayefsky's long-winded and heavy-handed screen adaptation of his own novel. Concessions here were less easily acquired. After all, no one, especially not a second-choice filmmaker with a less than spectacular recent batting record, rewrote "the great Chayefsky."

Instead a compromise was reached. The fantasies were Russell's, the script Chayefsky's, but it could be judiciously pruned, not rewritten. Having given in on this point (not without pressure), Chayefsky still exercised his unique (for a writer) power by overseeing Russell's direction. An outright ego clash was inevitable. Having enough problems to contend with, producer Howard Gottfried sided with Russell and instructed Chayefsky to "lay off," which the writer translated into "be discreet." This discretion took the form of Chayefsky spiriting the actors away from Russell and redirecting them. While Russell *might* have been able to work around this under other circumstances, the conditions on *Altered States* didn't allow for a bend-over-backwards attitude. Russell was making his first film in Hollywood bereft of his usual crew of technicians and stock company of supporting players; and he was working with two inexperienced leads (William Hurt and Blair Brown), who were being given conflicting instructions on how to play their roles by a man who openly distrusted (and seemingly disliked) Russell. Finally, Russell rang Chayefsky up and let him have it with both barrels. This resulted in the writer's

Director Ken Russell with Blair Brown and William Hurt on the set of *Altered States*.

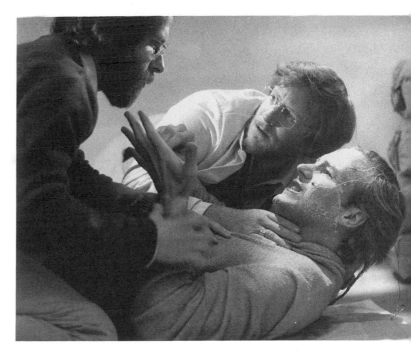

Jessup (William Hurt) tries to communicate with colleagues Bob Balaban and Charles Haid following an experiment that has altered his vocal chords.

Emily Jessup (Blair Brown) enters a whirlpool of
swirling energy to save her husband (William Hurt).

almost immediate departure from Hollywood and his
insistence that a *nom de plume* be used in his
screenplay credit (a somewhat empty gesture, since no
pseudonym was ever so highly publicized as
Chayefsky's "Sidney Aaron," his actual first and middle
names.)

What Chayefsky had given Russell in terms of plot
was a kind of high-tech *Dr. Jekyll and Mr. Hyde*. And
while Russell was quite willing to deliver the goods on
that score, the real attraction was the story's core of
personal salvation through human interaction. Nothing
is so central to Russell's work as this theme—and this
theme was *always* there, even though somewhat buried in Chayefsky's abundance of needlessly abrasive,
vulgar and sometimes incomprehensible dialogue.
Since Russell was not at liberty to rewrite Chayefsky's
dialogue, he worked around it—ignoring it altogether
here and there, then orchestrating it the rest of the

time, reducing much of what the characters say in the
film to the level of pure sound. As a result, much of the
film's emotional punch isn't conveyed by the words
themselves, but rather by the speed, pitch and volume
with which the words are delivered. [In contrast, the
emotional punch of Chayefsky's other filmed scripts
depend almost entirely upon his words, much like stage
plays.] Where the dialogue in *Altered States* is insightful
and incisive (and occasionally it is very much both),
however, Russell not only leaves it alone, but hands it
over with nary an intrusive flourish.

Truthfully, *Altered States* is rather oddly structured
for a horror film. By far the most terrifying sequence in
the film is the sensory deprivation tank fantasy that
opens it. Richly detailed, the sequence manages to
reveal most of Eddie Jessup's fears (the danger of his
reckless behavior on anyone who gets close to him) and
ghosts (the death of his father and Eddie's inability to
get away from the religious visions of his youth).
Amusingly—and oddly for an Eighties commercial hor-

ror film—the sequence utilizes one sure-fire bit of pure Eisensteinian montage in the sacrificial slaughter of a multi-eyed goat. What we *see* is a shot of the goat, a shot of a raised knife, and a shot of a quantity of theatrical blood being poured over the "Book of the Seven Seals." Nothing more. Yet audiences invariable gasp and cringe as if they'd just witnessed an actual throat-cutting.

The subsequent horrors in *Altered States* are designed quite differently and have different aims. The film's hallucinatory mushroom fantasy certainly has moments of terror (a giant boa constrictor wrapping itself around Eddie's head, for example), but Russell's primary goal here (as in the film's hell sequences, which are also quite terrifying) is to create a sense of awe and wonderment in the viewer.

Emily (Blair Brown) rescues Eddie (William Hurt) from "the pit."

Even more of a (pleasant) surprise is the relative simplicity of most of the film's special effects. Only the film's big set piece (where Eddie de-evolves back to primordial ooze) is given over entirely to effects. Huge and elaborate though this scene is, however, Russell makes it his own through editing, sound and his refusal to allow the pyrotechnics to overshadow the characters and their concerns. Never has so solidly budgeted a horror film been so less concerned with flaunting that budget on the screen. What seems to have shocked many—and shouldn't have—was that Russell's approach made *Altered States more* technically impressive than other flashier, but simplistic, special effects extravaganzas. Why was it more impressive? Because the film was *saying something* and used its state-of-the-art effects to say it.

As a curious footnote to the production, *Altered States* ran into even more trouble upon its release. Audiences expecting a simple Spielbergian display of razzle-dazzle special effects were wholly unprepared for the emotional force of Russell's film, which came down on them like a sledgehammer. This resulted in the unprecedented response of viewers finding themselves having difficulty standing up and exiting the theatre immediately after the film. Warner Bros. even went so far as to suggest that theater managers schedule additional "spill-over" time from one showing to the next, at which point bizarre allegations began being leveled at the film—rumors of "subliminal edits" and "unorthodox sound procedures" [similar allegations pervaded *The Exorcist* as well] and so on. Of course, this was all palpable nonsense. Nevertheless, these trivial allegations served to unfairly relegate—initially at least—this serious and important modern horror film to stunt status.

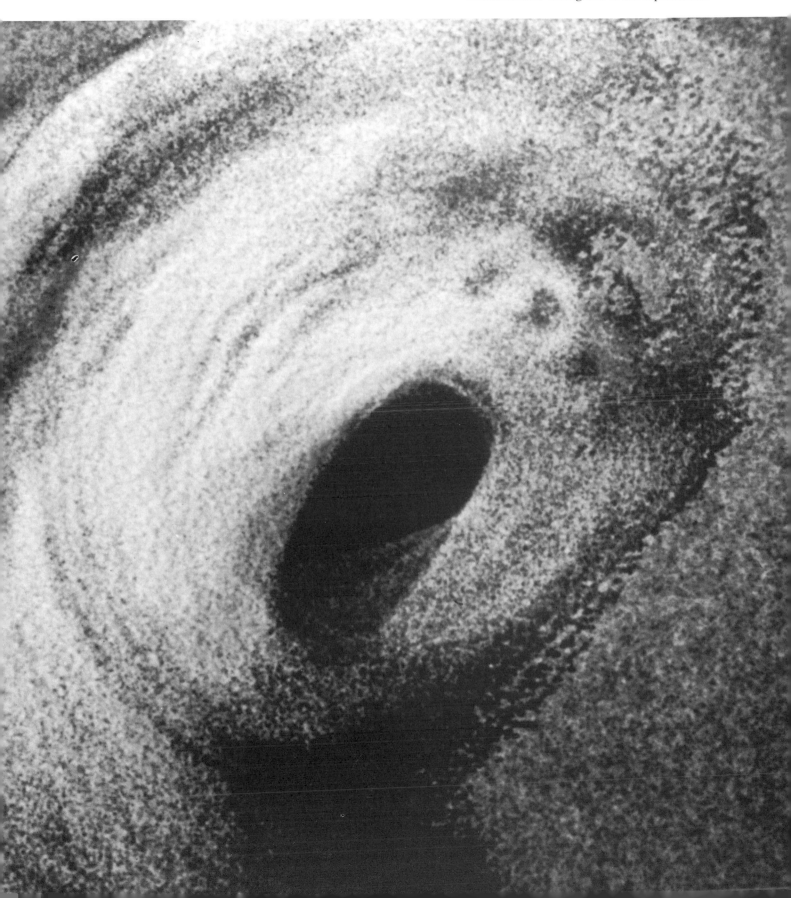

Eddie (William Hurt) undergoes an amazing
transformation during one of his experiments.

THE SHINING (1980)

A Warner Bros. Release
Color /142 minutes

Director Stanley Kubrick lines up a shot in "the gold room" for the *The Shining*.

Ullman (Barry Nelson) and Durkin (Tony Burton) share details of the Overlook's unsavory past with their newly hired winter caretaker, Jack Torrance (Jack Nicholson).

Credits

Director: Stanley Kubrick; *Producer:* Stanley Kubrick; *Screenplay:* Stanley Kubrick and Diane Johnson, based on the novel by Stephen King; *Cinematographer:* John Alcott; *Editor:* Ray Lovejoy; *Music:* Bela Bartok; *Production Designer:* Roy Walker; *Videocassette source:* Warner Home Video.

Cast

Jack Torrance: Jack Nicholson; *Wendy Torrance:* Shelley Duvall; *Danny Torrance:* Danny Lloyd; *Halloran:* Scatman Crothers; *Ullman:* Barry Nelson; *Grady:* Philip Stone; *Lloyd:* Joe Turkel; *Doctor:* Anne Jackson; *Durkin:* Tony Burton.

Stanley Kubrick's movie of Stephen King's best-seller *The Shining* has probably generated more controversy among horror fans than any horror film in history. Though it was a solid box office and commercial success, it was by no means the megahit that its distributor, Warner Bros., had hoped and, indeed, expected it would be in light of the high-powered combination of Kubrick and King. The reason it wasn't was that Kubrick fans, who liked the film, were far outnumbered by King fans, who mostly hated what Kubrick had done to the book and, as a result, refused to turn it into a smash by seeing it again and again. Though a few fans of King's book have since come to appreciate the film version on its own merits, I think it's still fair to say that if you love Stephen King's *The Shining*, you won't much like Stanley Kubrick's *The Shining*.

My own reaction to King's novel (which his fans consider to be one of his best if not *the* best) has always been somewhat mixed. The King novels I most admire tend to be his shorter and, I feel, comparatively more visceral works—*Carrie, Cujo, Misery*, none of which have an ounce of "flab" in them. His novels I admire least—*The Stand, It, The Tommyknockers*—strike me as *total* "flab," almost as if the author was financially compelled to turn out such fat, overblown books because he was literally being paid by the word. *The Shining* falls somewhere in between. When the novel focused on the character of Jack Torrance, the alcoholic writer whose self-destructive behavior and brooding self-hate find a welcome home in the haunted Overlook Hotel, I found myself riveted. Yet whenever the book moved away from Torrance into pure ghost and ghoul territory, I frankly got bored.

Apparently, Stanley Kubrick felt the same way, for in adapting King's book to the screen with the help of novelist Diane Johnson, he tossed out just about all of the ghost and ghoul stuff and made Jack Torrance's psychological inner struggle the film's primary focus. The result, for me, was not only a vast improvement upon the book but a modern horror film masterpiece—though I concur that most of the novel's legion of fans do not share my view. King, who wrote a screenplay based on his book that Kubrick elected not to use ("Let me see what I can bring to it," the writer-director tellingly suggested in return) tends to offer various opinions on the subject. On the one hand, he's said that Kubrick's screen version treated his book quite fairly. On the other, however, he's also said that Kubrick totally muffed the job by "thinking about it too long or not long enough." If one considers the film version not as a separate and wholly unique entity (an *interpretation* of King's book) but rather as a straight translation of it into another medium, one would have to concur with King's latter feeling—one which, as the author of the original source material, King has every legitimate right to feel. At the same time, however, film *is* a separate entity and filmmakers, like all other artist/adapters, have the legitimate right to treat their source material not as inviolate but as a jumping off point—even if they jump at their own peril, as Kubrick surely did with the book's many fans.

Essentially, Stanley Kubrick's *The Shining* is a modern dress ghost story of the "is it or isn't it?" school popularized by Henry James and other writers. Down on his luck and down on himself, the loser central character, Jack Torrance, takes on the job of winter caretaker at a remote Colorado mountain resort called The Overlook which has an unsavory history and may (or may not) be haunted. King's novel gradually reveals a number of horrific incidents that occurred within the hotel's walls over the years, but Kubrick basically includes just one of them—the previous caretaker's axe murder of his family after seemingly going crazy from cabin fever. [Usually meticulous about every detail in his films, Kubrick offers a strange lapse here. During Torrance's interview with Mr. Ullman at the outset of the film, Ullman refers to the previous caretaker as *Charles* Grady. And yet when Torrance later encounters the caretaker's ghost personally, he refers to him as *Delbert* Grady. Which is it?]

Danny's (Danny Lloyd) precognitive skills, the shining, give him a terrifying glimpse into what's happened—and what's going to happen—at the Overlook.

Halloran (Scatman Crothers) drives to the Overlook in a storm to rescue its beleaguered occupants.

The demented Torrance (Jack Nicholson) breaks
through the bathroom door to get at his wife and
son.

194

When the Overlook is cut off from the outside world by a blinding snowstorm, Torrance's already precarious psychological state deteriorates rapidly and he tries to kill his own family in a similar manner. Pursuing his son with an axe through the hotel's snow-covered hedge maze, he collapses, however, and freezes to death in the snow. As the film ends, the camera lingers over several photographs of the hotel's previous occupants and we see Torrance's smiling face among them—indicating that he too has now joined the hotel's benighted company, or that he was *always* one of them. (Grady suggests as much when he tells Torrance, "You were always the caretaker here.")

In the novel, there is never any question that the evil that befalls Torrance, his wife Wendy and their son Danny (whose precognitive gifts, the shining, enable the boy to "see" what's ahead for them) springs entirely from the haunted hotel. The film, however, is a lot coyer about coming straight down on the ghostly side of things. In fact, a good case can be made to support the opinion that *nothing* that occurs in the hotel is supernatural at all—that *everything* is due to Torrance's escalating madness. As with Henry James' *Turn of the Screw*, however, this opinion goes only so far before a number of fascinating questions arise that compel one to reassess it. Kubrick himself has stated that the hotel clearly *is* haunted and that Torrance's deteriorating state-of-mind is just a red-herring, albeit one that makes him quite susceptible to the hotel's evil influence. The film itself, however, offers no clear-cut answers, and this, I think, is its greatest narrative strength over the novel.

The film boasts a number of other strengths too—ones that even lovers of the source novel must admit to. These include John Alcott's breathtaking photography; the stunning and totally convincing recreation of the labyrinthine Overlook Hotel (which Kubrick's production designer, Roy Walker, built entirely on a studio soundstage); its brilliantly staged climax in the snow-covered hedge maze; and Jack Nicholson's creatively daring centerpiece performance as the flipped-out Torrance. Maybe it isn't the novel—not completely—but Stanley Kubrick's *The Shining* ranks right up there anyway as one of the most elegant, superbly crafted and intellectually challenging of all modern horror films.

Wendy (Shelley Duvall) snatches up butcher knife to defend herself—and her son—as the demented Torrance (Jack Nicholson) hacks his way through the bathroom door.

The possessed, psychopatic Torrance pursues his son through the snow-covered hedge maze, one of the many brilliant sequences in Kurbick's modern horror classic.

HOUSE OF THE LONG SHADOWS (1983)

A Cannon Films Ltd. Production
Released through MGM/UA
Color/96 minutes

The male members of the Grisbane clan. From left:
Vincent Price, John Carradine, Christopher Lee, Peter
Cushing.

Credits

Director: Pete Walker; *Producers:* Menahem Golan and Yoram Globus; *Screenplay:* Michael Armstrong, based on the novel *Seven Keys to Baldpate* by Earl Derr Biggers and the play of the same name by George M. Cohan; *Cinematographer:* Norman Langley; *Editor:* Robert Dearberg; *Music:* Richard Harvey; *Art Director:* Mike Pickwoad; *Videocassette source:* MGM/UA Home Video.

Cast

Lionel Grisbane: Vincent Price; *Kenneth MaGee:* Desi Arnaz, Jr.; *Sebastian Grisbane:* Peter Cushing; *Corrigan:* Christopher Lee; *Victoria Grisbane:* Sheila Keith; *Sam Allyson:* Richard Todd; *Lord Grisbane:* John Carradine; *Mary Norton:* Julie Peasgood; *Diana:* Louise English; *Andrew:* Richard Hunter; *Stationmaster:* Norman Rossington.

House of the Long Shadows is ostensibly a remake of Charlie Chan creator Earl Derr Biggers' hoary "old dark house" classic *Seven Keys to Baldpate*. Published in 1913, *Baldpate* was the prolific Biggers' first novel. It was adapted for the stage during the second decade of this century by George M. Cohan, who starred both in the play and in the first film version made in 1917. Another silent version starring Douglas McLean followed in 1925. Richard Dix appeared in the first talkie version made in 1929. In 1935, Gene Raymond starred in yet another version of the tale for RKO, which was remade again in 1947 starring Phillip Terry. Most of these adaptations were based equally as much on the Cohen play as on the source novel and *House of the Long Shadows* is no exception.

The Biggers/Cohan story centers around a popular novelist, William MaGee, who bets his publisher that he can grind out a new book in twenty-four hours given the proper ambience and solitude. The publisher knows just such a place, a resort called Baldpate Inn which has been closed for the winter. MaGee heads there and launches into his new novel, but is continually interrupted by the arrival of a host of suspicious characters—thieves, crooked politicians, a mysterious caretaker, etc.—in search of some stolen loot that has been stashed there. Murder and mayhem follow in rapid succession and MaGee must put his book away to save the day. The twist is that all this has been a ruse

The senile Lord Grisbane (John Carradine) mumbles into the car of his non-musical daughter, Victoria (Sheila Keith).

concocted by his publisher with the help of some local actors to make MaGee lose the bet. But then, in a subsequent turnabout, we see that all these events, even the twist, form the plot of the book MaGee is actually writing. He finishes in time, wins the bet and all ends well.

In *House*, best-selling American novelist Kenneth MaGee is goaded by his British publisher to write an "over the top" Gothic novel full of larger than life characters and grand passions on the order of *Wuthering Heights*. MaGee cynically agrees to do so and bets the publisher $20,000 that he can turn the book out in twenty-four hours. The publisher arranges for him to stay at an abandoned mansion, Baldpate Manor, in Wales. There, MaGee sets up his typewriter and begins work on a potboiler called *Midnight Manor*. Baldpate turns out to be anything but abandoned, however, and soon MaGee finds himself up to his ears in a bizarre family reunion. The manor's rightful owners, the aging Grisbanes, have all gathered together to release a homicidal family member they've kept locked away for over forty years. But when the room is opened, the maniac is found to have escaped. Soon, he starts killing off his relatives and some innocent bystanders one by

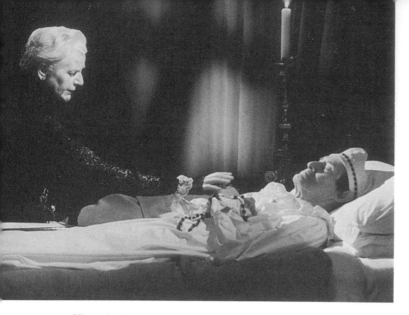

Victoria (Sheila Keith) laments the passing of her senile father (John Carradine), the first member of the family to be dispatched.

Writer Kenneth MaGee (Desi Arnaz Jr.) confronts the supremely theatrical Lionel Grisbane (Vincent Price) about the mysterious goings-on at Baldpate.

one. The identity of the maniac, whom no one has seen for years and whose face they wouldn't recognize, is revealed in a surprise twist. Confronted with this knowledge, MaGee finds himself locked in a struggle to save his own life. As this is a fun movie, all ends well, of course. The maniac-on-the-loose scenario turns out to be a plot hatched by the publisher. And that, in a final twist, turns out to be the ending of MaGee's novel. Ironically, he likes this new novel better than anything he's ever done because it's full of characters he found himself genuinely caring about. Tearing up his winning $20,000 check, he decides that the money and the bet are unimportant. His novel in the grand old tradition has found a place in his heart, and that is reward enough.

One gets the feeling that for director Pete Walker, this film too became a labor of love. Like MaGee's novel, *House of the Long Shadows* is a nostalgia piece played wildly "over the top." Walker's achievement is that he successfully involves us in the melodramatic proceedings and makes us care about the characters (as MaGee comes to do) even though we know we're having our leg pulled every inch of the way. The irony is that Walker began his career making modern dress splatter movies such as *Die Screaming Maryanne* (1970) and *House of Whipcord* (1974), films which stood in marked contrast to the British tradition of Gothic horror and the successful ones in that vein then being made by Hammer. *House of the Long Shadows* was not only a departure for him (as *Midnight Manor* is for Kenneth MaGee), but an affectionate return to that form. In fact, Walker has admitted that *House* is the "complete film buff's movie," a veritable catalogue of "old dark house" movie cliches which also offers a number of amusing references to everything from Hitchcock and Hammer to James Bond. All of this doesn't add up to mere parody, however, for *House of the Long Shadows* stands very nicely on its own. One doesn't need to be a film buff to appreciate its many knowing winks.

No small part of the film's success is due to its venerable cast of veteran scene stealers. As the fossilized head of the Grisbane clan, the late John Carradine is all smiles and senility. Peter Cushing's cowardly Sebastian Grisbane (he sounds like Elmer Fudd) is as endearing as he is pathetic. As the land developer who seeks to turn Baldpate into a series of condominiums, Christopher Lee is suitably arch, sinister, and very Dracula-like. And Vincent Price's grand entrance as the supremely theatrical Lionel Grisbane ("Please do not interrupt me whilst I'm soliloquizing!") is worth the price of admission alone. Sheila Keith, part of the Walker stock company, also registers strongly as the only female member of the clan, Victoria Grisbane, whose atrocious singing talent prompts the maniac to strangle her with piano wire. The only weak link is Desi Arnaz, Jr., as the wise-cracking MaGee. But as he has most of the film's best lines ("He *is* only a man—even if he *hasn't* cut his fingernails in forty years!"), Arnaz does manage to be amusing. And at the conclusion when he sums up the film's theme by confessing his unexpected affection for his new novel and its characters, he is both persuasive and convincing.

House of the Long Shadows is a small treasure.

Corrigan (Christopher Lee), the land developer who wishes to turn Baldpate into a series of condominiums, is revealed as the maniacal missing son. In his attempt to kill MaGee, he takes a fatal axe in the gut. His death, as well as all the other, will prove bogus, however.

Invited in out of the rain, a young traveler washes down and finds herself scalded with acid.

A NIGHTMARE ON ELM STREET (1984)

A New Line Cinema/Media Home Entertainment/
Smart Egg Picture
A New Line Cinema Release
Color /92 minutes

Greetings from hell—Robert Englund as the vengeful child killer Freddy Krueger in Wes Craven's *A Nightmare on Elm Street*.

Credits

Director: Wes Craven; *Producers:* Robert Shaye and Sara Risher; *Screenplay:* Wes Craven; *Cinematographer:* Jacques Haitkin; *Editor:* Rick Shaine; *Music:* Charles Bernstein; *Production Designer:* Greg Fonseca; *Videocassette Source:* Media Home Entertainment.

Cast

Lieutenant Thompson: John Saxon; *Marge Thompson:* Ronee Blakley; *Nancy Thompson:* Heather Langencamp; *Tina Gray:* Amanda Wyss; *Rod Lane:* Nick Corri; *Glen Lantz:* Johnny Depp; *Freddy Krueger:* Robert Englund.

Despite a silly and virtually incomprehensible tacked-on shock ending, to say nothing of the dilution of Freddy Krueger into a kind of stand-up maniac in a string of progressively more foolish sequels, Wes Craven's *A Nightmare on Elm Street* is certainly one of the most impressive of modern horror films. Here, in the midst of such faceless slice-and-dicers as *Friday the 13th*'s Jason Voorhees and *Halloween*'s less humorous Michael Myers, emerged a genuinely terrifying presence, one with—wonder of wonders!—a *personality*, something all the classic movie monsters have had. Moreover, Craven's teens-in-peril were considerably better drawn than the standard meat-on-the-hoof non-characters in most other slasher films, and his story was not only disconcerting, but often complex. Craven *appeared* to be working within the confines of the slasher sub-genre, but all the while he was standing that sub-genre on its head.

The astuteness of Craven's approach is immediately apparent in the opening sequence, which is played partly under the credits. The film starts out in what looks like hell, with the Freddy Krueger character introduced to us in fragmentary bits as he shapes the razor blade claw-glove he uses to dispatch his victims. Into this oddly lit, steamy netherworld comes a girl, who appears to be in mortal danger from this sharp-taloned creature. But the imagery is askew, distorted, even vague (as when a sheep inexplicably runs past). Of course, it all turns out to be a dream sequence, which explains the basic illogic of the images and occurrences. This sets the basic groundwork for the world in which the film takes place: the borderline between nightmare and nightmare reality. Ultimately, even these boundaries are blown away as the two worlds merge into one, whereupon the film becomes a nightmare from which one cannot wake.

Tina (Amanda Wyss) is pinned to the ceiling as the evil Freddy plays one of his nightmarish tricks.

"I'm your boy friend now," Freddy whispers to Nancy (Heather Langencamp) as he tries to French-kiss her through the phone.

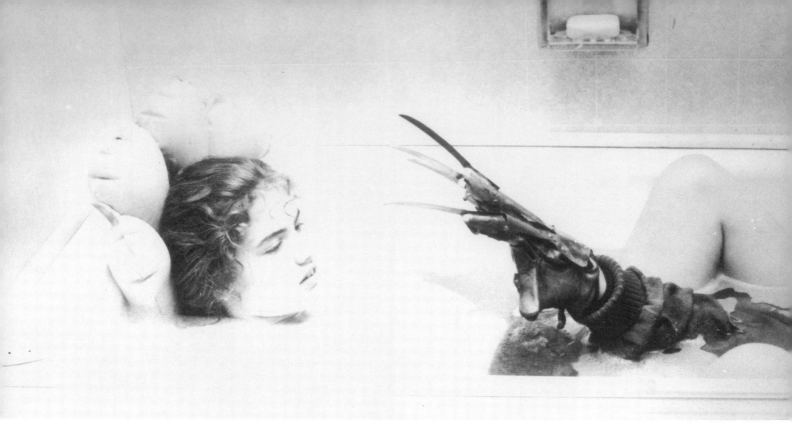

Nancy (Heather Langencamp) finds that's there's just no escape from the logic and geography-defying presence of Freddy (Robert Englund).

Mrs. Thompson (Ronee Blakley), who participated in the vigilante execution of Freddy, reveals a memento of the crime—the monster's claw glove.

Craven's basic concept—the evil spirit of a notorious child-molester/murderer revenges himself on the children of the people who took the law into their own hands and burned him alive—is itself shrewd and strangely out-of-step with the times. In an age where all too many films pander to the base notion of quick vigilante "justice," *A Nightmare on Elm Street* presents a bizarre and fantastic picture of the horrific results of this type of thinking. [Possibly the director was also purging himself of his own past vigilante "justice" picture, the execrable *Last House on the Left* (1972).]

But Craven's greatest coup lies in Freddy Krueger's vengeance being carried out in the nightmares of the children, giving the entire affair undercurrents of inherited guilt. Moreover, his screenplay is good enough that the "real" portions of the film don't come across as dull filler.

What the film is rightly remembered for, though, is Robert Englund's Freddy Krueger and the nightmare sequences that contain him. What is not remembered, especially by the sequel-makers, is *why* Krueger and the nightmare sequences worked so well in Craven's film. True, Craven gives Krueger a warped sense of humor and a personality, but, unlike subsequent films, the humor is not overused. Apart from his maniacal laugh and occasional calling out to his victims, Krueger's dialogue is very limited. Fairly early in the proceedings, he is pursuing the central character, Nancy, who is making an attempt to climb stairs that have turned to sticky goo. Nancy cries out, "Help! Save me from…"

"Freddy!" calls out Krueger, finishing the sentence for her. Later, letting her in on the impending demise of her boyfriend, he tells her over the phone, "I'm your boyfriend now, Nancy." When she starts to fight back, her very clever booby traps earn a variety of dark-humored Freddy threats. "I'm gonna split you in two!" He vows, after being sledge-hammered in the chest. "I'm gonna kill you...*slow*!" He announces when she nearly blows him up. And that's it. No elaborate one-liners, no silly puns—just honest, black-humored bits and pieces that flesh out Freddy's character without diminishing it.

Craven's handling of the nightmare scenes is also very different from that of subsequent directors. With precious little budget to work with, Craven's film is free of much of the technical razzle-dazzle of the later films. [*Nightmare IV*, in fact, plays like a series of effects sequences farmed out to different special effects companies and loosely assembled around a plot.] In part this was due to simple economics, but Craven's use of shifting perspective (Krueger seems able to expand his arm-length at will) and dislocation (characters move from one location to another simply by passing through a door in nightmarish defiance of geography) is quite unnerving. Some of his most disturbing effects are the simplest—as when the first victim mysteriously appears in the hallway in her body bag, beckoning Nancy to follow her. The bag then slides down the hallway as if being dragged by some unseen force, leaving a trail of blood like some gigantic, obscene slug. Instead of marveling at clever effects work and weird prosthetics, the viewer is caught up in the film's world, one in which sleep may well mean death and where nightmares are as real as—or more real than—reality.

So much of the film is so effective that it is unfortunate that New Line Cinema insisted upon the sleazy shock ending that disfigures much of what went before. In Craven's favor though, he did the best he could with this extended climax. He starts it with the same sense of dislocation used in the nightmare (Nancy leaves her mother's bedroom, emerging on the front porch as her friends arrive in a convertible to pick her up) and he wittily has the convertible top painted to resemble Krueger's dirty striped sweater. It isn't enough to stave off the feeling of being "had" by an ending obviously designed to leave room for sequels, but, false move and all, Craven's film readily deserves its classic status and popularity—even if what it wrought does not.

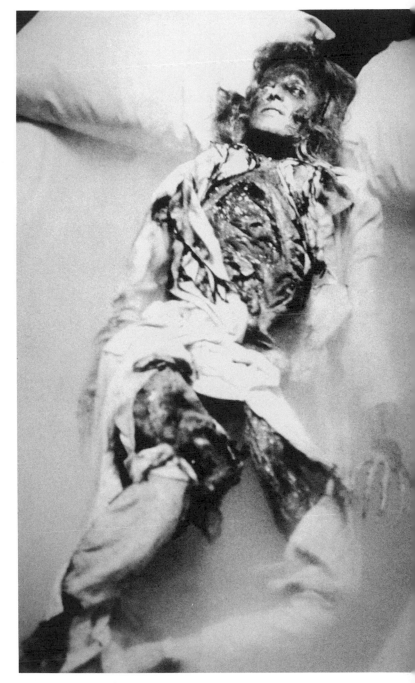

The ghoulish results of Freddy's handiwork.

203

THE RE-ANIMATOR (1985)

Empire Pictures
Color /86 minutes

With more ideas and gore per square inch than any
dozen movies, *The Animator* succeeds on sheer nerve
and invention alone.

Credits

Director: Stuart Gordon; *Producer:* Brian Yuzna; *Screenplay:* Dennis Paoli, William J. Norris and Stuart Gordon, based on stories by H.P. Lovecraft; *Cinematographer:* Mac Ahlberg; *Editor:* Lee Percy; *Music:* Richard Band; *Art Director:* Robert A. Burns; *Videocassette source:* Vestron Video.

Cast

Herbert West: Jeffrey Combs; *Dr. Carl Hill:* David Gale; *Meg Halsey:* Barbara Crampton; *Dan Cain:* Bruce Abbott; *Dean Halsey:* Robert Sampson.

Adapted from H.P. Lovecraft's relatively obscure "Herbert West, Re-Animator" stories, Stuart Gordon's *The Re-Animator*, for all its fanciful screwiness, is probably the closest anyone has yet come to putting Lovecraft on film—even if the results *are* as much cockeyed hommage as outright adaptation. Preserving the bare bones of Lovecraft's stories, Gordon and his co-writers flesh out the screenplay with Lovecraftian in-jokes [much of the action takes place at Lovecraft's fictional Miskatonic University in Arkham, Massachusetts] and wigged-out variations on ideas and descriptions from the original source material. For example, one of the "re-animated" in Lovecraft's story is described as having a wax-like head, a concept that takes on new meaning in Gordon's hands when his arch villain, Dr. Carl Hill, having been decapitated and revived in two pieces, plops a plastic model head on his shoulders so as not to draw attention to the fact that he's carrying his real head around in a gym bag!

For a modern horror film, *The Re-Animator* is almost shockingly old-fashioned in its attention to setting up characters and story development. The first section of the film carefully details West's antagonistic relationship with Dr. Hill, Hill's creepy attachment to heroine Meg Halsey, Meg's romance with student Dan Cain, and her father the Dean's dull-witted distaste for Cain and approval of Hill. When the film does get down to cases with the re-animating of Cain's dead cat, it does so in an equally surprising fashion. The sequence is played for a combination of gross-out disgust and self-spoofing humor.

Awakened by the cries of the deceased cat, Dan investigates and discovers West and the seriously anti-social zombie kitty in the basement laboratory. Shot in

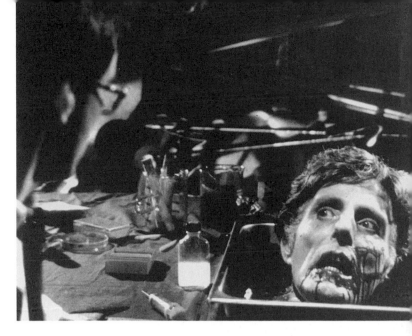

West (Jeffrey Combs) re-animates Dr. Hill's (David Gale) severed head.

Despite the amusing inconvenience of controlling his headless body, the animated Dr. Hill (David Gale) has designs on conquering the world.

Hill's (David Gale) re-animated torso straps the nude Meg (Barbara Crampton) to the operating table in preparation for a most unusual experiment.

half-darkness with a *Psycho*-like swinging light fixture, the scene is nothing more than two actors crashing about in the dark, trying to dispatch the unseen cat, until a wonderfully unrealistic stuffed cat gets splattered against a wall, only to be revived a *second* time ("Don't expect it to tango, it has a broken back," says West) to prove the validity of West's re-animation process.

Dan joins West in the experiments. Palming West off as a corpse, Dan sneaks him into the morgue for the Big Experiment on a Human Being. Choosing a suitable corpse, West injects the body with his green serum. When there is no immediate reaction, West increases the dosage. With Dean Halsey in pursuit, Dan is ready to call it quits when the added serum seems not to work. "We failed," Dan says to West. "*He* failed, not I!" West exclaims, whereupon the ill-tempered corpse clambers to its re-animated feet and runs amok. Dean Halsey picks this improper moment to arrive and the corpse bites off a couple of the Dean's fingers and beats him to death. Helping himself to a cranial power saw, West removes the offending horror by boring a hole through its chest. By now, all bets are off. The deliberately hokey cat business has given way to an over-the-top, graphically realistic display of state-of-the-art gore.

Rather than give the viewer a breather, Gordon takes his outrageousness even further. Immediately, West concludes that the corpse simply wasn't fresh enough, so he opts to do the natural thing: revive Dean Halsey. Not surprisingly, Halsey proves no more grateful for West's ministrations than previous subjects, and he proceeds to throttle both Dan and West—until his daughter Meg breaks in and sends him cowering into a corner in shame.

The smarmy Dr. Hill, who guesses the truth about what's going on, lobotomizes Halsey in order to control him and tries to blackmail West into turning over the re-animation formula. But West cuts off Hill's head with a shovel. More zealous than wise, West then decides: "Parts! I've never done whole parts!" And he proceeds to re-animate Hill's head *and* body, creating a split-level zombie. "I had to kill him," West confesses to Dan. "You mean he's dead?" Dan asks rather dimly. "Not anymore," admits West. "Herbert, this has *got* to stop!" Dan retorts with all the fervor of a kindergarten teacher.

Despite the amusing inconvenience of controlling a headless body [he bumps into walls and so on], Hill has designs on conquering the world with a zombie army— and having his way with Meg. This secondary ambition leads to the film's most notorious scene in which the zombified Hill—head in hand—performs an idelicate sexual act on the strapped-down Meg. Her screaming protests only serve to increase his enthusiasm. "That's it, my dearest Meg," he shouts. "*More passion!*" Lionel Atwill at his slimiest never had it so good.

With more ideas and gore per square inch than any dozen movies, *The Re-Animator* succeeds on sheer nerve and invention alone. Each time it seems that director Gordon can go no farther afield, or top this or that effect, he *does*. The results are both funny and horrific—if, obviously, not to everyone's taste. Fortunately, taste is subjective and Gordon was savvy enough not to have tried pleasing everyone. Instead, he allowed his creative juices to run riot and proved himself a master of the genre his first time at bat—a status he has continued to enjoy in subsequent films, though he has yet to outdo this unqualified gem.

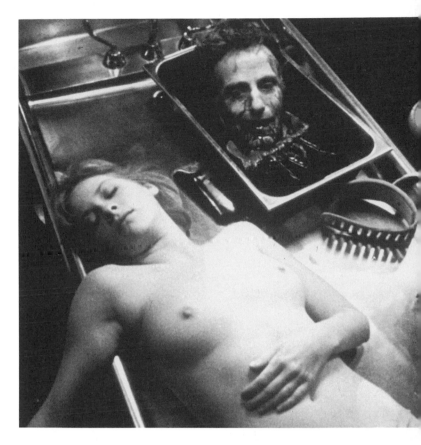

Hill (David Gale) leers at the delectable Meg (Barbara Crampton).

"That's it, my dearest Meg. *More Passion!*" Hill (David Gale) shouts in the film's most notorious scene.

THE FLY (1986)

A Brooksfilms Production
A Twentieth Century-Fox Release
Color /96 minutes

Using himself as a guinea pig, Seth Brundle (Jeff Goldblum) enters the telepod to begin the experiment that will turn him into *The Fly*.

Credits

Director: David Cronenberg; *Producer:* Stuart Cornfeld; *Screenplay:* Charles Edward Pogue and David Cronenberg, based on the short story by George Langelaan; *Cinematographer:* Mark Irwin; *Editor:* Ronald Sanders; *Music:* Howard Shore; *Production Designer:* Carol Spier; *Videocassette source:* CBS/Fox Home Video.

Cast

Seth Brundle: Jeff Goldblum; *Veronica Quaife:* Geena Davis; *Stathis Borans:* John Getz; *Tawny:* Joy Boushel; *Dr. Cheevers:* Les Carlson.

Like *The Blob* (1958), director Kurt Neumann's *The Fly* of the same year remains one of the most popular and memorable horror/SF films of the Fifties without being one of the best. Based on a short story by Canadian writer George Langelaan that caused quite a stir when it appeared in *Playboy* magazine the year before, it was given a larger budget than usual for films of its type and produced by a major Hollywood studio, Twentieth Century-Fox, which also lavished a considerable amount of advertising dollars on it. Though reviews at the time were mainly favorable, the film's reputation has fallen so considerably over the years that many now look upon it as little more than a camp classic. The truth falls somewhere in between. The film is not nearly as bad as its detractors now claim. It is fairly well made, but it is not especially well thought out and fails to make much emotional use of the human dimensions of the story. As a variation on the man-into-monster theme, however, it was, and still is, quite unique.

Apart from shifting the locale from France to Canada, Neumann's film (scripted by superstar novelist James Clavell) follows Langelaan's story fairly closely. Helene Delambre has murdered her husband, avant-garde scientist Andre Delambre, by crushing his head and torso in a flat bed press. In a lengthy flashback, she reveals to her skeptical brother-in-law Francois the situation that led up to the crime. It seems Andre had been involved in an experiment aimed at breaking down matter and transmitting it from one spot to another by means of a revolutionary matter disintegration/reintegration machine. Using himself as a guinea pig, he had entered the transmitter device unaware that a common housefly had gotten locked inside with him.

208

During the successfully-achieved transmission, his atoms had merged with the fly's, transforming him into a creature that was half man, half insect. Finding his efforts at correcting the mistake unsuccessful and feeling his human self being more and more overwhelmed by his fly self, he burned all records of the experiment and enlisted Helen's aid in destroying himself in a way that would render his transformation undetectable.

Though I haven't re-read the story in many years, my memory of it is that Helene's bizarre tale falls on deaf ears and she too commits suicide out of anguish and despair. In the film version—which is only slightly less downbeat—Francois and the inspector on the case don't believe her either. But they quickly change their minds when they hear the inexplicably human cries of "Help me!" emanating from a fly trapped in a spider's web in the backyard of the Delambre home, and, discovering that the fly has Andre's head, put the pitiable creature out of its misery by crushing it with a rock.

Probably the biggest reason why Neumann's film misses the mark is that its characters are fairly one-dimensional and the film evokes very little feeling in the audience for them. Because of the horrific situation, the viewer can't help but be caught up in it, of course, but that's a far cry from actually being *involved* with Andre, Helene and their desperate plight. In addition, there is the problem of the transformation itself. The horror inherent in such a situation is severely diluted because—except for his inexplicable retention of his own brain—Andre transforms right away. More problematic still, his newly acquired fly head is hundreds of times larger than the real fly's and several times larger than his own. Even for a horror/SF film, this pushes credulity too far.

Because the original *Fly* had so much potential for horror film greatness—yet missed it—it was an ideal subject for remake treatment. And to their credit, director David Cronenberg and his co-writer, Charles Edward Pogue, didn't blow the opportunity. In effect, they started from scratch [Cronenberg is surely the least imitative and homage-obsessed horror director of his generation] and completely rethought the story— not only in terms of the potential afforded by today's more advanced special effects, but in terms of the tale's

Seth Brundle (Jeff Goldblum) find that he is undergoing a terrifying transformation.

Realizing that he's no longer quite himself, Seth (Jeff Goldblum) warns his girlfriend Veronica (Geena Davis) of the danger if she stays with him.

Seth Brundle (Jeff Goldblum) fully transformed as
The Fly. Three views of the horrific fly/man created
for the film by Chris Walas.

character and thematic potential as well. The result was
a brand new work that far eclipsed the original and
stands as the definitive screen version of *The Fly*.

Cronenberg's *The Fly* is a compelling mixture of love
story, medical horror film and Kafkaesque nightmare
about the loss of identity. As played by Jeff Goldblum,
scientist Seth Brundle is a lanky, offbeat and thoroughly
likable character. And the love that builds between this
essentially lonely man and the equally appealing Veronica—the reporter to whom he reveals his scientific
marvel—is very convincingly sketched in. As a result,
Brundle's inevitable descent into flyness is far more
emotionally wrenching than it was either in Langelaan's
story or the earlier film.

Though Cronenberg had built his genre reputation
as a *goremeister* par excellence, he maintains that the
grislier aspects of the film were already present in
Pogue's first draft screenplay and that the story's emotional undercurrents were his major contribution to the
film. This is especially evident in the director's treatment of Stathis Borans (Veronica's boss, her former
lover and Brundle's rival) who was portrayed as an
outright villain in Pogue's script, but given more three-
dimensional shadings in the director's revised version.
Putting it simply: there are no cardboard characters in
this film, and no villains either. There are only victims.
Even science itself is portrayed as a victim, for unlike
the earlier film, Cronenberg's *Fly* is no cautionary fable
about the evils inherent in "tampering with things best
left untampered with." Brundle's teleportation device *is*
a scientific marvel with potentially great benefits for

mankind. The experiment goes wrong only because of a tragic accident that can easily be avoided next time around. It is for this very reason that Brundle, unlike Andre Delambre, makes no attempt to destroy what he has wrought. What would be the purpose? The device *worked*.

The bulk of the film is given over to Brundle's gradual (rather than abrupt) transformation into a creature that is neither human nor insect but biologically unique (Brundlefly)—and the impact of his transformation not only on himself, but on Veronica and Borans, both of whom are transformed in very different, human ways themselves. As much in awe as he is frightened of his metamorphosis, Brundle becomes a monster—and a threat—only when he begins to accept what's happening to him. Knowing he can't reverse the process on himself, he sees but one logical—albeit grotesque—alternative: repeat the experiment by going through the machine with Veronica (who is pregnant with their baby), thereby merging them all into one. His attempt to do this, however, is frustrated when Borans, whose chauvinistic bitterness towards Veronica for having ended their sexual affair has evolved into genuine love and concern for her, shows up with a shotgun. Borans is almost killed, but he gets Veronica out of the machine, and as the now completely transformed Brundlefly crawls out after them, the teleportation device triggers and the creature fuses with the machine itself.

Then, in one of the most moving conclusions in genre film history (which does tie to the original story and earlier film), the misshapen creature gazes up at the distraught Veronica, who is now holding the shotgun, and clasping a claw around the barrell of the shotgun and lifting it to its head, makes one final, *human* request with its sorrowful eyes: to be put out of its misery. A request she sobbingly grants.

GOTHIC (1986)

A Vestron Pictures Release
Color /90 minutes

The morning light outside the Villa Diodati drives
away the night's horrors for Dr. Polidori (Timothy
Spall), Lord Byron (Gabriel Byrne) and Mary Shelley
(Natasha Richardson).

Byron (Gabriel Byrne) prepares to conduct a seance to conjure up a ghost with the help of his houseguests.

Byron (Gabriel Byrne) comforts his laudanum-besotted friend (and object of his affections), the poet Shelley (Julian Sands).

Credits

Director: Ken Russell; *Producer:* Penny Corke; *Screenplay:* Stephen Volk; *Cinematographer:* Mike Southon; *Editor:* Michael Bradsell; *Music:* Thomas Dolby; *Production Designer:* Christopher Hobbs; *Videocassette source:* Vestron Video.

Cast

Lord Byron: Gabriel Byrne; *Percy Shelley:* Julian Sands; *Mary Shelley:* Natasha Richardson; *Claire Clairmont:* Myriam Cyr; *Dr. Polidori:* Timothy Spall; *Fletcher:* Andreas Wisniewski; *Murray:* Alex Mango; *Rushton:* Dexter Fletcher; *Justice:* Pascal King; *Tour Guide:* Tom Hickey; *Mechanical Doll:* Linda Coggin; *Mechanical Woman:* Kristine Landon-Smith.

Sometimes described as a "thinking man's" *Nightmare on Elm Street*, Ken Russell's *Gothic* is quite possibly the most accomplished and multi-layered modern horror film of all because in it Russell dares the near impossible: to unearth "the horror *beneath* the horror." In so doing, he created a genre film worthy of the best of Universal and Hammer while simultaneously furthering his own experiments in understanding (and making understandable) the artist behind the art, the relation of the creator to his creation, and the nature of art as a separate entity beyond the control of the artist. While all these diverse, yet related, elements exist in Russell's work prior to *Gothic*, this film brings a new focus to bear on them. For in *Gothic*, one is constantly asked to ponder the unanswerable question: did these people create worthwhile, even great, works *in spite of* their foibles, or *because of them?* (The same question would pop up again in Russell's next film, *Salome's Last Dance* (1988).)

Gothic telescopes the events leading up to Mary Shelley's writing of *Frankenstein* into one nightmarish evening. It is a nearly perfect companion piece to James Whale's two Frankenstein films, which it echoes in its time-honored "It's alive!," its use of eye imagery (recalling the swirling eyes behind the credits of *Frankenstein*) and its casting of Elsa Lanchester lookalike Myriam Cyr. There is a great deal of thematic connection between the films also. At bottom, *Gothic* centers upon the characters' deepest personal fears made real ("Conjure up your deepest, darkest fear—now call that fear to form," says Byron). The emphasis here is on

Mary Shelley though the fears of all the characters interconnect in the use of the same "monster creation" pulled from the emotional baggage of their subconscious minds. Stephen Volk's screenplay has Mary state outright that her great fear revolves around her desire—at any cost—to have her dead baby restored to her, but Russell's handling of the film places a far greater, more complex emphasis on her sexuality and sexual fears. Here, after all, we have a young woman defying convention by living openly with a still-married man (Shelley) who, in turn, is a bisexual in love with another man (Byron) to whom Mary herself is drawn. Complicating this already overheated situation is the fact that Byron is also the father of the unborn child of Claire (Mary's half-sister)—unless, that is, Shelley himself is the father! Without question, the fear of the realization of ones own sexuality and the sexuality of those with whom one is involved are central to the film. For Russell, the monster *behind* "The Monster" is a combination of sexual awakening and sexual fear.

Much of this underlying meaning was quite lost on most critics, who could not see beyond the film's horror film trappings, nor its conceit of presenting important historical figures as drug-taking, over-imaginative, sexually entangled young bohemians involved in an elaborate mind game that overtakes them in its intensity until the boundaries between reality and imagination cease to exist—for them *and* the viewer. That we know these people did take drugs, did have overheated imaginations and were sexually entangled is one thing. Seeing it on the screen is another—or so it seemed for the majority of mainstream critics. That neither Volk's screenplay nor Russell's film presents these people as characterless hedonists, but rather as haunted, tortured, passionate, driven beings who are forced into their roles by the restrictions and repressions of the society in which they lived, was overlooked—as was the fact that the historical persons were far more petty and childish than their cinematic incarnations.

Instead, the bulk of critics with enough historical knowledge to do so insisted on wrestling with the depiction of Byron as fairly open about his bisexual nature (which he in fact wasn't in 1816) and the presentation of Shelley as somewhat closeted about his sexuality (which he never much seems to have been). If

Director Ken Russell confers with Gabriel Byrne on the set of *Gothic*.

Gothic were a history lesson, there would have been some validity in this, but the film isn't history and the objections overlook the fact that *Gothic* is seen primarily through Mary's eyes—eyes that see into Byron's true nature yet wish to avoid that of Shelley.

As with Russell's previous foray into the overtly fantastic, *Altered States* (1980), *Gothic* is a film that is accessible and comprehensible without a working knowledge of the cinematic world of Ken Russell, but it is also a film that gains immeasurably from such knowledge. The cross-references to his non-genre works add a sense of texture and depth. The powerful image of Shelley standing naked on a rooftop during a thunderstorm shouting, "Lightning is the fundamental force of the universe—the spirit, the ether!" is a heart-stopping moment in its own right. However, its unified significance of the communion of Man with the forces of nature as presented in Russell's work overall is brought into focus for the viewer familiar with the climactic image of Roger Daltrey atop the mountain, reaching to embrace the sun (as here Shelley reaches into the darkness) in *Tommy* (1975) and the attempts by Eddie Jessup in *Altered States* to "know the unknowable"—or "to get it off with God," as Jessup puts it.

Since *Gothic* is plotwise a film about the creation of *Frankenstein*, the major focus is what Mary sees and what she and others see about her. Everyone is treated to a vision of the truth about her or himself. Polidori has to face up to his homosexuality and his guilt about it. [Apparently, this was to have been a more involved and fantastic sequence featuring a giant penis that sprouted leeches and a baby's skull that was deleted.] Shelley has an obsession with a dream in which he saw

Claire Clairmont (Myriam Cyr), Percy Bysshe Shelley (Julian Sands) and
Mary Shelley (Natasha Richardson) arrives at the villa of the infamous
Lord Byron (Gabriel Byrne) for an evening of drugs, fun and games.

a woman with eyes in her breasts (an historically documented fantasy of Shelley's, by the way). He has to see his breast dream in the flesh, witness his self-destructive tendencies (a stunning scene in which he runs toward and shoots a masked man who turns out to be his reflection in a mirror), and his love for Byron. Byron sees his incestuous love for his sister (and, worse, it is seen by others), his growing homosexuality (no longer deniable when he realizes Mary has seen its expression), and his innate, yet egomaniacal, destructive tendencies toward those around him. Claire—somewhat more catalyst than character—sees the destructive nature of the group's collective self-delusions. Yet it is Mary who sees the most.

She first recognizes the danger beneath Byron's cynical charm, her fears about her dead child, her fears about Shelley's love for her. She sees Byron's romantic pass at Shelley firsthand ("Forget your women, Shiloh. Don't waste your brilliant words upon them. Poets were made for each other," Byron says.) Most significantly, she witnesses—forces into being—Shelley's pent-up passion for Byron when she attacks the unconscious Byron with a jagged piece of shattered skull,

and Shelley fends off her attack by blocking her with his own body—after which he heatedly kisses his male love on the mouth. With this realization, Mary finds herself plunged into a lengthy phantasmagoric vision of the self-induced destruction of all those around her. She envisions all this as the result of their excessive behavior, of their tampering with things beyond their knowledge and reason in their quest for both an ultimate truth and a new thrill.

At bottom, what she foresees is the rejection and destruction of themselves by their own creation—the monster they conjured up—just as they have rejected and destroyed the concept of God in their own minds. Most important of all, Mary is the only one of the group who will be *consciously* haunted ("to the grave") by these visions and realizations—precisely because she is the only one not playing an hysterical, induced game. The others are, to varying degrees, stoned out of their minds on laudanum, while Mary has eschewed the drug at each offering. She is the sole sober character in the group—an unwilling spectator to the truth brought on by the chemically-shed inhibitions of her friends.

216

EVIL DEAD II: DEAD BY DAWN (1987)

Renaissance Pictures
Rosebud Releasing Corporation
Color /84 minutes

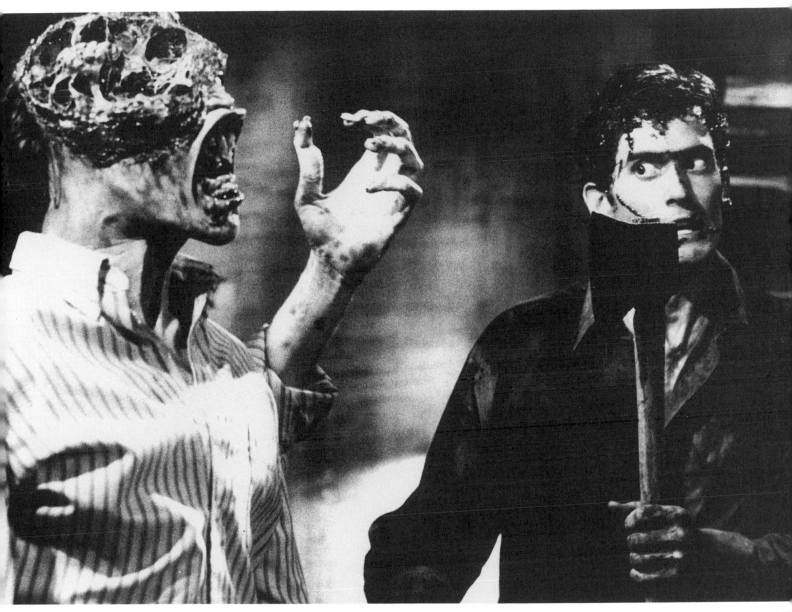

The axe-wielding Ash (Bruce Campbell) fights off one of many, *many* grotesque creatures in Sam Raimi's gory extravaganza, *Evil Dead II*.

Credits

Director: Sam Raimi; *Producers:* Robert G. Tapart and Bruce Campbell; *Screenplay:* Sam Raimi and Scott Spiegel; *Cinematographers:* Peter Deming and Eugene Schlugleit; *Editor:* Kaye Davis; *Music:* Joseph Lo Duca; *Art Directors:* Philip Duffin and Randy Bennett; *Videocassette source:* Vestron Video.

Cast

Ash: Bruce Campbell; *Annie:* Sarah Berry; *Jake:* Dan Hicks; *Bobbi Jo:* Kassie Wesley; *Possessed Henrietta:* Theodore Raimi; *Linda:* Denise Bixler; *Ed:* Richard Domeir; *Professor Knowby:* John Peaks; *Henrietta:* Lou Hancock.

Before getting into why I think Sam Raimi's *Evil Dead II* deserves a spot in a book about modern horror film classics, let me first explain my reasons for including the sequel rather than the first film—and not both films as I did with *Psycho, Psycho II* and *Psycho III*, Romero's zombie trilogy and Tobe Hooper's two *Texas Chainsaw Massacre* films. The reason is simple. Hitchcock's *Psycho*, Romero's *Night of the Living Dead* and Hooper's *The Texas Chainsaw Massacre* were separate and distinct films whose various sequels treated the story told in those films as basically unfinished and proceeded to continue on with it, taking the story in new and sometimes surprising directions. Sam Raimi's *The Evil Dead* (1982) and its sequel, *Evil Dead II*, regardless of their merits individually, just don't do that. Raimi's sequel, in fact, is basically a bigger budget *remake* rather than continuation of the first film, which not only treats the first one as if it didn't exist but leaves one with the impression that it is the movie Raimi had really wanted to make the first time around. Though the earlier one was extremely inventive (especially given its shoestring budget), the elaborate sequel is more polished and professional, more technically dazzling—and even more outrageously amusing. In short, it is essentially the *same* film, done better. It also leaves the door open for a bona fide continuation of the story, which, as of this book goes to press, writer-director Raimi has announced he will be making.

Financed independently by a group of Detroit investors and shot on location in Michigan and Tennessee, *The Evil Dead* was the then 23-year-old Raimi's debut theatrical feature [he had made a number of Super 8 and 16mm films in college]. Spurred by a rave review from Stephen King, who called it "the most ferociously original horror film of the year" after seeing it at the Cannes Film Festival, *The Evil Dead* was picked up for theatrical release by New Line Cinema and went on to become a minor hit. Ballyhooed as "the ultimate experience in grueling terror," the virtually plotless film focused on five vacationing college chums who come

It may appear that his malevolent demon is down for the count, but don't be too sure.

upon a ramshackle cabin deep in the woods and decide to party there. They find a musty old volume called *The Book of the Dead* that was left in the cabin by its former occupants, a professor and his wife. One of the chums flips the book open for a little leisure reading, not realizing that its mystical passages are aimed at raising the evil spirits of the dead that lurk in the woods outside. As night wears on, several of the chums are possessed by these spirits and attack the others. By morning, only one of the five, Ash, manages to survive, having destroyed his possessed former chums in all sorts of graphically horrible ways, and having set fire to the dreaded tome that released the evil dead. One supposes that Ash is now safely out of the woods, literally, but in a cliche shock epilogue, the camera swoops down upon him as he leaves the cabin and we realize that he too is about to be claimed by yet another demon—thus rendering the destruction of *The Book of the Dead* meaningless.

Wildly implausible and practically incoherent at times, *The Evil Dead* did not succeed as a cult hit on the basis of a solid script. What did set it apart was the energy, wit and amazing technical virtuosity Raimi and his meager cast and crew were able to bring to the film. Despite its very low budget, the film manages to employ just about every known cinematic trick available, piling one ghastly special effect scene of horror and carnage upon another, each one topping the last, in much the same manner that the slapstick comedians of the silent film era built and then topped gags (no pun intended).

Raimi followed up the splattery slapstick of *The Evil Dead* with a blackly humorous, but far less funny, comedy of murders called *Crimewave* (1986, a.k.a. *The XYZ Murders*), co-written by the Coen brothers (*Blood Simple*). Negatively reviewed and barely released, the $3-million film was a box office failure, prompting Raimi to return once more to *Evil Dead* country. Instead of picking up where *The Evil Dead* left off, *Evil Dead II* starts all over again with a much smaller group of people, including Ash and the daughter of Professor Knowby, the man who unearthed *The Book of the Dead*, stumbling upon the same cabin in the woods. They find a tape recorder inside, turn it on and hear the voice of the late professor reading some of the spirit summoning passages from the book. The evil spirits roaming the woods outside are once again given license to return and possess the living—which they do with even more ghastly malevolence than before.

The demon-bedevilled Ash (Bruce Campbell) gets a not-so-helping hand in *Evil Dead II*.

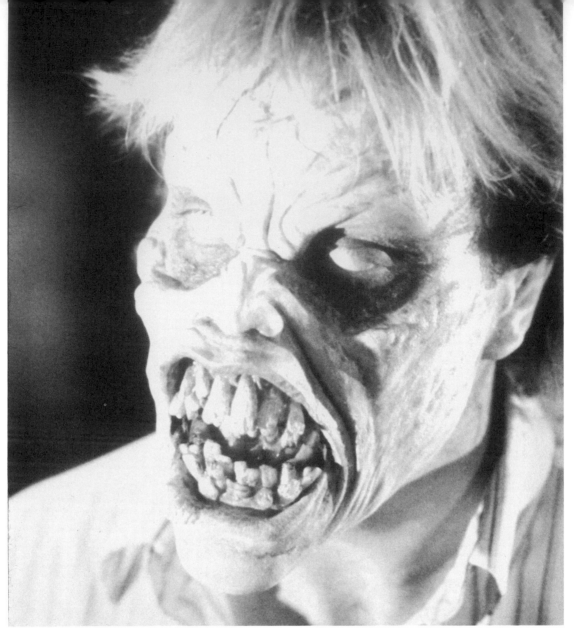

Another of *Evil Dead II's*
creatures galore.

As soon as the evil passages are read, the film launches into a freewheeling display of ever-more outrageously bizarre and horrible images and situations. Headless corpses dance in the woods, people are possessed and summarily chainsawed and shotgunned in order to be exorcised, and the survivors of all this mayhem are faced with doing battle with the film's grandaddy of a wood demon, a gigantic tree creature with a bloodshot eyeball. The job of returning the evil spirits to where they belong falls once more to the intrepid Ash, who loses his hand along the way, but compensates by rigging his mutilated limb to wield a chainsaw—an accomplishment he pronounces "Groovy!" He also snaps a shotgun to his back so that he can whip it out with his other hand and fire it at a moment's notice.

The key to sending the dead back to where they belong rests in finding and torching some missing pages to the burned *Book of the Dead*, which Ash succeeds in doing only to find himself hurtled through a time warp back to the dawn from whence the evil sprang—circa 1300 A.D. There, our blood-caked and uncomprehending hero is surrounded by a band of medieval knights who view the man as some sort of uniquely armored God come to save them. Which is probably what the impending *Evil Dead III* will be about.

Though just as plotless and narratively incoherent as the first film, *Evil Dead II* is so energetic that it seems to go by in a flash. It is, as was the first film, a riotous—but this time much more accomplished—celebration of cinematic technique, over-the-top sight gags, ghoulish humor and every conceivable type of screen special effect. And it's directed with astonishing visual flair, gusto and command by a young man who seems to share the late Orson Welles' attitude toward the medium: that it's "the best electric train set a boy ever had."

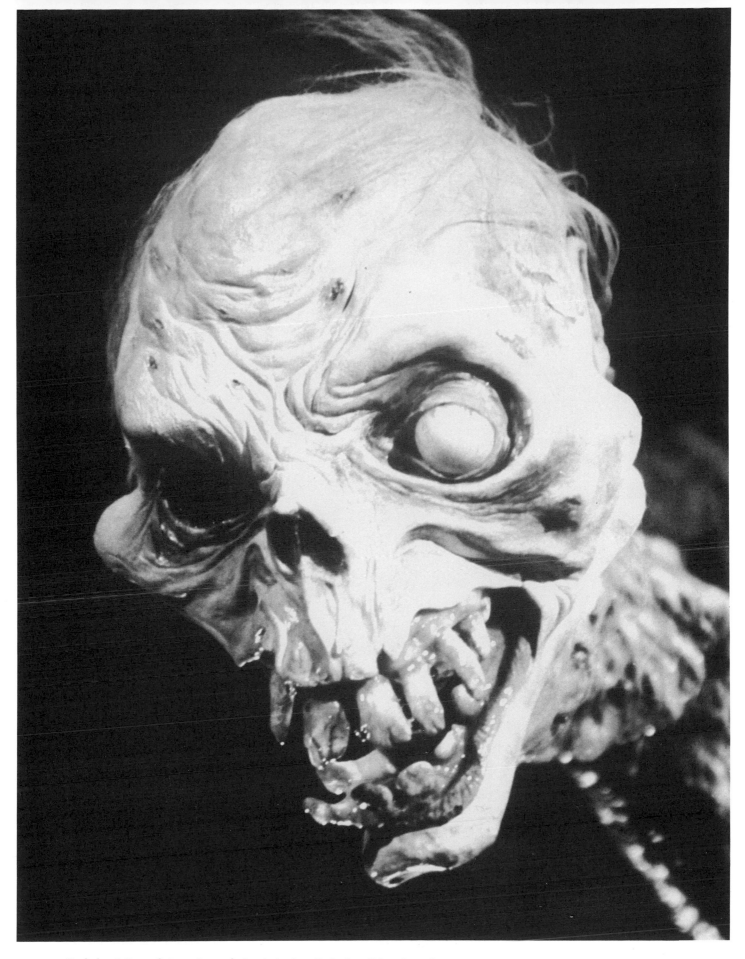

Peekaboo! One of the galaxy of ghouls in Sam Raimi's wild-and-wooly splatter show, *Evil Dead II*.

THE WITCHES OF EASTWICK (1987)

A Warner Bros. Release
Color /118 minutes

Jack Nicholson as Daryl Van Horne ("Just your
average horny little devil") with the three *Witches of
Eastwick* (Cher, Susan Sarandon, Michell Pfeiffer).

Credits

Director: George Miller; *Producers:* Neil Canton, Peter Guber and Jon Peters; *Screenplay:* Michael Cristofer, based on the novel by John Updike; *Cinematographer:* Vilmos Zsigmond; *Editors:* Richard Francis-Bruce and Hubert C. De La Bouollerie; *Music:* John Williams; *Production Designer:* Polly Platt; *Videocassette source:* Warner Home Video.

Cast

Daryl Van Horne: Jack Nicholson; *Alexandra Medford:* Cher; *Jane Spofford:* Susan Sarandon; *Sukie Ridgemont:* Michelle Pfeiffer; *Felicia Alden:* Veronica Cartwright; *Clyde Alden:* Richard Jenkins; *Walter Neff:* Keith Joakum; *Fidel:* Carel Struycker.

One of the reasons John Updike says he wrote *The Witches of Eastwick* was to expand the reading audience for his type of "literary fiction." Though most of Updike's output had consistently scored well on *The New York Times* best-seller list, it was obvious to the author that the reading public's overall greater preference for popular horror and fantasy fiction indicated that these readers were not getting something important from authors such as himself. *The Witches of Eastwick* was his attempt to acknowledge this "flaw" in contemporary "literary fiction" and to tap into the larger readership's consciousness in his own very distinctive style. Combining social satire, metaphor, sophisticated comedy and broad fantasy, *The Witches of Eastwick* emerged as one of Updike's most accessible works and became his most popular novel to date.

What was true of readers was even more true of moviegoers, whose insatiable demand for fantasy, horror and science-fiction movies in the past two decades had propelled genre films to the top of the list of the most financially successful movies ever made. It was logical therefore that a major Hollywood studio, Warner Bros., would consider Updike's sophisticated, yet very popular, excursion into genre territory to be an ideal subject for big screen treatment. What seemed less logical was the studio's choice of George Miller, the Australian director of the action-oriented *Mad Max* movies, to bring Updike's bizarre but subtle comedy of sexual manners and mores to the screen. The choice proved to be inspired, however, for Miller's topsy-turvy treatment of the material is, along with the hilariously

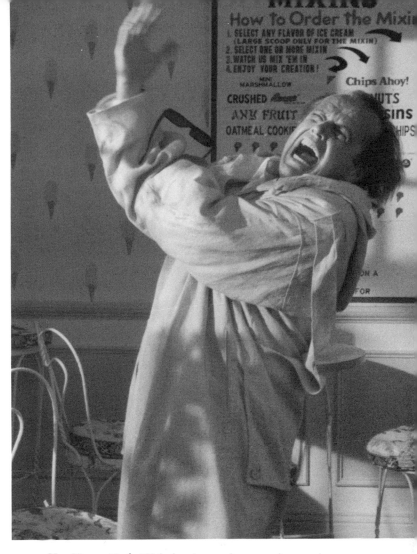

Van Horne (Jack Nicholson) experiences a sharp pain as his vengeful paramours stick pins into his waxen image.

The vengeful witches of Eastwick mount another supernatural attack on their devilish suitor (Jack Nicholson), causing him to puke up feathers and get buffeted about in a conjured-up windstorm.

The satanic Romeo Daryl Van Horne (Jack Nicholson)—as scarifying yet hilarious a screen devil as we are ever likely to see.

over-the-top performances of Jack Nicholson and Veronica Cartwright, the film's major asset. Veering wildly from outright slapstick to full-throttle horror, Miller's direction of the film is a real tour-de-force.

Three New England divorcees (two of whom are also single mothers) discover that when they are together and thinking the same thing, they have the ability to conjur up that thing. Bored with the routine of their dull and romance-less small town lives, they decide to put their heads together and "create" their dream man. They do and—presto!—he turns up in the form of a wealthy but bizarre Romeo named Daryl Van Horne, whose arrival in town causes an immediate stir. First he buys a prime piece of real estate, the foreboding Castle Dracula-like Lennox Mansion, an historical landmark where witches were supposedly burned during the days of the Salem witch trials. Then he shows up at a high school recital, where he proceeds to fall asleep and drown out the music with his overbearing snores. Finally, he zeros in on the women who brought him there through their conjuring. By tapping into their psyches and getting them to expose their needs ("Who are you?" They ask. "Anybody you want me to be," he replies.) and worst fears—growing old, pain, snakes— he succeeds in seducing each of them.

The recently divorced Jane, a shy, sexually-repressed music teacher, undergoes the most startling transforma-

tion as a result of his attentions, turning into a vain, flaming-haired floozy. Though the aptly named Van Horne does little to disguise his true identity ("I'm just your average horny little devil"), it is Felicia, the nosy wife of the town's newspaper publisher, who first catches on to his real identity and purpose: impregnating the women and populating the earth with his devilish spawn. The outraged Felicia ("I have nothing against a good fuck, but there is danger here!") begins spreading the word about the orgies taking place at the mansion and the three women become outcasts in the community.

When the trio opts to cool it with Van Horne for awhile, he decides he must get the meddlesome Felicia out of the way and employs an ingenious curse to accomplish it. As he and the women consume quantities of cherries, Felicia begins vomiting streams of cherry pits and bile in front of her astonished husband. Knowing who's responsible and why, she launches into a tirade against Van Horne and the women in between bouts of cherry puking until her disbelieving husband can't take it anymore ("Let's call it a day") and dispatches her with a fireplace poker.

Felicia's death finally clues the women in to what they've wrought and they refuse to have anything more to do with their charmingly devilish suitor. Enraged, he reveals his true self—talons, cloven hooves and all— and proceeds to snap the women back into line by conjuring up their worst fears. Jane is allowed a frightening glimpse of herself as an aging crone. Sukie is overcome by a strange malady that wracks her body with pain. And Alexandra wakes up to find her bed crawling with snakes (for sheer eye-closing, creepy-crawley horror, this slithery sequence eclipses anything in Spielberg's "Indiana Jones" films).

Each of them now pregnant with his child, the women cave in to Van Horne's demonic influence and go back to him. Their seeming capitulation is only a ruse, however, for the women have a plan up their collective sleeve to save their babies and rid themselves of this devil once and for all by retaliating with the same supernatural tricks they learned from him. In a protracted sequence that mixes gross out humor with wild stunt action and special effects, Van Horne is almost killed by his own runaway car, buffeted about in a conjured-up windstorm, doubled over in pain when the women stab his waxen image with pins, and

The bizarre seedling puppet of Nicholson created for the film by special effects master Rob Bottin.

subjected to a violent spell of cherry pit and feather puking. Taking refuge in a church of all places, he regales the open-mouthed worshippers with a hilarious monologue about how unfair mankind has treated him ("When *we* make mistakes, they call it evil. When God makes mistakes, they call it nature") and denounces the three women for their ingratitude. Then he returns to the mansion to get even. He transforms into a giant and starts knocking down the house, but is subsequently reduced to the size of a seedling and disappears when his waxen image breaks apart and burns. The film concludes with an even more bizarre epilogue taking place some years later that makes no sense whatsoever except to pave the way for a sequel.

Michael Cristofer's screenplay is a fairly loose adaptation of Updike's novel. For example, in the novel, the three women are the leading characters and Van Horne, though he acts as catalyst and is pivotal to the plot, is very much a supporting character. This is why the novel was titled *The Witches of Eastwick* and not "The Devil of Eastwick." In the film, however, Van Horne's role is the dominant one—a concession, perhaps, to the multi-million dollar salary demanded and gotten by star Jack Nicholson [producers *do* like to get their money's worth, after all], who not only delivers most the film's wittiest lines but proves as scarifying yet hilarious a screen devil as we are ever likely to see.

Loose adaptation though it may be, Cristofer's sharply satiric "battle of the sexes" screenplay—and George Miller's all-stops-out direction of it—does successfully follow the novel's same strategy: which was to employ the basic ingredients and generic conventions of popular horror/fantasy entertainment to create a unique piece of audience-pleasing *adult* entertainment in the same horror/fantasy vein.

LADY IN WHITE (1988)

A New Sky Production
A New Century/Vista Film Company Release
Color /112 minutes

Locked in the school cloakroom on Halloween night.
Frankie (Lukas Haas) witness the ghostly reenactment of a
murder that took place there ten years ago.

Frankie (Lukas Haas) describes the mysterious figure that tried to strangle him in the school cloakroom to his brother Geno (Jason Presson) and his father (Alex Rocco).

Angelo (Alex Rocco) expresses his anguish over what almost happened to Frankie to his longtime friend and co-worker Phil (Len Cariou).

Credits

Director: Frank LaLoggia; *Producers:* Andrew G. La Marca and Frank LaLoggia; *Screenplay:* Frank LaLoggia; *Cinematographer:* Russell Carpenter; *Editor:* Steve Mann; *Music:* Frank LaLoggia; *Production Designer:* Richard K. Hummel; *Videocassette source:* Virgin Vision.

Cast

Frankie: Lukas Haas; *Phil:* Len Cariou; *Angelo:* Alex Rocco; *Amanda:* Katherine Helmond; *Geno:* Jason Presson; *Mama Assunta:* Renata Vanni; *Papa Charlie:* Angelo Bertolini; *Melissa:* Joelle Jacobi; *Donald:* Jared Rushton; *Lady in White:* Karen Powell.

Critics who constantly assail the modern horror film for its splattery excesses and yearn hopefully for the genre to return to the good old days B.C. (Before Carnage) received Frank LaLoggia's valentine to the kinder, gentler days of horror, *Lady in White*, with welcoming arms. Though the film received virtually no theatrical distribution domestically, the well-deserved applause of such critics—and others like myself who *don't* have a problem with modern horror's "blood and gore"—helped to generate solid word of mouth for the film and launch it as a "sleeper hit" on video and pay cable TV.

Lady in White is a return to the past, not only in terms of its style, but its story as well—which is part memory piece, part coming-of-age tale, part detective yarn and part ghost story, all woven together in a leisurely and nostalgic manner reminiscent of *To Kill a Mockingbird*, one of LaLoggia's favorite movies. *Lady in White* even takes place in the year of *Mockingbird's* release, 1962.

The setting is Willowpoint Falls, a small upstate New York town where, over the past decade, ten children have been slain by an elusive madman. When two prankster chums lock him in the school cloakroom—the site of the first murder—on Halloween, young Frankie Scarlatti, a budding writer with a fondness for monster tales, sees the ghost of the victim, a little girl named Melissa, whose murder is replayed before him. As Frankie witnesses the child's ghostly manifestation being strangled by an invisible assailant, her barrette and the killer's ring fall into the furnace grate. The image fades and, moments later, the actual killer, who has learned that the furnace system is to be refurbished, returns to reclaim the lost ring that will reveal his identity. When he spots Frankie observing him, he throttles the boy and leaves him for dead.

Frankie revives, however, and when Melissa's apparition appears to him several more times ("I've lost my mommy. Will you help me find her?"), he sets out with his older brother Geno to snare the killer and unite the restless spirit of the child with that of her dead mother, who committed suicide after discovering her daughter's body. According to local superstition, the ghost of the mother—the lady in white—still haunts the cliffs above which the child's body was found. As Frankie proceeds to unravel the mystery and unite mother and child—almost at the cost of his own life—he not only finds out who the ghostly lady in white *really* is, but traumatically discovers that the elusive child murderer is a beloved family friend. Though this revelation doesn't come as any great surprise, it still works because LaLoggia, who also wrote the film, paints the killer as a fundamentally nice guy (except for his "off-moments,"

Frankie (Lukas Haas) meets the ghost of the murdered girl, Melissa (Joelle Jacobi).

Geno (Jason Presson) is dumbstruck as the ghost of the murdered girl reappears before him and Frankie (Lukas Haas).

of course) whom we come to like, and because he doesn't pin the whole finale upon the revelation itself.

Lady in White is *primarily* a ghost story—and a dandy one at that, which ranks along with Val Lewton's *Curse of the Cat People* (1944), Lewis Allen's *The Uninvited* (1944), the British *Dead of Night* (1945) and Jack Clayton's *The Innocents* (1961) as one of the best and most persuasive such tales ever brought to the screen. Like those earlier films, *Lady in White* does not beat the audience over the head with a lot of spectral blood and thunder (a la *Poltergeist*, for example). But LaLoggia's approach is by no means a total departure from that of other directors of his generation. LaLoggia is just as forthright about presenting his film's numerous fantasy elements as realistically as possible via a wide variety of special effects. Unlike many of his contemporaries, however, he does not indulge in these effects for their own sake, but rather uses them only to support, flesh out and add emotional weight to his story.

Not all the ghosts in the film are of the supernatural kind. *Lady in White*, like *To Kill a Mockingbird*, is also largely autobiographical—a tender and nostalgic reflection on the writer-director's own past. LaLoggia has admitted that he did take some liberties in recreating that past, but not many. The characters of Frankie's bickering ethnic grandparents, his warm-hearted iron worker father (played effectively against type by the underrated Alex Rocco), his impish but devoted older brother Geno—and even Frankie himself (LaLoggia's alter ego)—were all based on real-life LaLoggia family members, some of them now deceased. As a result, the film's characters have a flesh and blood dimension to them that is quite rare in genre films.

Not all of the film's autobiographical reflections on life back in the early Sixties are so rosy, however, for LaLoggia also includes a subplot dealing with racial intolerance and unrest—as when Frankie sees TV news footage of black student James Meredith being escorted by federal troops into the segregated University of Mississippi. Also in the course of the film, a black janitor in Frankie's school is falsely accused of being the elusive child killer. Released for lack of evidence, the innocent man is shot down anyway by one of the dead children's grieving parents in the film's most shocking scene.

With *Lady in White*, LaLoggia was determined not to repeat any of the mistakes he'd made with his first feature film (and first excursion into genre territory), *Fear No Evil* (1981), which was taken out of his hands and altered considerably by its distributor, Avco-Embassy. To maintain full control of the project from conception through final cut and distribution, LaLoggia and his cousin Charles financed *Lady in White*'s $4.5-million budget independently through a penny stock option. LaLoggia's determination paid off. Funny, frightening and shot through with feeling, *Lady in White* is a modern horror film classic made with consummate skill and taste.

The ghostly lady in white (Katherine Helmond).

THE BLOB (1988)

A Tri-Star Pictures Release
Color /95 minutes

A tramp comes across the crashed capsule containing *The Blob*.

Credits

Director: Chuck Russell; *Producers:* Jack H. Harris and Elliott Kastner; *Screenplay:* Chuck Russell and Frank Darabont; *Cinematographer:* Mark Irwin; *Editors:* Terry Stokes and Tod Feuerman; *Music:* Michael Hoenig; *Production Designer:* Craig Stearns; *Videocassette source:* RCA/Columbia Home Video.

Cast

Brian Flagg: Kevin Dillon; *Meg Penny:* Shawnee Smith; *Paul Taylor:* Donovan Leitch; *Sheriff:* Jeffrey DeMunn; *Fran:* Candy Clark; *Dr. Meddows:* Joe Seneca.

In the Seventies and Eighties, big budget remakes of six of the best known, most popular and, in some cases, classic horror and science-fiction films of the past were brought to the screen in fairly rapid succession: *King Kong* (1976), *Invasion of the Body Snatchers* (1978), *Cat People* (1982), *The Thing* (1982), *The Fly* (1986) and *The Blob* (1988). Of the six, I believe David Cronenberg's *The Fly* [see separate chapter] is not only the best, but also the most moving and complex—and Chuck Russell's *The Blob* is the most fun. While it may be heresy to say so, I think the main reason why these two particular films are not only as good as they are but why they eclipse the originals is because each improves upon concepts that were not handled especially well the first time around, something that clearly cannot be said of the other four remakes—although, admittedly, Phil Kaufman's *Body Snatchers* does come close.

In his rationale for tackling a remake of *The Blob* in the first place, writer-director Chuck Russell affirms this. "I was turning the [TV] dial and all of a sudden I changed the channel and there was *The Blob*," he told *Fear* magazine at the time of the new film's release. "I really got excited about the potential that film had and the fact that it left so much room to elaborate on the premise. I've never believed that *The Blob* was a full-blown classic. I loved the film, but the truth was that the original was a low budget throwaway cheapie."

Made independently of the Hollywood studio system for an estimated $240,000—which, by comparison to some low budget films being made at the time, was a fairly high price tag—the 1958 *Blob* is best remembered today as the film that gave Steve (then billed as Steven) McQueen his first starring role in a theatrical feature. Picked up for distribution by Paramount, the film was cleverly merchandized, clicked at the box office and launched McQueen on his way to superstar status. This, combined with the film's unique concept for a monster—a huge, deadly glop of Jello-like ooze from outer space—is what helped *The Blob* achieve its enduring status as one of the quintessential monster movies of the Fifties. The remarkable thing about Russell's purportedly $20-million remake is that while it clearly updates *The Blob* in terms of state-of-the-art gore effects, trendy language and so on, it also retains a considerable amount of the earlier film's innocence and charm. This even extends to the locations. The first film was shot in a small town in Pennsylvania, while the new one was shot thirty years later in a small town in Louisiana—and yet both towns look remarkably the same. Even the remake's mostly high-tech special effects occasionally take on a Fifties appearance—as when the tentacles of the huge, marauding new blob lash out and grind victims into the sidewalk. Many of these process shots look exactly like the early, and not always convincing, work of Ray Harryhausen in such films as *It Came From Beneath the Sea* (1955)—an effect, I'm sure, at which the new *Blob* was purposely aiming.

Part of the tramp's torso is eaten away by the *The Blob*.

In the original *Blob*, McQueen plays a rebellious teen named, appropriately enough, Steve—although he and all the other teenagers in the film scarcely appear all that rebellious or non-conformist. They're all too neat and clean cut—even McQueen himself. Nevertheless, most of the adults—including the parents of his goodie-two-shoes girlfriend Jane (Aneta Corseaut)—consider him practically a juvenile delinquent. When the quick-thinking Steve saves the day by freezing the marauding blob into immobility (after which it is transferred to the Arctic for storage), he earns the respect of all the the fat-headed authority figures who must finally admit that if it hadn't been for "the kids," they'd all have been "blobbed." No doubt about it, despite all its monster movie trappings, the original *The Blob* was little more than a teenage fantasy—sort of a "Rebel *With* a Cause," the cause in this case being to save the world from the blob.

The remake not only retains this same subtext, but pushes it to the limit. The McQueen part is divided into two characters: Paul, the high school football star, and Brian, the teenage punk in a leather jacket [even though it's 72 degrees outside] who's always in trouble with the law ("I'm a broken man," he sneers at the cops when

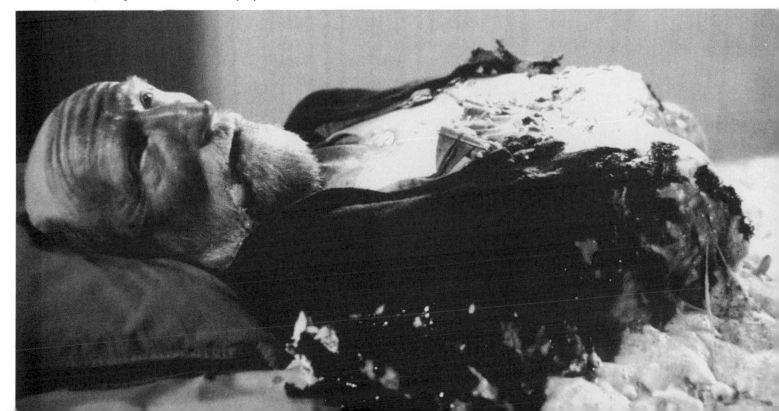

Paul (Donovan Leitch) becomes victim of *The Blob*.

they taunt him about his troubled home life). Paul is "blobbed" early on, leaving the way clear for Brian to take up with Paul's cheerleader girlfriend, Meg (who, unlike Jane, is not only quite plucky but turns into a female Rambo at the end of the film). As amusingly played by Kevin Dillon, the rebellious, motorcycle-riding Brian owes less to the original character played by McQueen than to McQueen himself, whose off-screen rebelliousness and on-and-off screen fondness for motorcycles and fast cars were part of the actor's mystique.

In addition to fleshing out its two central characters more—and giving them each more heroic things to do—the remake also provides a stronger rationale for the blob's existence. In the original, it was just something that crashed on earth from outer space and "blobbed" people. In the remake, the blob is actually a man-made experimental virus which, after being shot into outer space, undergoes a strange mutation and accidentally returns to earth. The government moves in and quarantines the town to contain its new and improved biological warfare weapon, but their mutated

handiwork proves too much for them. Despite all military efforts to "frag the sonofabitch," the blob appears unstoppable, until Meg and Brian discover that it can't stand the cold and blow up a snow making machine in order to freeze it—after which the ever-unflappable Brian breathlessly announces: "What a rush!"

Though some of the film's effects, as I've mentioned, were designed to recreate a Fifties look, the major set pieces of people being broken in half, sucked into drain pipes, crushed inside telephone booths, gobbled up inside their protective space gear and dissolving into pus-like ooze push this *Blob* firmly into the high-tech present so that modern horror film fans won't be disappointed. These effects and many others are as ingeniously well executed (by Lyle Conway and an army of other technicians and makeup artists) and suitably ghastly as any genre aficionado could possibly

The blob.

wish. But what really gives the film its charm is its tongue-in-cheek, but not deprecating, sense of humor (the movie theater scene, in which the showing of a parodied *Friday the 13th* clone called "Garden Tool Massacre" is fatally interrupted by a massive blob attack, is both a comic and scary high point) and the very real feelings of warmth its makers so obviously hold for the film that spawned it. This new *Blob* may out-do the old in just about every way, but it bends over backward neither to ignore nor trash the original—nor the era in which the original was made.

A little boy in the advanced stages of being blobbed cries out for help.

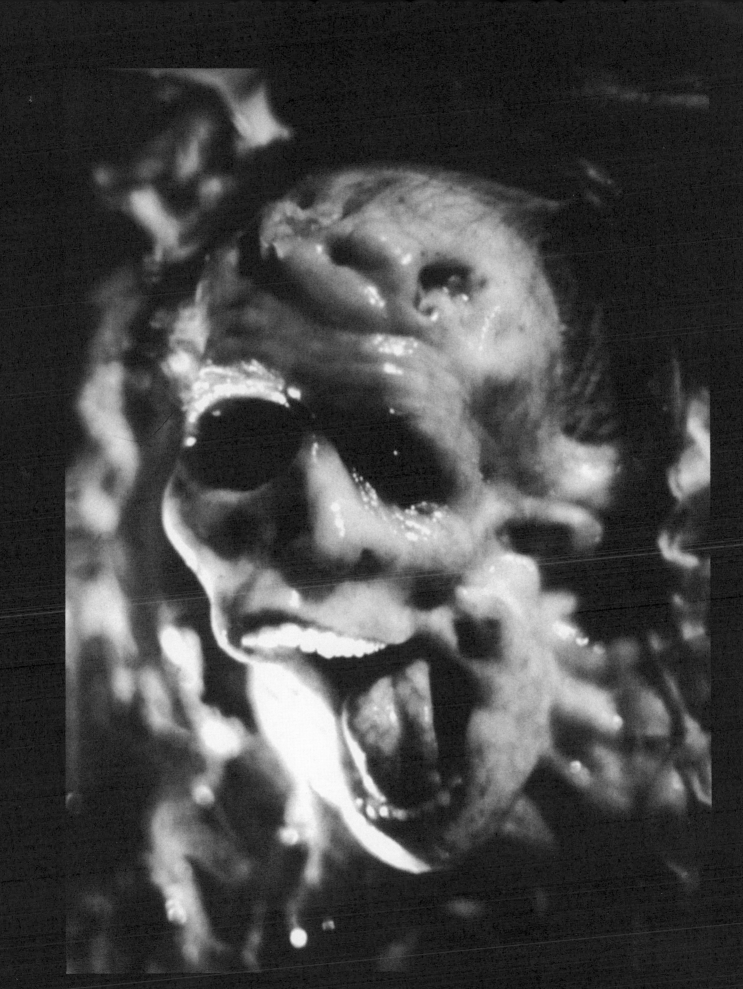

The ravaged face of yet another victim is absorbed by the blob.

THE LAIR OF
THE WHITE WORM (1988)

A Vestron Pictures Release
Color /94 minutes

Amanda Donohoe as
Lady Sylvia Marsh,
Derbyshire's
sophisticated snake
woman.

Credits

Director: Ken Russell; *Producer:* Ken Russell; *Screenplay:* Ken Russell, based on the novel by Bram Stoker; *Cinematographer:* Dick Bush; *Editor:* Peter Davies; *Music:* Stanislas Syrewicz; *Set Designer:* Anne Tilby; *Videocassette source:* Vestron Video.

Cast

Lady Sylvia Marsh: Amanda Donohoe; *Lord James D'Ampton:* Hugh Grant; *Eve Trent:* Catherine Oxenberg; *Angus Flint:* Peter Capaldi; *Mary Trent:* Sammi Davis; *Peters:* Stratford Johns; *P.C. Erny:* Paul Brooke; *Dorothy Trent:* Imogen Claire; *Kevin:* Chris Pitt; *Nurse Gladwell:* Gina McKee; *Joe Trent:* Christopher Gable; *Jesus Christ:* Lloyd Peters.

There is a certain rightness that this book on modern horror film classics should conclude with Ken Russell's *The Lair of the White Worm* since it is one that despite certain connections to Jacques Tourneur's *Curse of the Demon* (and Hammer's underrated *The Reptile* [1966]) is very close in spirit to the beloved horror classics of yore, particularly James Whale's *The Bride of Frankenstein.* The tendency in many of the best modern horror films to use large doses of stylish comedy, satire and/or outright camp certainly follows the Whale lead, but Russell is the first filmmaker since Whale to blur elements of horror and comedy into an inseparable unity.

The locale of the Bram Stoker novel upon which the movie is based appealed strongly to Russell. "It wasn't set in Transylvania," he commented in *Fangoria* magazine, "but in deepest Derbyshire, which hasn't been seen too much in horror films, and it had a particularly English quality about it." [Regardless of the fact that his films are not often thought of as *properly* British, Russell—with his non-stop celebration of British eccentricity, the British countryside and British music—is probably the most *British* of all filmmakers.] The Derbyshire setting (both the physical location and the sociological aspects) provided Russell with the raw material to create his most intensely English film to date. To some extent, this is the result of *The Lair of the White Worm's* unusual—almost unique—use of English folklore. Pagan and Roman mysticism and their impact on Christianity have not been much explored by filmmakers. The idea is present in Stoker's novel, but Russell

Eve Trent (Catherine Oxenberg) participates in the annual pantomime of the slaying of the D'Ampton worm.

has taken it and, typically, run with it, fleshing out the material with additional folklore and a heady aura of "last of the Empire" humor. Though updated to the 1980s, the movie has the definite air of a mock "England Swings" film of the Sixties. The campy Lady Sylvia Marsh prowls the countryside looking for victims in her 1960s Jaguar, while dressed in a variety of kinky leather outfits that make her come across like a voracious (sexually and otherwise) version of Diana Rigg in *The Avengers* TV series. But when Lady Sylvia wants a little music, she pulls out a compact disc. Similarly, she occasionally rests in a coffin-like tanning machine and has a taste for heavy metal head-banging music.

Having fashioned the world of the film, Russell gives himself free reign to create (or re-create) the myth of the D'Ampton worm—a gigantic, carnivorous snake-like creature lorded over by the immortal high priestess snake woman, Lady Sylvia. This fantastic creature was originally slain by an ancestor of Lord James D'Ampton (a feat acted out in an annual pantomime dance at the D'Ampton estate). But worms being what they are, the beast seems to have regenerated itself and has been

Lady Sylvia (Amanda Donohoe) reveals her true reptilian colors.

living at the bottom of a secret well for a thousand years, kept alive by the odd sacrificial virgin provided by Lady Sylvia. The unearthing of the skull of the original worm by Scottish archeologist Angus Flint while he's excavating an area of the Trent Farm (one time location of an ill-fated convent and earlier site of the snake cult) brings the secret of the legend to light again, setting off the chain of events that form the story.

When Russell first wrote the screenplay for *Lair*, he described it as "an off-the-wall adaptation" of the novel, and it certainly is that. Mindful of the fact that Stoker's novel (his last) was the work of a man suffering from the ravages of Bright's Disease (with incipient madness creeping into its pages at every turn), Russell opted to use the intriguing premise of the book as a springboard for an updated morality play. At the core of the film is a very personalized depiction of an ongoing conflict between Christianity and paganism. This conflict dates back to the idea of the Garden of Eden (hysterically recreated in the film with Lady Sylvia up a tree tempting Eve Trent, a virgin, back to her house as a sacrifice). It was Lady Sylvia who engineered the downfall of the convent that had the temerity to build on the foundations of the snake cult's temple. Time hasn't mellowed her. She has only to see a crucifix on the wall of the Trent home to sprout fangs and spray venom all over the offending object. On the other end of the scale, Eve (who *could* be *the* Eve) is less conscious of her role in the whole thing. It is only when her racial memory is pricked that her mind is flooded with images of the horror of the conflict—spawned by knowledge of her previous existence as one of the nuns at the ill-fated convent.

Morality play, horror film, tongue-in-cheek satirical romp. *The Lair of the White Worm* manages to be all three, working on all these levels at one time. Mostly, this is the result of Russell's decision to handle everything—even the most bizarre episodes—with a sense of gravity. The screenplay may be very funny and wildly improbable, but Russell's players inhabit it with the utmost seriousness. Lady Sylvia's immediate problem may be in finding a virgin for the worm, but this is only symptomatic of her overall greater dilemma: being the only stylish and sophisticated person in an area populated by dullards and rubes. Not only does this make her rapier wit go unappreciated, but the stolid minds of her foes are constantly undermining her by their very dullness. Even a homely boy scout named Kevin can

Lord James (Hugh Grant) awaits news that Lady Sylvia has left her lair—summoned by the snake charming music he's playing over an elaborate speaker system.

Lord James D'Ampton (Hugh Grant) gives Eve (Catherine Oxenberg) a watch belonging to one of her missing parents—which was found in a cave.

A victim of snake bite, Angus (Peter Capaldi) examines his wounds in a mirror, wondering if the serum he's taken will work.

throw her off. When she suggests a little music to heighten the romantic mood, he gamely whips out his harmonica and inadvertently strikes up snake charmer music—with devastating results. Thinking that stylish looking Lord James D'Ampton, descendant of a worthy opponent, might be a different matter, she coolly jokes with him. "Name your poison," she coos, sliding up to the bar. "Do you have any children?" He asks. "Only when there are no men about," she quips. Discussing

The D'Ampton worm rises from its lair.

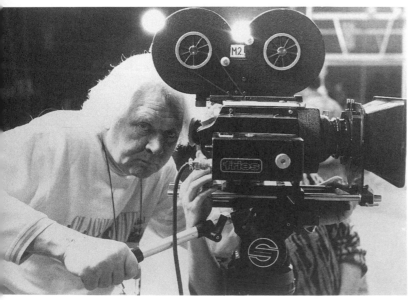

Director Ken Russell on the set of his "off-the-wall" adaptation of Bram Stoker's *The Lair of the White Worm*.

the disappearance of the Trent girls' parents, she takes a line from Oscar Wilde: "To lose one parent may be regarded as a misfortune; to lose both looks like carelessness"—only to be upbraided for her coldness in the matter. Explaining the quotation helps not at all.

Lair is an unforced, unpretentious, and very much "fun" film that takes a surprising number of risks along the way. The snake charmer gag with the boy scout is, for instance, merely a harbinger of more elaborate developments—as when Lord James rigs up a speaker system, digs up a proper tape (a souvenir of an ancestor in India) and uses it to summon the snake lady. Later, co-hero Angus Flint (complete with kilt and a handy mongoose) uses a set of bagpipes to do the same thing.

The hilarious and horrific spectacle that is *The Lair of the White Worm* is left open-ended, making the possibility of a sequel (at which Russell has hinted) a serious consideration. In this era of endless sequels to *Friday the 13th*, such a prospect is enticing indeed.

About the Author

John McCarty is the author of numerous film books, including the cult classic *Splatter Movies: Breaking the Last Taboo of the Screen* which *Fangoria* magazine called: "The definitive history of the gore film." His companion volume, *The Official Splatter Movie Guide*, has been hailed by Michael Slade (author of *Headhunter* and *Ghoul*) as "a splatterpunk's gourmet feast." His other books include *Deadly Resurrection* (a novel); *The Films of John Huston*; and *Psychos—80 Years of Mad Movies, Maniacs and Murderous Deeds*. He lives in upstate New York.

FREE!

Citadel Film Series Catalog

From James Stewart to Moe Howard and The Three Stooges, Woody Allen to John Wayne, The Citadel Film Series is America's largest film book library.

Now with more than 125 titles in print, books in the series make perfect gifts—for a loved one, a friend, or yourself!

We'd like to send you, free of charge, our latest full-color catalog describing the Citadel Film Series in depth. To receive the catalog, call 1 800 447 BOOK or send your name and address to:

Citadel Film Series/Carol Publishing Group
Distribution Center B
120 Enterprise Avenue
Secaucus, New Jersey 07094

The titles you'll find in the catalog include:
The Films Of...

Alan Ladd
Alfred Hitchcock
All Talking! All Singing!
   All Dancing!
Anthony Quinn
The Bad Guys
Barbara Stanwyck
Barbra Streisand:
   The First Decade
Barbra Streisand:
   The Second Decade
Bela Lugosi
Bette Davis
Bing Crosby
Black Hollywood
Boris Karloff
Bowery Boys
Brigitte Bardot
Burt Reynolds
Carole Lombard
Cary Grant
Cecil B. DeMille
Character People
Charles Bronson
Charlie Chaplin
Charlton Heston
Chevalier
Clark Gable
Classics of the Gangster
   Film
Classics of the Horror Film
Classics of the Silent Screen
Cliffhanger
Clint Eastwood
Curly: Biography of a
   Superstooge
Detective in Film
Dick Tracy
Dustin Hoffman
Early Classics of the
   Foreign Film

Elizabeth Taylor
Elvis Presley
Errol Flynn
Federico Fellini
The Fifties
The Forties
Forgotten Films
   to Remember
Frank Sinatra
Fredric March
Gary Cooper
Gene Kelly
Gina Lollobrigida
Ginger Rogers
Gloria Swanson
Great Adventure Films
Great British Films
Great French Films
Great German Films
Great Romantic Films
Great Science Fiction Films
Great Spy Films
Gregory Peck
Greta Garbo
Harry Warren and the
   Hollywood Musical
Hedy Lamarr
Hello! My Real Name Is
Henry Fonda
Hollywood Cheesecake:
   60 Years of Leg Art
Hollywood's Hollywood
Howard Hughes in Hollywood
Humphrey Bogart
Ingrid Bergman
Jack Lemmon
Jack Nicholson
James Cagney
James Stewart
Jane Fonda
Jayne Mansfield

Jeanette MacDonald and
   Nelson Eddy
Jewish Image in American
   Films
Joan Crawford
John Garfield
John Huston
John Wayne
John Wayne Reference
   Book
John Wayne Scrapbook
Judy Garland
Katharine Hepburn
Kirk Douglas
Lana Turner
Laurel and Hardy
Lauren Bacall
Laurence Olivier
Lost Films of the
   Fifties
Love in the Film
Mae West
Marilyn Monroe
Marlon Brando
Moe Howard and The
   Three Stooges
Montgomery Clift
More Character People
More Classics of the
   Horror Film
More Films of the '30s
Myrna Loy
Non-Western Films of
   John Ford
Norma Shearer
Olivia de Havilland
Paul Newman
Paul Robeson
Peter Lorre
Pictorial History of Science
   Fiction Films

Pictorial History of Sex
   in Films
Pictorial History of War
   Films
Pictorial History of the
   Western Film
Rebels: The Rebel Hero
   in Films
Rita Hayworth
Robert Redford
Robert Taylor
Ronald Reagan
The Seventies
Sex in the Movies
Sci-Fi 2
Sherlock Holmes
Shirley MacLaine
Shirley Temple
The Sixties
Sophia Loren
Spencer Tracy
Steve McQueen
Susan Hayward
Tarzan of the Movies
They Had Faces Then
The Thirties
Those Glorious Glamour Years
Three Stooges Book of Scripts
Three Stooges Book of Scripts,
   Vol. 2
The Twenties
20th Century Fox
Warren Beatty
W. C. Fields
Western Films of John Ford
West That Never Was
William Holden
William Powell
Woody Allen
World War II